THE NEW COMMERCIAL ARTIST'S HANDBOOK

THE NEW COMMERCIAL ARTIST'S HANDBOOK

JOHN SNYDER

WATSON-GUPTILL PUBLICATIONS, NEW YORK

Copyright © 1986 by Watson-Guptill Publications
a division of Billboard Publications, Inc.,
1515 Broadway, New York, N.Y. 10036

Manufactured in the U.S.A.

Library of Congress Cataloging-in-Publication Data
Snyder, John.
  The new commercial artist's handbook.
  Includes index.
  1. Commercial art—Technique—Handbooks, manuals,
etc. 2. Artists' materials—Handbooks, manuals, etc.
I. Title.
NC1000.S684 1986   741.6   86-15856
ISBN 0-8230-3160-8

Senior Editor: Julia Moore
Associate Editor: Victoria Craven-Cohn
Designer: Harry Chester & Associates
Production Manager: Hector Campbell
Typesetting and Page Makeup: Westview Press
Jacket Designer: Damien Alexander

Set in 10 point ITC Garamond

ACKNOWLEDGMENTS

I would like to express my long-standing gratitude to Don Holden and Susan E. Meyer, who were instrumental in shaping and developing this book, and to acknowledge, with thanks, the cooperation and expert assistance of Glorya Hale, Julia Moore, and Victoria Craven-Cohn. Thanks are also due my students, who directly and indirectly helped formulate the approach and presentation. This book is dedicated to Rowena Reed and to the memory of Alexander Kostellow.

PREFACE

This book is specifically for commercial artists. Its exclusivity is intentional. It is a recognition that commercial artists have very few resources that deal comprehensively with the raw materials of their professional lives, namely, the materials and processes of commercial art. Whereas fine artists and illustrators have shelves of books that cover their needs, commercial artists have been left to figure things out for themselves.

It is not difficult to find the reason for this disparity of resources. Fine artists and illustrators make pictures. Over time, many new materials, techniques, and styles have been introduced, but the essential function has not changed. Even the appearance of new outlets for their creations—galleries, publications, and other media—has hardly affected the basic principles of picture making. Books can and do dwell at length, and with some confidence, on how fine artists create, design, and render their compositions. Such books are timeless.

Commercial art, by contrast, is closely related to technology. Born in this century, commercial art has flourished and grown with each new technological introduction. Photography, moving pictures, offset lithography, television, computers—among others—have created jobs and functions that, although related, have quite distinct requirements. True, there are a few generalized job categories, such as graphic design and art direction, that embrace many of the areas of commercial art. But the specifics of what any one commercial artist does are extensive and particularized. For beginning professionals, such diversity is mysterious and confusing.

It is hard to define what commercial art is, and there has never been a completely accurate and acceptable definition. Here is mine: Commercial art encompasses every kind of graphic employed in every form of communication for advertising, industry, education, and entertainment; it is conceived, designed, laid out, and produced by one or more artists using whatever tools, materials, and techniques are demanded by the physical properties of the medium involved. In adapting to the technical requirements, each segment of this vast communications profession has differing procedures that are dictated by deadlines, budgets, and the nature of the material that has to be communicated. No school or education can cover every aspect of the field, and selecting goals and adapting to commercial employment can be difficult.

How is the professional to adjust to this complexity? What aims and aspirations are compatible with the continuous change in technology and materials? What preparations are necessary to blend hard-won experience with the opportunities of the future? Perhaps the best way to answer these questions is to examine the history of the profession. Each innovation has increased the number of occupational categories and has modified materials and procedures—without completely replacing them. For every job or tool that has been eliminated, dozens have been created. The successful professional is the one who can anticipate and respond to these changes, one whose knowledge is broad enough to adapt quickly. While the field demands specialization and expert proficiency, survival and success depend on this adaptability.

The purpose of this book is to assist the commercial artist in acquiring necessary knowledge as easily and efficiently as possible. By sharing my years of experience and teaching in the form of instructions and caveats about common pitfalls and difficulties, my intention has been to present the wide picture of what is possible in commercial art and, more than indirectly, to indicate the many avenues of employment open to an eager learner.

To the beginning commercial artist I say, Don't be discouraged by initial setbacks. Understand that every artist has experienced difficulty at first. Realize that many art tools and techniques have been borrowed or adapted from other sources and that your innovations can be as good as anyone else's. The true artist never stops learning or growing. Most importantly, remember a basic truth about all art—of any age: What you communicate is as significant as how you communicate it.

CONTENTS

Preface   6

A

Abrasives   13
Acetate   13
Acetate Ink   14
Acetate Mediums   14
Acetate Paints   15
Acetone   15
Acrylics   15
Adhesives   15
Agate Ruler   17
Airbrushes   17
Amberlith   23
Anatomical Casts   23
Anatomy Charts   23
Animation   23
Animation Cels   25
Architect's Scale   25
Art Gum   25
Art Markers   25
Artype   25
Atomizer, Mouth
    Type   25
Attaché Cases   26

B

Beam Compass   27
Benday   27
Bindings   28
Blotting Paper   28
Blueprint Files   29
Blueprints   29
Bond Paper   30
Bourges   30
Bow Compass   30
Brayer   30
Bristol   31
Bronzing Liquid
    Medium   31
Bronzing Powders   31
Brush, Lettering   32

Brush, Stencil   33
Brush Washer   33
Brushes, Paint   33
Bulletin Boards   36
Burnisher   36

C

Calligraphy   37
Camera Lucida   37
Carbon Paper   38
Carbon Pencil   39
Carborundum   39
Cartoon Colors   39
Casein   39
Casein Shellac   40
Cel   40
Cel-Grip   40
Cellophane Tape   40
Celluloid   40
Center Bow Compass   40
Chalks, Layout   40
Chalks, Oil   41
Chamois   41
Charcoal   41
Charcoal Paper   42
China Markers   43
Chip Board   43
Chisel-Point Pencils   43
Circle Cutter   43
Coated Papers   44
Cold Type   44
Color-Aid   44
Colorama   44
Color Charts   45
Color Keys (3M)   45
Color Wheels   45
Compasses   45
Compasses, Technical
    Pen or Marker   48
Compressors   48
Computer Animation   49
Computer Graphics   51
Computer Type   59

Concentrated
    Watercolors   60
Construction Paper   60
Copy Casters   60
Copying Machines,
    Color   60
Coquille Board   61
Correction Tape   61
Corrugated Paper and
    Board   61
Cotton   61
Cover Paper   62
Crayons, Conté   63
Crayons,
    Lithographic   63
Crayons, Wax   63
Crocus Cloth   64
Crop Marks   64
Cross Section Paper   64
Curves, Adjustable   64
Curves, Irregular   65
Curves, Prepared   65
Cutter, Dual   66

D

D'Arches Paper   67
Dazor   67
Designer's Colors   67
Direct Positives   67
Display Letters   68
Dividers   68
Drafting Machines   68
Drafting Sets   70
Drafting Tables   71
Drafting Tape   71
Drawing Board   71
Drawing Boards   72
Drawing Ink Pens   72
Drawing Inks   73
Drawing Tables   73
Drop Bow Compass   73
Dry Cleaning Pad   73
Dryers, Mechanical   73
Dry Mount   74

Dusting Brushes 75
Dye Markers 75
Dyes 75

E

Easel, Display 77
Easel, Painting 78
Egg Crates 78
Electric Eraser 78
Ellipse Machines 79
Ellipse Templates and
    Guides 79
Enamels 80
Engineer's Scale 81
Enlarger-Reducers 81
Epoxy 81
Eraser, Electric 81
Erasers 82
Erasing Shields 85
Etching Paper 85
Etching Press 86

F

Fiberglass Eraser 87
Filing Cabinets, Flat 87
Fixative 87
Flap Paper 89
Flex-Opaque 91
Flint Paper 91
Flip Charts 91
Flock 91
Flo-Paque 91
Fluorescent Light 91
Foamcore 91
Formatt 92
Fount Ink 92
French Curve 92
Frisket Knife 93
Frisket Paper 94
Friskets 94
Friskets, Liquid 99
Frosted Acetate 99

G

Gels 101
Gesso 101

Glitter 101
Glue 102
Gouache 102
Graph Paper 104
Graphite Paper 104
Graphite Sticks 104
Graphos 104
Guide Lines 104

H

Haberule 105
Handlettering 105
Halftone Screen 105
Hand Cleaners 105
Hand Rests 106
Hot Type 106

I

Illuminating 107
Illustration Board 107
Imaging Systems 107
Inch Rulers 107
India Ink 107
India Ink
    Dispensers 109
India Ink Pens 110
Ink Erasers 110
Ink, Manuscript 110
Inks, Acetate 110
Inks, Drawing 111
Inks, Printing 111
Instant Lettering 112
INT (Image 'N'
    Transfer) 112

J

Japan Colors 113

K

Kerning 115
Key Line 115
Kneaded Erasers 115
Knife, Frisket 116
Knife, Mat 116

Knife, Stencil 118
Knife, Swivel 119
Knife, X-Acto 119
Kodalith 120
Kraft Paper 120
Kroy Lettering
    Machine 120

L

Lacey Luci 121
Lacquer Thinner 121
Lamp, Daylight 121
Lamp, Fluorescent 121
Layouts 122
Layout Chalks 124
Layout Paper 124
Lead Holders 124
Lead Pointers 125
Leads 125
Leads, Colored 125
Leroy 126
Leroy Lettering
    Pens 126
Letraset 126
Lettering Guides 126
Lettering,
    Mechanical 126
Lettering Pens 127
Lettering Stencils 127
Lettering Templates 128
Light Boxes 129
Lighting 129
Light Tables 130
Linen Tester 130
Line-Up Board 130
Linoleum Blocks 130
Liquid Watercolors 130
Lithographic
    Crayons 130
Luci 130
Lucite 130
Lucite Cement 131

M

Magic Markers 133
Magnifier,
    Illuminated 133

Magnifying Glasses 133
Mahlstick 133
Mannequins 134
Manila Paper 134
Map Pins 134
Markers 134
Marking Pencils 136
Maskoid 136
Mat Board 136
Mat Cutters 136
Mat Frames 137
Mat Knife 137
Mechanical
    Lettering 137
Mechanicals 137
Mineral Spirits 138
Models (Live) 138
Mounting Board 138
Multiliner 139
Mylar 139

N

Newsprint 141
Non-Crawl 141
No-Seam Paper 141

O

Oak Tag 143
Oil Can 143
Oil Chalks 143
Oilstones 143
Opaque Projector 143
Opaque White 144
Osmiroid 145
Overlays 145
Overlays, Tinted
    Acetate 147

P

Paint 149
Paint Cups 152
Palette 152
Palette Knife 153
Pantograph 153
Pantone Matching
    System 154

Paper Clips 154
Paper Cutter 154
Papers and Boards 155
Parallel Ruling Straight-
    Edge 165
Parchment 167
Paste 167
Pastel 167
Pastel Holders 170
Pastel Paper 170
Paste-Up 170
Pen Cleaner 170
Pen Filling Inkstand 171
Pen Holders 171
Pen Points 171
Pencil Pointer,
    Metal 174
Pencil Sharpeners 174
Pencils, Charcoal 175
Pencils, Colored 176
Pencils, Lead 176
Pencils, Marking 177
Pencils, Sketching 177
Pens 178
Pens, Bamboo 180
Pentel 181
Perforating Wheels 181
Perspective Lineads 182
Photo Dulling Spray 182
Photolettering 182
Photo Prints 183
Photograph
    Cleaners 183
Photographic Tape 184
Photostats 184
Pica Ruler 186
Pink Pearl 186
Plastic Films 186
Point Ruler 187
Polaroid 187
Polyethylene 188
Portfolios 188
Poster Board 189
Poster Paint 189
Pounce Powder 189
Pounce Wheels 189
Press, Mounting 189
Pressure Graphics 189
Prestype 189
Printing Inks 189

Progressive Proofs 189
Projector, Art 190
Projectors,
    Overhead 190
Proportional Divider 191
Proportional Scale 191
Protective Coverings 192
Protractors 192
Pushpin 192

Q

Quadrille Paper 193

R

Rapidograph 195
Razor Blades 195
Red Rope
    Envelopes 196
Reducing Glasses 196
Register Mark 197
Retouching Colors 197
Rice Paper 198
Ross Board 198
Roto Tray 198
Roulettes 198
Rubber Cement 198
Rubber Cement
    Dispenser 201
Rubber Cement Thinner
    Dispenser 202
Rubdown Type 203
Rub-Off Type 203
Rubylith 203
Rulers 204
Ruling Pen 206

S

Saddle Stitching 211
Sandpaper Pad 211
Saral Paper 212
Scaling Wheel 212
Scaleograph 212
Scissors 212
Scotch Tape 212
Scrap File 213

Scratch Board 213
Screen Determiner 214
Scriber Pens 214
Separations 214
Serigraphy 214
Shading Sheets 214
Shellac 214
Showcard 215
Showcard Lettering 215
Sign Cloth 215
Sign Writing 215
Silkscreen 215
Skeletons 215
Sketch Box 216
Slide Rules 216
Solvents 216
Speedball 217
Splines 217
Sponges 217
Spray Adhesives 219
Spray Can Handle 219
Spray Guns 219
Sprayers 219
Squeegee 220
Staplers 220
Stencil 221
Stencil Brush 222
Stencil Knife 222
Stencil Paper 222
Stencils, Lettering 222
Stipple Brush 222
Stomps 223
Straight-Edge 223
Studio Markers 223
Stylus 223
Swatchbooks 223
Swiss Cheese 225
Swivel Knife 225

T

Tables, Drawing 227
Taboret 227
Tackers 228
Tape, Cellophane 228
Tape, Chart 228
Tape, Cloth 228
Tape, Correction 229
Tape Dispensers 229
Tape, Drafting 229
Tape, Gummed
    Paper 230
Tapes, Photographic 230
Tape, Two-Sided 230
Technical Pens 231
Tempera 231
Templates 231
Templates, Lettering 232
Textile Paints 232
Textured Boards 232
Tissue Paper 232
Tongs 233
Top Sheet Shading
    Films 233
Tortillons 233
Trace Wheels 233
Tracing Boxes 233
Tracing Cloth 233
Tracing Paper 233
Transfer Type 233
Triangle 236
Triangle, Adjustable 237
T-Squares 239
Turpentine 240
TV Mats 240
TV Pads 240
Tweezers 240

Two-Sided Tape 241
Type 241

V

Van Dykes 243
Varnish 243
Vellum 243
Velox 243
Viewers 244
Vinyl Films 246
Visualizer Paper 246

W

Watercolor 247
Watercolor Paper 249
Watercolors, Dr. PH.
    Martin Radiant
    Concentrated 250
Watercolors, Dr. PH.
    Martin Synchromatic
    Transparent 250
Watercolors, Liquid 250
Wax Coater 250
Wax Crayons 250
Welders, Hand 250
Whetstones 250
Wrico 251

X

X-Acto Knife 253

Z

Zipatone 255

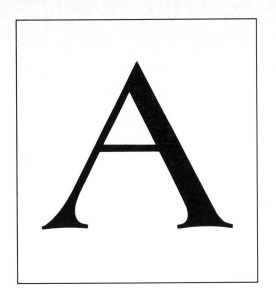

ABRASIVES

A substance used to wear away another substance by friction. Commercial artists use abrasives in all phases of their work—to shape, sharpen, or polish. Three abrasives are described here.

Whetstones. Used to shape and sharpen metal tools, drawing instruments, and knives. Fine-grained whetstones are also used to polish the surfaces of these tools and instruments.

Sandpaper. Used to shape and sharpen pencils and similar drawing materials. Sandpaper is also used to a limited degree for sharpening metal instruments when whetstones are not available.

Crocus cloth. Used to polish metal surfaces. Crocus cloth is too fine to produce any shaping or sharpening; it is used only to remove oxidation, stains, or very light scratches.

In a sense, erasing is accomplished by means of abrasion, and the various methods used to make corrections with abrasives are covered in the entry *Erasers.* (See also *Crocus Cloth, Erasers, Sandpaper Pad,* and *Whetstones.*)

ACETATE

Common term abbreviation for cellulose acetate, the most often used plastic film in commercial art. The term has come to represent any transparent plastic film.

Specifically, acetate refers to clear, comparatively stable plastic sheets that are sold in art stores in two thicknesses, .003″ and .005″. These sheets are sold in many sizes, in both pads and rolls. Two surfaces are also provided. The normal acetate is very smooth and shiny, and paint and ink tend to chip or peel from the surface. Frosted acetate and prepared acetate have one side that has been treated to provide a measure of "tooth." Frosted acetate and prepared acetate are used when conventional ink, paint, or adhesives must be applied to the surface.

Acetate is used to prepare overlays for artwork, separations, and paste-ups. Acetate is also used to provide protection as a removable covering.

Common Difficulties

Spreading. The surface of the acetate, even if prepared, tends to allow any liquid to spread out, and causes a line that is wider than planned. Adding acetate mediums, which are designed to help paint adhere to glossy surfaces, only increases this tendency. Therefore, work with the paint as thick as possible, and avoid using an acetate medium when you can. Test the line first to determine the width; ruling pens will usually have to be set closer for work on acetate.

Wrong side. Frosted acetate is only frosted on one side; the other side is glossy. However, the frosted coating does not interfere with the transparency at all. This makes it difficult for beginners to determine which side has been treated. It's even hard to tell by feeling it. It may be necessary to practice with your ink or paint on a remote corner of the acetate to determine which side takes the medium best.

Errors. Mistakes on acetate are frequently made, particularly by beginners, but these errors are easily removed. Most mediums will wash off, leaving no trace. Strong pigments may stain frosted acetate, but the stain can be removed by scraping the surface gently with the flat of a razor blade. This scraping does not change the character of frosted acetate, but will show on clear acetate.

Cutting. Trimming art is difficult once it has been mounted on acetate. If the blade penetrates the acetate, it will cause a small opening that will grow with the slightest touch, eventually producing a long slice or even a lost piece. Trim all artwork before mounting it on the acetate. If a cut is made, cover it immediately with a transparent tape to prevent its spreading.

ACETATE INK

Flexible, nonpeeling medium for working on plastic films. Since these films resist shrinking and other distortions, they are used extensively when complete transparency and accuracy are necessary. Film animation, for example, requires the use of these films. The animation is drawn on the "cels" (the common name for these plastic sheets), placed over opaque background art, and photographed with an animation camera. Regular inks and paints, meant for use on drawing papers and boards, will not adhere to plastic. These mediums will bead, crack, or peel away from the surface. Acetate inks and paints are used instead. (See *Cel, Inks, Acetate* and *Paint, Acetate.*)

ACETATE MEDIUMS

To increase the ability of water-based paints to adhere to a glossy surface, an acetate medium is added to the paint. Paint that has been mixed with an acetate medium will remain flexible and less brittle when dry, reducing the possibility of flaking or chipping from a glossy surface in normal handling.

Through trial and error, you may discover a number of household substances that can perform this function with some success. Common bar soap, for example, can be quite satisfactory. However, these homemade substitutes do not work as well as the commercial products and should only be used in an emergency. There are a number of these products on the market. Your art store's supply depends on the store's location and the judgment of the buyer. The products may not be referred to as acetate mediums, because there is no common generic name for this class of mediums. However, brand names—such as Non-Crawl, Flex-Opaque, and Cel-Grip—will instantly identify the item. A dealer who does not have one of these products will probably have another that will work as well. (See *Inks, Acetate,* and *Paint, Acetate.*)

Follow the instructions on the bottle; with most brands, you add one part medium to several parts prepared paint. Try to keep the amount of medium as small as possible; if too much medium is added, the paint tends to become thin, lose its opacity, and become bubbly.

Common Difficulties

Sudsing. Using any of these mediums (particularly soap) will cause the paint to bubble and froth if you stir in too much. This froth will not subside and when dry will leave the paint rough and pitted. The froth will also prevent the paint from being opaque. Always have your paint thoroughly mixed and at the desired consistency before you add the acetate medium. Avoid excess brushstrokes (or scrubbing) when applying the paint.

Stickiness. The acetate mediums will slow the drying time of the paint and leave the dry paint tacky. This will make the art difficult to handle or to overpaint. Use as little of the medium as possible.

Experiment to determine how much is necessary. You may find that you can work satisfactorily with considerably less medium than the instructions recommend. Try placing a drop of the medium in a clean spot and moisten your brush in it lightly before dipping the brush in the paint. This way you can avoid adding too much medium to the paint, and you can correct any excess amount by wiping the brush on a cloth between strokes.

Thinness. Any substance added to paint will thin it, reducing its covering power. Use as little medium as possible.

ACETATE PAINTS

Descriptive name for a series of paints, often acrylic, that is used for work on acetate and similar plastic films, as well as other glossy surfaces. Referred to by such names as Cartoon Colors, Cel-Flex, etc., these paints are not directly labeled as acetate paints, but their specific qualities are directed for such work. (See *Paint, Acetate.*)

ACETONE

A common organic solvent that is capable of dissolving many fats, resins, and plastics—including cellulose acetate. It is particularly useful to the commercial artist for dissolving lacquers, varnishes, and fixatives when they must be diluted or removed. Acetone can be purchased in art stores, hardware stores, and drugstores (where it is found as the principal ingredient of nail polish remover). (See *Solvents.*)

ACRYLICS

The most successful of the synthetic paints, acrylics are water-soluble, fast-drying, waterproof when dry, and bond to many surfaces. Acrylics offer an alternative to oils and watercolors, although they have not been used in as many ways as the two older mediums. Perhaps the most common applications are in fine art and illustration. There, the generally lower cost, quick drying time, and wide range of supporting mediums, coupled with acrylics' versatility of technique—including thin washes, airbrush, and heavy impasto—have made it popular. Acrylics can be damaged by extremes of temperature.

Acrylics have not been broadly accepted by commercial artists. Their tendency to ruin sable hair requires special brushes of nylon, and their quick-drying quality is actually a hindrance to reworking. Acrylics also require special handling when being used in ruling pens, airbrushes (of the fineness preferred by commercial artists), and other conventional tools. Therefore, the profession uses more of the gouache-style paints.

One area of commercial art, animation, has adopted acrylics almost exclusively. Acrylics' ability to bond to acetate cels with a smooth, flat, opaque color that resists chipping makes them ideal for rendering animation art. Commonly called Cartoon Colors, after the California firm that is a leading manufacturer of them, acrylic paints dominate the animation field.

ADHESIVES

Any substance that bonds one surface to another. The primary adhesive used by commercial artists is rubber cement. Because of its importance, rubber cement has been given an entry in this book. Familiarize yourself with this medium before you use any other adhesive because rubber cement is the best adhesive for your purposes, and solves most of the adhering problems that occur in commercial art. Rubber cement is clean, non-staining, strong, and easily removed. However, there are occasions when another adhesive might be preferable. The following are some of the other products available that may fit your specific needs.

Epoxy. The epoxy glues are the strongest adhesives made. Epoxy glues come in two tubes, the contents of which can be stored indefinitely since they do not begin to react until they are mixed before using. After the glue is mixed, it is applied to both surfaces, which are then pressed together and held firmly for a specified time while the glue sets. You may have to hold the pieces with weights or clamps to prevent them from moving during this drying period, which may be as short as five minutes. Once the glue is set, heat, chemicals, or strain will not weaken it; nothing can destroy an epoxy bond. This makes epoxy an excellent medium for models, displays, etc., where great strength and permanence are necessary. Since epoxy cannot be removed, you should apply it with care.

Everyday glues. This is a rather arbitrary title for a wide range of products that serve much the same purpose as epoxy for the commercial artist. These glues may be resins, chemicals, plastics, or natural substances that come in tubes or bottles and are advertised as being effective for bonding all kinds of materials together. Their chief advantage is that they require no mixing, and several glues dry instantly. Although they may need some clamping or weighting before they set, their main disadvantages are that they are not as strong as epoxy, they may dry out in storage, and they may be flammable. There are far too many of these everyday glues to list by name or advantage. Any housewares counter, hardware store, or stationery store can recommend dozens of them.

One-coat cement. One-coat cement is stored and applied in much the same manner as rubber cement. Unlike ordinary rubber cement, one-coat cement does not need to be applied to both surfaces. It makes a comparatively weak bond that permits you to mount, remove, and reposition a piece of art. One-coat cement does just about everything that rubber cement can do in mechanicals and paste-ups with few of the difficulties. However,

this cement creates a weaker bond than rubber cement, it always remains tacky, and it leaves behind a residue each time the mounted piece is moved. This means that handling the pasted pieces is sticky; and the residue, which cannot be removed easily, picks up dirt—creating a messy mechanical. In addition, each movement reduces the adhering strength of the coated piece, so that eventually it will not stick at all.

To avoid the difficulty of handling sticky paste-up material that has been coated with one-coat cement, many artists coat the entire back of the sheet with cement, place it on a glossy surface (glass or acetate, for instance), and then cut out the individual pieces from the sheet. This procedure keeps the bulk of the coated surface out of contact with hands, tools, and materials, and the individual pieces may be peeled from the surface quite easily when they are needed.

Rabbit skin glue. This is not a true adhesive but is used as a binder. Applied to canvas or mixed with gesso, rabbit skin glue helps to size a surface in preparation for painting. However, the fact that this glue does not shrink or discolor, as many everyday glues do, makes it valuable for mounting thin pieces of paper without wrinkling or staining the rendering. Rabbit skin glue comes as a water-soluble powder.

Vegetable paste. Vegetable paste (or library or school paste) is another adhesive recommended for normal use when adhering paper. Although it comes as a paste, it may be thinned with water. This allows the paste to be softened when it begins to dry out in the container. Thinning with water may also prevent the paste from becoming too thick during application, a condition that may make the mounting of thin papers difficult. Too much paste can also cause shrinking, cracking, or discoloration.

Vegetable paste is excellent for stretching watercolor paper, particularly in conjunction with gummed paper tape. Being water soluble, the paste mixes with and reinforces the adhesive on the tape. The tape serves to hold the paper until the drying paste has a chance to set. Together, the tape and paste will withstand the tremendous pressure generated by the shrinking, drying paper.

Spray adhesives. Spray adhesives are very similar to one-coat cement, except that they come in the familiar aerosol spray can. The spray can offers a simple, convenient method of application, which provides the opportunity to build up the adhesive through repeated sprayings. The more coats applied, the stronger the adhesion will be. Stronger adhesion may be necessary if the piece being mounted must be moved several times to ensure proper position.

One warning: some spray adhesives tend to bond permanently if allowed to stand for any length of time. If you need to reposition the art, be sure to do so promptly. If you attempt to remove the adhered piece after a prolonged delay, you may tear the paper or damage the art. (See *Spray Adhesives.*)

Common Difficulties

Most adhesives have characteristics that make them difficult to handle. Usually these involve either their drying time or a lack of solvents for cleaning them from the finished art. There are no solutions to these problems. Except for rubber cement, no glue can be removed with ease. Work as cleanly as possible and avoid applying too much of any glue. Read the isntructions on the container to see if a solvent exists for the adhesive you are using, and keep a supply handy. It will probably not help to remove a stain, but it may make it possible to correct an error.

If the adhesive you are using causes stains, discoloration, or wrinkles, experiment with other adhesives until you discover one that serves your purpose more successfully. Try as many adhesives as you can. It is not easy to predict what problems you may face in the art field. The more you are familiar with the various products, the better your chance of finding one that works in any given situation.

AGATE RULER

A ruler containing the agate scale (fourteen units to the inch) used in measuring the depth of a column of copy. Most periodicals base their advertising rates on line counts, that is, so many lines for so many dollars. The lines referred to are agate lines. An artist, preparing an ad for such a publication, must measure the ad size in agate lines. (See *Rulers.*)

AIRBRUSHES

This is a device for applying paint by means of a controlled spray. The airbrush works on the same principle as the atomizer. A stream of air is directed over a tube which creates enough suction to draw paint out of a cup and then blows this paint out through a nozzle. The size of this spray may be controlled by withdrawing a needle which is seated inside the nozzle. As the opening is enlarged, a greater amount of paint is released.

The airbrush has had a varied history. Originally promoted as a replacement for conventional art techniques, it enjoyed a period of intense popular acceptance in the late 1920s and early 1930s. This was slowly replaced with indifference and ultimately rejection. In the beginning airbrush was a rather strange and unnatural

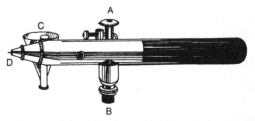

The parts of the airbrush are (A) paint and air control button, (B) air hose connection, (C) paint cup, and (D) needle seated in the tip.

technique that required comparatively expensive equipment and much instruction and practice. The first airbrushers were mostly technical people who delighted in dazzling virtuoso displays. Before traditional artists incorporated the airbrush into their work, the novelty waned and the highly stylized illustrations lost their appeal. For some years, the airbrush was avoided by artists except for photo retouchers and technical illustrators, until a newer generation rediscovered the value of the airbrush and the marvelous effects it could produce in combination with other techniques. The second generation also provided the creative input that had been missing earlier, with fine artists some of the most enthusiastic converts. Oddly enough, a device that may ultimately eliminate the airbrush has been a major reason for its new popularity: The computer has proved to be an excellent simulator of airbrush technique. (See *Computer Graphics.*) For those with no access to a computer graphics system, airbrush is an inexpensive alternative and is still valuable for all commercial artists.

Types of Airbrushes

There are several brands of airbrush on the market, each with a number of models. These range from inexpensive hobby tools that do not stand up to professional requirements to specialized equipment, such as the Paasche Model AB ("turbine") which only produces an extremely fine-line, cannot cover large areas, and requires extensive care and practice even for those familiar with airbrushes. The choice of an airbrush is a difficult decision that should be based on the amount of work to be done, the nature of that work, and the comparison of a number of models and makes. In general, the commercial artist should choose a professionally proved brand and select the top-of-the-line model. These will have double action control of both air and paint and will produce extremely fine-line to moderately wide coverage. Larger models are for sign

and poster work that need greater area coverage and for use with oil-based paints. The greater costs of these professional models is easily amortized over a lifetime of commercial work.

The most common complaint of artists who buy airbrushes is that of wrong selection. Seek advice from a professional or from a qualified airbrush service representative.

Assembling the Airbrush

Since the airbrush operates when air is passed through the mechanism, some method of creating pressure to force the air is required. The cheapest "air" is a tank of CO_2 (compressed carbon dioxide). However, these tanks may be difficult to obtain. They are often unavailable at art supply stores and must be acquired from the manufacturer. These companies will lend the tank and refill it for a reasonable charge but often require a large deposit. Other disadvantages of the tank are the impossibility of knowing when the tank is nearly empty, and the need to return the heavy tank to the plant for refilling.

The alternative is an electric motor-driven air compressor, with or without a storage tank. Tanks and compressors are initially expensive, but require no further servicing other than normal maintenance. Compressors with tanks turn themselves on and off automatically to maintain the proper pressure range, while the less expensive, tankless models run continuously. This annoying feature of the tankless model may be avoided by the addition of a foot switch, so that the compressor may be turned on only while the actual airbrushing is being done. A valve to control the pressure, optional with a compressor, is necessary on a CO_2 tank to maintain a steady flow of "air." Some valves have a moisture trap, simply a tube into which water may fall and be drained by means of a spigot. This is handy with a compressor on a muggy day. Damp air, when it is compressed, condenses drops of water which are collected by the moisture trap. You will have no moisture problems if you use compressed CO_2, which cools as it expands and is very dry at all times.

A length of hose is needed to connect the airbrush to the air source. A special kind, made for this use, has cloth woven around a rubber tube to protect it from the constant flexing received in normal use. This hose is sold by the foot; get as much as you need to work comfortably. Remember that you may wish to work on a large surface, and there must be sufficient hose to allow you to move freely.

The airbrush is a delicate tool. Although any thin liquid will go through the mechanism, care must be taken or the airbrush will be damaged. Use only high-grade watercolor paints, retouching colors, and dyes. India inks may be used, but only if diluted with a drop or two of clear ammonia (which slows the drying), and the airbrush must be cleaned thoroughly with ammonia immediately after using. Colored drawing inks of good quality are too thin to be diluted, so extra care must be taken to clean the airbrush. If you are going to be using inks for any length of time, clean the airbrush frequently while working. The proper way to clean the airbrush is discussed later in the section and should be read carefully.

Using the Airbrush

With the airbrush rig assembled, prepare your paint by thinning it with water. The thinner the paint, the better it will go through the airbrush. However, if the paint is too thin and watery, it will not cover properly and will soak and wrinkle the paper. Practice will determine the best proportion: probably around one-half paint to one-half water. Mix at least three times as much paint as you feel you will need, as the thinned paint will need several coats to cover, and the fine spray dissipates a great deal into the air. Once you have run out of paint, it is difficult to prepare a new mixture that will match properly. Prepare your working surface so that it is completely clean, otherwise the spray will settle unevenly on bits of dirt, grease, and fingerprints, discoloring the finished painted surface. (There are several products on the market for cleaning photographic prints. See *Photograph Cleaners.*)

As the spray diffuses in the air, it is necessary to protect exposed surfaces. Individual friskets are adequate when you are working on small areas. If a great deal of spraying is needed, block out the remaining surface of the art with pieces of newspaper, held in place with drafting tape or heavy weights. Avoid masking tape, since its adhesion will damage the surface of the paper when the tape is removed. (See *Friskets.*)

Fill the paint cup no more than half full, so that it will not spill when moved. Grasp the airbrush lightly, in the same manner as you hold a pencil. It should rest on the third finger, with the thumb pressing gently next to and even with the button. First, press the button down with the index finger to allow air to flow through the airbrush. Then, pull the button back with the index finger and paint will be released into the spray. The farther back you pull the button, the more paint will flow.

These movements of the button are very small and subtle. Any initial awkwardness and tendency to exaggerated movement can be counteracted if the button is moved with the *joint* of the index finger and not the tip. This procedure will bring the tip of the index finger in contact with the thumb. Adjusting the position of the thumb will enable it to form a rest for the index finger, which assures a steady flow of paint and makes it possible to return to this exact position on future strokes of the airbrush. (See illustrations.) Use a practice sheet to determine the amount of paint and the distance from the paper that will produce the desired effect.

When working on the finished art, keep the brush in constant, steady motion so that you get an even tone. This is more easily done if you work in short bursts of a second or two, hence the value of the thumb as a guide and rest. To get a graded tone, keep up the steady movements, but gradually increase the distance from the paper. For the beginner, this is easier than trying to cut down the amount of paint.

For retouching photographs, try to work without friskets on portraits and other soft-edged subjects. Friskets produce an unrealistic, hard edge. When you have finished your retouching, you may find that some areas have received an undesired "spill." To clean these areas, use a slightly moist piece of cotton. Do not use a dirty one; change it after every two or three strokes. With practice and care, you will be able to clean off excess paint without leaving a telltale edge.

Care and Maintenance

After using the airbrush, or when changing colors, rinse the cup thoroughly and flush the airbrush by spraying several cups of clean water through it, until the spray shows no trace of paint. Dyes are difficult to clean entirely and may require liquid chlorine bleach to remove the last remnants of the dye color. Make sure the bleach is flushed out thoroughly with fresh water, or it will act on the next dye color used in the airbrush. After cleaning, as a precaution, remove the needle or pull it part way out, so that it will not dry and stick to the nozzle. The needle will be hard to remove if it has become stuck, and forceful removal may damage the delicate tip. Remember to use ammonia to clean an airbrush that has used India ink, particularly black.

Once or twice a year, remove all the accessible parts, particularly the small springs in the air valve and behind the button. The manufacturer encloses a set of illustrated instructions showing which parts can be handled by the nonexpert.

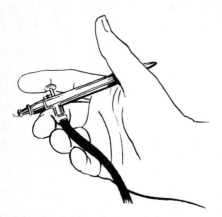

The airbrush is held gently, in much the same manner as a pen, but with less pressure. The thumb and index finger should be free to move without disturbing the airbrush.

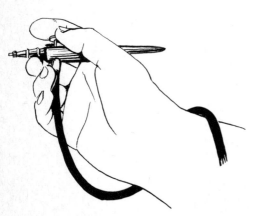

The thumb rests against the airbrush just behind the operating button and acts as a post against which the index finger can press when operating the airbrush. This grip prevents too much pressure on the button and permits subtle control of the airbrush.

(Do *not* touch the nozzle; this is a job for a skilled professional.) Moisten your hands with light oil and thoroughly rub all the parts to lubricate and protect them from rust and wear. This method will not leave so much oil that it gets into the spray.

Even with proper care, parts of the airbrush may become damaged or worn out. Although you can reorder parts by checking them against the parts list that comes with your airbrush, it is advisable, whenever possible, to let a skilled airbrush repairperson do such replacement. As a matter of fact, many airbrush artists take the airbrushes in for repair and readjustment periodically.

There is nothing so satisfying as working with an airbrush that, after a period of difficulty, works like new again. When the airbrush is returned from repair, the case will contain a small slip of paper on which the repairperson has tried several test strokes to be sure that the airbrush is functioning properly. Your art supply store will be able to tell you where such repairs are available.

Common Difficulties

Little or no air. Check your system to make sure the air pressure is sufficient; about twenty to twenty-five pounds is proper for most work. Be sure that all air passages are clean and in working order. The air valve and spring are particularly susceptible to age and decay. Often they may be cleaned and oiled, but occasionally they must be replaced. Check the tip of the airbrush. The tip is adjustable and may be screwed on too tightly, stopping the air.

Little or no paint. Make sure your paint mixture is not too thick and that it has not dried out in use. Thick paint cannot be sucked through the airbrush; the pressure is not that strong. Clean the cup and all the tubes through which the paint must pass. The needle and the hole in which it sits must be clean at all times. Paint will dry out while in use and block

these small, delicate openings. Try adjusting the screw tip. If it is closed too tightly, it slows the air flow, reducing the suction.

If the stoppage has occurred while you are working, try operating the airbrush with only clear water in the cup. Remove the plastic handle and loosen the screw that holds the needle. Now operate the airbrush by holding the air button down and moving the needle in and out by hand. This opens the paint flow to its maximum and will clear minor obstructions.

Paint splattering. If the needle doesn't sit perfectly or if the air flow is the *least bit* uneven, paint will cake on the inner surface of the tip. This will further deflect the air and cause a splatter. Wash this surface with a paintbrush and water.

Check the needle. The point of the needle is quite soft and bends easily. Even normal handling of the airbrush can bend that small part of the needle that protrudes. This will deflect the paint and cause splatter. Remove the needle and roll the point against the flat of your thumbnail. If this is done carefully, the bend can be removed. If a small kink remains, it may often be smoothed down by lightly grinding the point on a fine oilstone. Place a drop of oil on the stone and press the point of the needle flat against the stone with your thumb. With the other hand, rotate the needle gently while withdrawing the needle from under your thumb. Do not do this too much or you will destroy the shape of the needle. If this shaping does not work, replace the needle.

If the paint mixture is too thick or too thin, paint will bead on the end of the needle between strokes. When you start a new stroke, the air will blow this accumulation off all at once, causing a splatter. Change the mixture if you can. If not, test the brush on a piece of scrap before using, or begin the air flow away from the work and start the paint only when you are in proper position.

Water splotch. If your paint has not been mixed thoroughly in the cup, water may unexpectedly come through in the middle of a stroke. Often when you are changing colors and rinsing the cup, water will be left in the system and react the same way. In both cases, an ugly water splotch will result. Always mix your paint *before* putting it into the cup and test the airbrush on a piece of scrap until the color flow is proper.

On compressor systems without a moisture trap, water can condense on a muggy day as the humid air is compressed. When enough water collects, it will be blown into the airbrush, causing a sudden dilution of the paint and resulting in the same ruinous splotch on the artwork. To eliminate this problem, disconnect the airbrush from the hose and run the compressor by itself for a minute or two. If water condensation was your problem, you will see a light fog coming from the hose; this fog will dampen a scrap of paper or the back of your hand. Hold the hose so that all of it hangs below the level of the compressor. This will allow gravity to assist in draining all the water in the system. Continue to run the compressor until this fog disappears and the air feels dry when directed against the back of your hand.

When the air looks and feels dry, reassemble the airbrush and continue working. If considerable work must be done under muggy conditions, repeat the draining process often to prevent water from accumulating.

Uneven strokes. The airbrush does not weigh much and the hose is flexible. Yet they will not respond as smoothly as you might think. The drag of the hose as you move the airbrush over your artwork may be sufficient to disturb your normal rhythm. To prevent any difficulty, drape the hose *over* your wrist by reaching around and under the hose before you grasp the airbrush. This will allow you to maintain a much more sensitive grip.

Clogged paint cup. If paint has been allowed to dry in the cup, remove the small screws that appear on the top and bottom of the tube next to the cup. Straighten out a paper clip and run it through the openings from all directions. This will remove most of the blockage. Rinse the cup under a stream of water and clean the tubes by closing two of the openings at a time and allowing the water to flow through the remaining one. When the cup is clean, oil the screws and reassemble them. Be careful; they're small and easily lost.

Stuck needle. Drying paint will firmly lock the needle in the brush so that it cannot be withdrawn by any normal procedure. In this event, remove the plastic handle and the screw holding the needle. Grip the needle firmly with a pair of pliers and gently pull and twist at the same time. Increase the pressure until the needle comes free. Sometimes it may take a considerable amount of effort to accomplish this.

When the needle is finally removed, it will probably be damaged to some degree. If the point is bent, straighten it by rolling the point against the flat of your thumbnail. Clean the shaft with water and polish it with a piece of crocus cloth. Flush the inside of the airbrush with clean water. This will take some time, as the dried paint must first be dissolved.

If the paint has dried so completely that it resists washing, use a reaming needle. These needles, available as part of your airbrush supplies, are like regular airbrush needles except that a portion of the point has been flattened so that the edges can cut away dried paint. Twist the reaming needle gently two or three times inside the airbrush. Remove the reaming needle and wipe off the paint that has been collected. Repeat this operation until the reaming needle no longer brings out any residue.

Be careful about this procedure. If the reaming is done too vigorously, or too often, it will deform the fragile tip in which the airbrush needle must be seated. Then even a new needle will not fit properly and the damaged part will have to be replaced. Keep the parts list that comes with the airbrush so that you may reorder parts when necessary.

AMBERLITH

Transparent, orange plastic film bonded to a sheet of acetate which is used to prepare overlays for color separation mechanicals. (See also *Rubylith.*)

ANATOMICAL CASTS

Plaster or plastic reproductions of the human body. Heads, torsos, hands, and even full figures are available and offer students and commercial artists an accurate reference for the study of detail. The one limitation is the inflexibility of such casts; they cannot be shifted into a variety of poses or positions. Therefore, they should not be copied slavishly, but used to further your understanding of the structure of the body. (See *Skeletons, Mannequin, Anatomy Charts,* and *Models.*) These sources, used in conjunction with anatomical charts, can help artists fill in detail that may not be clearly visible or easily understood when working from a live model.

ANATOMY CHARTS

Consist of detailed renderings of the muscle and bone structure of the body in a wide variety of poses and views. These charts are usually included in good books on figure drawing, but they are also available individually in separate works or in loose sheet form.

The study of anatomy is perhaps the most important subject art students undertake. All drawing and design is based upon thorough familiarity with the human body. Therefore, the choice of an anatomical reference is extremely important.

Be sure to avoid the cheap, superficial, and often inaccurate material that floods the field. A good, comprehensive anatomical reference is expensive to prepare and will be relatively expensive. But such an investment is worthwhile since it will save you from acquiring faulty or incomplete knowledge which may well lead to the formation of bad habits, or from having to purchase supplemental material.

It is not the place of this book to make specific recommendations of any text or product. It is advisable to consult with a well-established, knowledgeable artist or teacher who can guide your choice of material.

ANIMATION

Animation, in the commercial art field, is creating motion by photographing still-art sequences one picture at a time and projecting the resulting film in a movie projector. This vast field, exemplified by Walt Disney, is responsible for films for education, entertainment, and TV advertising. Its techniques, procedures, and materials are highly specialized and complex. It is one of the few art fields that has unions for its members. This means that the skills necessary to produce animation are not easy to acquire, though this has not prevented a strong resurgence of interest in the profession. One stimulus has been the computer and the amazing special animation effects it can produce. Television (with its commercials) is also providing an expanded audience for the technique.

Special training in school or an apprenticeship are necessary to become familiar with the procedures, tools, and materials. Some books give sufficient information to begin practicing animation, and, fortunately, the medium lends itself well to amateur efforts with 8 mm film equipment.

A brief description will give you a general idea of the animation process. First, layout drawings are produced in

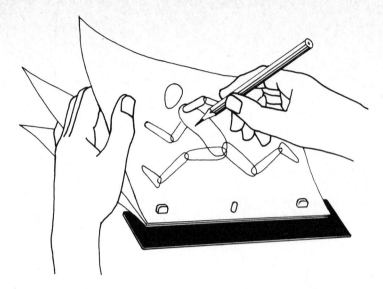

Typical animation situation. Three drawings on punched bond paper are firmly registered on a peg bar. The top two sheets are held so that the drawings can be fanned in sequence to allow the animator to review the action.

pencil. Each succeeding drawing is nearly identical to the previous one, with only a slight alteration of the portion that is to move. To insure exact register of these layout drawings, the paper that they are drawn on is punched with holes at the top and the paper is placed over corresponding pegs on an animation disk. The animation disk is a circular metal frame with a glass face, lighted from beneath, thus the previous drawing can be seen through the top paper and acts as a guide to subsequent drawing. The disk rotates so that work can be done on all parts of the paper without disturbing the pegs.

Once a sequence of action is laid out, the drawings are traced with ink or paint on acetate animation cels that have been punched with identical holes. Any rendering or coloring is added, and the finished animation cels are taken to an animation camera. The animation camera is a motion-picture camera that can be operated one frame at a time. A separate background drawing is placed on a stand beneath the camera, and a single animation cel is placed over it on pegs that are identical to those on the animation disk. Both the camera and the pegged portion of the stand, which can be moved in many different ways, are adjusted to the proper position and a single picture is taken. The cel is removed, replaced with the next cel in the sequence, the camera is adjusted if necessary, a picture taken, and the process repeated until all the cels have been photographed. When the resulting film is projected, the drawings appear to be moving.

This is only a general summary of the entire animation process. It does not mention any of the problems of synchronizing sound with lip movements, preparing instructions for the camera operator, or any of the other myriad considerations that make this one of the most exciting and difficult professions. More than any other branch of commercial art, animation requires thorough technical preparation as well as artistic skill. (See *Computer Animation.*)

ANIMATION CELS

Sheets of acetate (see *Plastic Films*) that have been cut to a standard size (10¼″ × 12½″) and punched with standard holes that conform with pegs used by various animation systems. (See also *Animation*.)

ARCHITECT'S SCALE

Prismatic-shaped rule containing several scales used for translating dimensions in preparing scale drawings. (See *Rulers*.)

ART GUM

Soft, crumbly eraser (sometimes called a soap eraser) used for removing pencil and other light marks from paper. (See *Erasers*.)

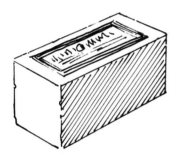

Art gum eraser.

ART MARKERS

(See *Markers*.)

ARTYPE

Product brand name of a transfer type. One of the first products of this nature to become available commercially, its name has become generic, referring to all kinds of transfer type whether similar to artype or not. (See *Transfer Type*.)

ATOMIZER, MOUTH TYPE

The mouth-type atomizer is made with two small tubes that are simply hinged

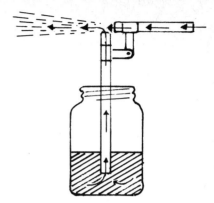

Mouth-type atomizer, showing the flow of air and liquid.

on a pivot so that they may be placed at right angles to each other. The end of the longer tube is placed in a jar of liquid, and air is blown by mouth through the opposite end of the smaller tube. The air, blowing over the open end of the tube in the liquid, causes the liquid to rise in the tube and scatter over the working surface.

The atomizer may be used with any fluid such as paint, shellac, etc. Fixative is practically the only medium sprayed in this manner today, since the large, coarse spray of an atomizer is unsuitable for most other purposes. The aerosol spray can has replaced the atomizer in virtually all the mediums, including fixative. However, in an emergency, when no other device is available, the atomizer will do.

Common Difficulty

Spattering. This kind of atomizer produces a spray that is coarse, with relatively large droplets. For this reason, always place the surface to be sprayed upright and hold the atomizer about 1–1½″ away. This will cause the larger droplets to fall before they reach the surface, and prevent them from collecting on the surface and running. Similarly, an unevenness in the spray can be caused by the difficulty of maintaining a constant force of air when blowing with the mouth. Practice a few times to determine the proper distance and amount of force that will produce the best results in each different situation.

ATTACHE CASES

Since everyone now carries an attaché case, you are probably familiar with them. These cases—whether ultra slim, soft leathered models or bulky, covered-cardboard bargains—offer attractive alternatives or supplements to portfolios. There are almost as many choices of cases as there are individuals, and although the attaché case is not one of the artist's required pieces of equipment, its versatility makes it very useful.

In the medium price range, there are cases that come with deep storage space and contain folding files. These models are helpful for the artist who must travel to the client. In them can be carried layouts, artwork, and enough drawing materials to perform discussion layouts or art corrections on the spot.

Art stores carry some attaché cases, but you can probably find them more easily in luggage stores and department stores (See also *Portfolios.*)

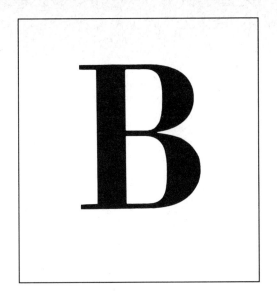

Look closely at a picture in the newspaper where a coarse screen is used, and you can see these dots very clearly. But when an area of flat tone must appear, this process will not work.

Optically, more light seems to bounce off certain areas and creates a splotchy effect that makes large, even-colored areas look very messy. Day created a mechanical screen that was completely even and that could produce dots on the plate directly without using the photographic screen. Eventually he created many other textual patterns that could be applied in the same manner, which lent variety to the tones produced.

Today when the bulk of our printing is done by offset lithography, these tones are added to the photographic negatives on the stripping table, but the process is still referred to as benday. For the most part, these tones are limited to the dot pattern. These value screens are available at any platemaking establishment, and are usually ordered by percentage. An area to be tinted in this manner is outlined in blue (so that the outline will not photograph) and a notation is included on the overlay above the area. For instance, an area marked "20% B.D." is an instruction to the platemaker to place a screen of dots over the marked area that will produce a tint that is 20% of the solid color being printed on the plate. Some organizations use a letter code, which means that you must have a sample card to compare. However, if you give the percentage, any platemaker can match it without trouble. Different art studios and printers may have different ways of denoting these screens. Become familiar

BEAM COMPASS

A form of compass distinguished by a bar of metal upon which the legs are moved independently. (See *Compasses.*)

BENDAY

Ben Day is the name of the man who invented a process of creating halftone effects on printing plates by mechanical means. If you are familiar with the printing processes, you know that values cannot be achieved on a printing plate. Only a solid color can be imprinted, so that values must be approximated by using a series of small dots that create a visual mixture on the printed paper. With photographs and other continuous-tone art, the dots are created by using a photographic screen when the plates are made.

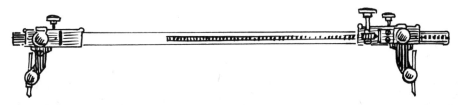

A high-quality beam compass with a wormgear mechanism to eliminate slippage.

with all the printing processes and learn to cooperate with your printers. They will be able to explain their operation and teach you the way they prefer instructions to be prepared.

BINDINGS

There are many occasions when several sheets of material must be bound for presentation. Flip charts, booklets, folders, are often produced in small quantities, by hand, and need to be bound. Such binding is most often accomplished today by using plastics in strap, tube, or continuous spiral form. These plastics are passed through holes punched in the presentation sheets, holding them together attractively. For the most part this binding service is best performed by a commercial bindery. Check your classified telephone directory for the name and location of such a bindery. If none are listed, a local printer may either perform the service or know where it is available.

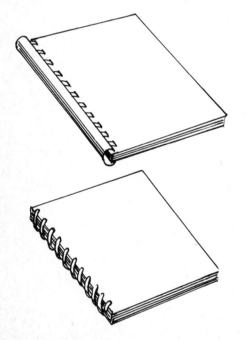

Two examples of binding. Top is a common plastic binder. Bottom is spiral binding.

You can purchase kits that allow you to punch the holes and form the plastic into a binding. (See *Saddle Stitching*.)

Common Difficulties

Margins. All plastic binding techniques require a minimum ¼" space. Make sure that you have allowed for this dimension in planning your margins.

Gutter. The gutter, the space between two facing pages, is widened by a plastic binding. In addition to the space occupied by the binding holes, there will be an opening caused by the size of the plastic spine itself. Material that must read across the gutter is, therefore, interrupted. Design your pages accordingly. Some bindings are less distracting then others. Check your binding beforehand, with an actual sample if possible, so that you can take this factor into account.

BLOTTING PAPER

Soft, felt-like paper used for conventional blotters, and valuable to artists for several purposes.

Wash drawings. Washes are applied with copious amounts of liquid. When the wash has been completed, a large pool of excess liquid remains. If this liquid is not removed, it may drip over the rest of the drawing, or dry unevenly, creating a mottled appearance. The excess liquid can be sucked up with blotting paper. Take care that the paper touches only the liquid, not the drawing. In this way, the drawing will not be harmed, even though the excess liquid is eliminated.

Correcting ink mistakes. Errors that have been made with ink, even India ink, can be removed quite easily if they are treated quickly. The longer the ink lies on the paper, the deeper into the fibers it penetrates. If the ink can be dried before penetrating too deeply, it can be scraped off with a razor blade, or rubbed off with a clean ink eraser.

(See *Erasers.*) If the ink has penetrated too deeply, these same actions will dig into the paper, fraying the paper fibers and creating a torn surface that is just as ugly as the original error. Blotting paper can speed the drying of such ink without spreading the error, making the swift, clean correction possible.

Cleaning tools. Lettering pens, ruling pens, etc., are much easier to use if ink or paint can be removed from them quickly before they cake or harden. Since the openings in these tools are small and hard to get at, this is not easy to do without stopping to do a complete cleaning, and the tendency is to avoid trying to clean them while you are working. Blotting paper fits into the small openings easily and the absorbency of the paper draws the fluids out without difficulty. Keep a few scraps of blotting paper handy while you are working to keep the tools clean and functioning properly.

Blotting paper, without the hard paper backing found on conventional advertising blotters, can be purchased at most art supply stores and stationers.

BLUEPRINT FILES

Usually a wooden or metal storage cabinet with large, shallow drawers, designed to hold blueprint drawings and materials for architects and engineers. The shape of the cabinet drawers makes them suitable for holding artists' drawings and materials as well. (See *Filing Cabinets, Flat.*)

BLUEPRINTS

Simple paper negatives produced by exposing sensitized papers to light and developing with heat and chemical fumes. The nature of the paper is such that the negative areas are colored blue and the lines are left white, hence the name. The most common blueprints are used by engineers, architects, and construction workers. These blueprints are produced by preparing drawings in pencil or ink on transparent cloth or paper. These original drawings are placed over a sheet of unexposed blueprint paper and exposed to strong light. The exposed paper is developed in a machine that automatically subjects the paper to the chemical fumes, producing a dry copy. The process is repeated for each additional copy.

Printers use the blueprint process to proof, or test, their negatives prior to making plates for the printing press. All the negatives representing one printed piece are assembled in accurate register. The assembled package is exposed simultaneously on one negative, and the print developed. The resulting copy may be difficult for the nonprofessional to read, for any areas being overprinted will cancel each other out. Depending on the printing method used, the blueprint may appear as a positive or negative. This copy gives the printer and the client the chance to make one last check for errors and position before the plates are made.

You must be familiar with the process for you will be asked by the printer if you want "blues." ("Blues" is the common term used in the trade.) Any error discovered after the blues have been okayed is your fault, and you must pay the printer for the correction. If the job is more than one color, or if it contains many pieces that have to be stripped into position by the printer, be sure to check the blues. Some printers will try to avoid the step if they are rushed. Any errors that occur without blueprint checking will be blamed on you as the result of faulty artwork. Make sure everything is correct on the blues before the job goes to press.

A similar process produces a brown and white negative, and these copies are called "Van Dykes"—probably due to the deep brown color. These are the same as blueprints in all respects and are used for the same purposes.

When your job involves four-color, process color (photographs and full color renderings, for example), a blueprint will allow you to check for position only. The result of printing four negatives at once, each with some material on it, produces a white hole the size and shape of the original. While this will allow you to discover positional errors, it will not let you check the quality of the color printing. (See *Progressive Proofs.*)

BOND PAPER

Name given to a series of lightweight papers used commercially for stationery and writing, as well as for layout and drawing in the art field. Art bonds are sold in sheets or pads in just about any size at all art stores. Bonds are referred to as layout, visualizer, drawing, or sketching papers. These terms may also apply to other papers, as well. Although the names may not indicate their composition, bond papers are distinguished by their light weight and their near opacity. There are a limited range of colors available, usually through commercial paper houses or printers. (See *Papers and Boards.*)

BOURGES

Brand name (pronounced burgess and named after its inventor) of a line of tinted acetate overlays. Because it was the first of its kind, the name is associated with any of the subsequently introduced tinted acetate overlays. Today, the name has lost some of its earlier connotations and the products no longer have their prior availability.

The distinctive characteristics of Bourges sheets are their limited range of colors, their gradation in a set progression of tint percentages that correspond to benday designations, and their creation of these tints with the use of actual benday screens. These factors permit a layout that accurately resembles the effect of a printed piece. Bourges sheets are

coated with an adhesive backing. Desired shapes are cut, removed from their protective backing, and adhered to art work and mechanicals. (See also *Shading Sheets, Overlays, Tinted Acetate,* and *Pressure Graphics.*)

BOW COMPASS

Name given to a group of compasses whose legs are held together by a C-clamp. These are the most effective and durable compasses produced. (See *Compasses.*)

BRAYER

A rubber roller, the axle of which is connected to a handle, permitting free turning of the roller. The brayer is used primarily to apply printing ink on a metal, wood, or linoleum printing plate. Printing ink, from either a tube or a can, is placed on a flat, nonabsorbent surface. The brayer is rolled over the surface many times in different directions to spread the ink evenly on both the surface and the roller. The brayer is then rolled over the plate, transferring ink to the printing surface. (See *Inks, Printing.*)

The brayer is also a good painting tool. Many artists create unusual and delightful effects by working with a brayer. Variations can be made by applying the paint directly from the tube to the brayer, or by rolling the brayer over paint on a

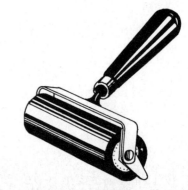

Brayer, or roller, for applying ink and paint.

palette first. Several colors may be applied at one time, and mixed or scattered by the rolling action of the brayer. Use the brayer with different mediums and on different surfaces for various effects.

Extremes of heat and cold and chemical reactions caused by leftover paint and ink can damage the rubber roller, so always clean the brayer carefully after each use. Always store the brayer so that the roller is free from any pressure or flat sides will result.

Common Difficulties

Ragged edges. The pressure of printing will squeeze excess ink from the plate beyond the desired printing areas. Never overload a brayer or a printing plate with ink. Roll the inked brayer over the plate only once or twice. If there is still too much ink, wipe the brayer with a cloth and repeat the inking procedure.

Uneven coverage. If too little ink is applied, the impression may appear mottled. Try rolling the brayer two or more times over the plate. If this does not improve the impression, increase the amount of ink and repeat the inking procedure. If the impression is still imperfect, check the brayer, plate, and source of pressure. Any unevenness existing on these surfaces will impair the proper transfer of ink.

BRISTOL

Name for a series of heavy, opaque, commercial printing or drawing papers and boards. Commercial bristols are sold in bulk to printers; drawing bristols are available in different size sheets in any quantity at art supply stores. Drawing bristols offer two surfaces: kid—a natural, matte texture—and plate—a smooth, glossy surface. These drawing bristols are also sold in three weights: single ply, two ply, and three ply. Single ply is similar to a heavy bond paper, while three ply is just short of being a fairly rigid board and is called bristol board. Bristols make up the largest category of commercial drawing papers for finished artwork. Bristols are also the papers used to provide the surface for illustration boards. (See *Papers and Boards.*)

BRONZING LIQUID MEDIUM

A clear lacquer used for applying metallic pigments in powdered form. (See *Bronzing Powders.*)

BRONZING POWDERS

Metallic pigments in powdered form. These powders are mixed with a bronzing liquid medium, a form of lacquer, and applied with a paintbrush. Artists use bronzing powders in order to obtain a metallic effect with paint. Although most paint lines include a range of already prepared metallic colors, the best effects are created and the widest range of hues are available with bronzing powders. These powders come in more than dozen metallic shades and hues, from silver to gold.

To prepare the medium for painting, a portion of the powder is placed in a dish and an equal amount of the bronzing liquid medium is added. When stirred, the powder is taken in suspension by the fluid (not dissolved) and the resulting mixture may be handled like lacquer or paint. As the lacquer dries, it binds the powder thoroughly without destroying any of its metallic sheen or allowing it to flake or dust off. Bronzing powders can be used on any surface that will take lacquer: plastics, glass doors, wooden signs and displays, and heavy papers.

Common Difficulties

Thinness. Since the powder is not dissolved, clear or thin areas may result when too little powder is suspended in the mixture. In this case, add more powder. If such thinness happens only after a period of use, settling has occurred. Stir the mixture to restore the powder into the suspension. The bronzing powders are heavy and settle quickly, so stirring may have to be done frequently.

Another cause of thinness can be the addition of solvents. As the mixture dries, it may become too stiff to be used easily. The natural tendency is to thin the mixture with a solvent. However, solvents tend to destroy the suspension qualities of the medium, and the powder will settle out much faster—even while it is being applied. Try to mix only as much as can be used in a short time. More can always be mixed as needed.

Caking. If too much powder is added to the medium, it cannot be taken into suspension fully and will lump and cake. Once again the tendency is to thin the mixture with solvents, but this is incorrect. Thin the mixture only by adding more medium. If the mixture becomes too hard and dry, the medium may not be able to return the mixture to a smooth consistency. In this case, discard the mixture and prepare a fresh batch.

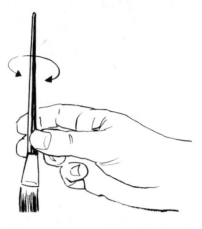

The best way to hold a lettering brush to take full advantage of the chisel-edge characteristics. The brush is easily turned by twirling the fingers so that the broad face of the brush is always facing the direction of the stroke.

BRUSH, LETTERING

Any brush can be used for lettering, but several are constructed primarily for lettering. These brushes, similar to conventional brushes in all other respects, have a chisel-shaped point. Like the chisel-point pencil, these brushes are excellent for single-stroke lettering.

These brushes may be called lettering brushes, sign writing brushes, show card brushes, riggers, or stripers; they come in a wide range of sizes, materials, and prices.

The entire field of brush lettering is not easy, and requires extensive study and practice. For example, although the illustration shows the preferred way to hold a lettering brush, this grip is unnatural and awkward for most people. The brush itself is only part of the lettering procedure. If you wish to pursue this specialty, you should enroll in a good course on the subject, read the various

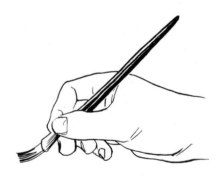

The conventional method of holding a drawing tool. This grip prevents the brush from turning with the stroke and makes creating strokes of even width difficult if not impossible.

publications that describe the methods, or apprentice yourself to a sign writer. In all cases, you will need a good understanding of letter forms and a large amount of patience.

The lettering brush is similar to any fine paintbrush and should be cared for in the same way. (See *Brushes, Paint*.)

BRUSH, STENCIL

Stiff-bristled, round-headed brush made specifically for use with *stencils*. In the stencil technique, paint is applied through an opening in a mask or stencil. Allowing the paint to flow too heavily during this process permits the paint to seep under the edges of the stencil. Therefore, a little paint at a time must be blotted or dabbed with quick vertical strokes so that the paint is not forced under the edges. The stiff bristles of the stencil brush withstand the strenuous action and do not bend easily. Such bending would force paint under the edges of the stencil.

The stencil brush is useful for creating stippled paint techniques with or without the stencil. Dabbing paint from the brush on paper produces a round mark with soft edges caused by the small dots left by the bristles on the edge of the brush. Overlapping strokes will create many blending variations. (See *Stencil Brush* and *Stipple Brush*.)

BRUSH WASHER

A metal coil affixed to an inverted metal U. The ends of the U are inserted into tubes attached to the sides of a metal can that forms the base of the unit. Water (or a cleaning solution) may be placed directly into the can or into a glass jar that fits into the can. Inverted brushes, held by the coil, will remain suspended with only the tips immersed in fluid, soaking and preventing the paint from hardening and damaging the brushes.

The coils also allow brushes to be held without touching the liquid, and thus are

safely out of the way while working.

The glass jars may be purchased separately to replace breakage, or the jars may be used alone for storing plenty of fresh water.

Common Difficulties

Brush damage. Prolonged soaking in any liquid destroys the "spring" or "snap" of the hairs, causing the brush to lose its shape. Avoid leaving the brushes in the soaking position. After each work session remove brushes from the washer and clean them thoroughly. (See *Brushes, Paint*.)

Breakage. The metal coil is inserted into tubes in the base of the brush washer, but it is not fastened. The friction of these parts makes it seem as though the joint were permanent. Do *not* pick up the washer by the coil, because it may come apart and drop, breaking the glass water jar or spilling fluid on the working area.

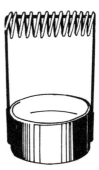

Brush washer with metal coil for holding soaking brushes.

BRUSHES, PAINT

Paintbrushes are important tools for artists, and therefore should be familiar to them. Paintbrushes are made from a wide range of materials, natural and synthetic, depending on the intended use of the brush. A brush is evaluated primarily by its ability to retain its shape during and after use. A good brush will perform equally well when used with most any medium. For these reasons, you should

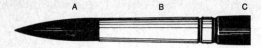

Typical paintbrush with (A) bristles, (B) ferrule, and (C) handle.

only select brushes that are made of the finest materials.

Paintbrushes come in two general shapes—flat and pointed. The flat brushes are not used much by the commercial artist with the exception of lettering, both comprehensive layout and sign writing (or showcard). (See *Lettering Pens.*) Other than these specialized lettering brushes, flat brushes are used for oil painting or laying large, flat areas in watercolor. Since these are not subjects to be covered by this book, we are more concerned with the pointed brushes that are commonly used by the commercial artist.

The finest paintbrushes are constructed of fine natural hairs, preferably sable, hand-picked, trimmed, shaped, and bonded to a wooden handle by glue and a metal ferrule. Other materials, including bristles, hairs from other animals, and synthetic fibers, may perform simple tasks satisfactorily and are cheaper to use when the painting action is destructive. A prime example is the nylon brush that has been introduced for use with acrylic paints. These paints do not perform well with, and are very destructive to, the conventional brushes. But since acrylic paints are more useful to the fine artist and illustrator, there will be little need for the commercial artist to make use of such materials.

In any event, use the finest brand you can afford. Your art supply dealer can inform you about the best available. Oddly enough, the quality of brushes may vary considerably. A brand that has enjoyed a fine reputation for a time may suddenly perform in an inferior manner. Similarly, a lower-priced brand may become highly prized. This is due to the supply and cost of available hairs. Two of the most enduring, dependable, and popular brands have been Winsor & Newton and Grumbacher. Both of these firms, as well as many other reputable manufacturers, offer a wide range of brushes in many sizes, lengths, and thicknesses for use with any medium. There is no standard for choosing any one of them; cost, personal preference, habit, availability, etc., will all affect your choice. The nature of the work in the commercial art field and the mediums involved (India ink and water-based paint for the most part) usually make sable the best choice. These brushes come in sizes from the smallest (00 or 000) up to the largest (usually 12 or 14, although some brush lines may offer large brushes up to size 28 or larger). Few commercial artists need very many of these latter sizes. Perhaps a typical commercial art studio would have very small brushes (0, 00, or 000) for fine detail work and corrections, a medium size (2 or 3) for the most general work, and a few very large brushes (8 to 14) for the rare occasions when large areas must be covered. Although these brushes are expensive, they can last for many years, if used with care.

There is little to be said about the use of a paintbrush. Individuals develop their own mannerisms quite early, and they tend to stay with them for the rest of their lives. Most people grip a brush as they would a pen or pencil, and this seems to be adequate, although many people tend to clench the brush too hard. This overly firm grip reduces the possible size of a stroke to a very small and choppy slash that is performed completely by the fingers. Such a stroke is hard to control and causes the artist to press even harder. The best results are obtained when the action is governed by the full arm and shoulder, requiring a very gentle (but firm) hold on the brush. Try drawing a long, curved stroke with only your fingers. To do this, you will plant the heel of your hand firmly on the drawing surface and make a cramped arc of an inch or so. Then lift your hand, move it, and repeat the sequence until the curve is completed. Now try the same curve *without* using your fingers. Mentally *lock* your elbow, wrist, and fingers, but hold the brush lightly. Now start to paint the curve, but mentally try to draw it with your *shoulder.* You will find that even your body will move slightly as the stroke progresses, *but* you will produce the curve with one continuous, rhythmic sweep. Granted, you may not be very accurate the first time, but the line you do produce will look more graceful and accurate than the series of tight little jerks that the fingers produced. With practice you will develop confidence, and with confidence and experience you will be able to produce any line with complete control and accuracy. This method allows the character of the brush to come into play. A good sable brush has what is called snap or body. This means that the brush tries to retain its original shape. As the hairs are bent in a drawing stroke, they do not limply relax; they fight to return to their normal position. This action, if not interrupted, produces a very smooth sweep that the artist uses and dominates. Let's use an analogy. Watch a new driver handle a car. Unfamiliar with the mechanics of the action, an inexperienced driver will oversteer. Trying to turn, he/she will make the steering wheel control every inch of the turn and grip the wheel too tightly. As a result, the turn will be jerky and uneven. An experienced driver *knows* that the car will always try to right itself in a turn, and will *lightly* hold the wheel in a turn to permit the motion to do most of the turning, producing a smooth, graceful turn. It's the same with a paintbrush. Don't over control. Learn to use the brush's characteristics.

Like all good tools, brushes require care. Never leave a brush uncleaned, but also never leave a brush in water. Rinse the brush thoroughly while using it, and wash it carefully with warm water and mild soap when you are finished. First stroke the brush lightly over a cake of soap until it lathers, then place the bristle portion of the brush against your open palm and scrub gently, but firmly, to work the suds into the heel of the brush. Rinse in running warm water, never hot. Repeat this process until the brush is clean. Point the brush against your palm, or point it with your fingers or with your lips. Allow the brush to dry completely in an open position so that the hairs do not become bent. If brushes are to be stored or a long time or carried about, leave a very small residue of soap in the bristles. The soap will harden and protect the point, but will dissolve easily when next used. If you are storing brushes for long periods of time, place a few mothballs in with the brushes to protect them from moths.

Common Difficulties

Splitting. The point of a brush will become undependable if paint accumulates in the heel or if the character of the bristle is destroyed. Always clean the brush as described above. When using inks or similarly corrosive media, clean the brush often and add a little ammonia to the water in order to dissolve the harmful agents. Any brush that is used with ink will deteriorate rapidly. Plan on having several on hand for replacement.

Shedding. Hairs will fall out of the ferrule if you scrub too much with the brush. Hot water will weaken the glue in the ferrule, forcing the hairs to come loose. In some cases this will not destroy the brush, merely diminish the size of the bristles, and the brush may still be used. Once the hairs begin to fall out, however, nothing can be done and the brush must be replaced. Keep old brushes on hand to mix paints and to perform other tasks that might harm a new brush.

Looseness. Extended usage or harsh cleaning may cause the ferrule to come unglued from the handle. Such a brush may not be damaged. Temporarily take a piece of tape and wrap it around the handle and ferrule. If the tape is kept small, the feel of the brush will not be altered. Later, you can reattach the ferrule with an adhesive like epoxy glue.

Streaking. Large areas of paint are difficult to apply without leaving streaks. For this operation, always use as large a brush as possible. Outside of the normal range of brush sizes, there are very large brushes called "background brushes." These will handle large areas with comparative ease.

Drying. When doing fine detail work, it may be unwise to use the smaller sizes of brushes, as they are too small to hold sufficient amounts of paint and dry out quickly. Even very fine detail can be accomplished with a 2 or 3 brush, while this larger brush size permits enough paint to be carried to prevent fast drying. Practice and experience will tell you which size works best under varying conditions.

BULLETIN BOARDS

Any penetrable surface to which items may be attached with pushpins or thumbtacks. These boards may be bought in a variety of sizes and materials, with and without framing borders. The materials may also be purchased separately and the boards constructed to fit any area or decorative scheme. Artists use bulletin boards to post assignments, scrap, memos, inspirational materials, etc., in convenient view without cluttering up the work area.

If you wish to fill an extensive area with bulletin boards, check your local lumber yard. There will be a larger selection of materials at lower costs than at the art or furniture stores. For instance, homosote, a cardboard conglomerate, is available in sheets of 4' x 8' and is very inexpensive. This material is light, can be cut with a mat knife, and holds tacks and pins very well. Homosote can be mounted with nails, screws, or glue, and a little paint will turn its drab gray color into an attractive surrounding for your work area. Lumber yards sell cork board in many sizes and shades which also works very well as a bulletin board. These cork boards are easily attached to any surface; many of them come with a pressure sensitive backing, and the texture is handsome and needs no painting.

These are only a few suggestions among a range of unlimited possibilities. Your own imagination will allow you to produce an environment conducive to creative work, while affording you an area upon which you can continually and impulsively attach items that have stimulated you.

BURNISHER

A smooth plastic tool, not unlike a cuticle stick, that is used to supply rubbing pressure to transfer and adhere material from wax-coated sheets. The nature of these sheets is such that any sharp pressure from a hard point, like a pencil or ballpoint pen, can damage the film or the material on it. The burnisher, or any rounded surface such as a spoon bowl or the flat of a fingernail, diffuses the pressure, protecting the delicate transfer material and insuring a firm bond. The burnisher is not to be confused with a similar metal tool used to prepare engraved printing plates. (See *Transfer Type* and *Shading Sheets.*)

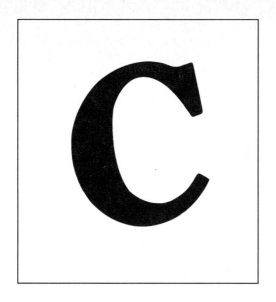

CALLIGRAPHY

The practice of handlettering with a single stroke of a pen, brush, or other writing instruments using antique cursive styles and flourishes. Although practiced primarily as a fine art or hobby, calligraphy finds many applications in modern commercial art, from greeting cards to advertising. Calligraphy requires little more than tools, materials, style books, and much practice. Although sparingly used by professional commercial artists, production of calligraphic testimonials, mottoes, and invitations can be a profitable and satisfying sideline. (See also *Handlettering and Illuminating.*)

CAMERA LUCIDA

Enlarges or reduces artwork by permitting the artist to trace an apparent projection of the image. It is a simple stand equipped with an interchangeable set of prismatic lenses. These prisms bend light rays at a right angle, so that the image of a piece of art placed vertically in front of the camera lucida stand is projected into the eyes of a viewer above the stand.

To the viewer, however, it appears that the art is actually on the table beneath the lens. If a piece of paper is placed there, beneath the lens, the viewer may copy the art by tracing the apparent image on the paper. By varying the lens and the distance from the lens to the art reference, the apparent image may be enlarged or reduced to any desired size. Other lenses and changes in the angle of the artwork will allow you to flop the image or correct perspective distortions of photographs. The instructions for these procedures are provided with the camera lucida, which can be purchased at art supply stores.

In its simplest form, the camera lucida may be found as a child's toy and costs very little. Such a set usually contains only a single lens of limited quality, is incapable of any appreciable size variation, and has little use for the commercial artist. Professional camera lucida sets are very well constructed, contain a wide range of lenses, and are packaged in durable, velvet-lined cases. These sets are quite expensive, as is any high-quality optical instrument. For this reason, they must be handled with care.

The professional camera lucida takes some time to set up properly and to make the adjustments necessary to arrive at the desired size. However, this limitation is balanced to a degree by its convenient size. The camera lucida is quite portable, can be set up anywhere, and takes no permanent space in a studio. Its cost is only a fraction of the bigger, more permanent enlarger-reducers. (See *Lacey Luci.*)

Despite these advantages of the camera lucida, most professionals prefer to work with the enlarger/reducers or with photostats, since these can be used immediately without preparation. If it is inconvenient for you to use these more expensive alternatives, ask your art supply dealer for a demonstration of a camera lucida. There is probably one in the price range you can afford. (See *Projector, Art.*)

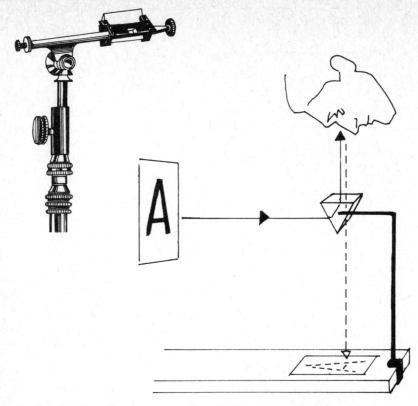

The camera lucida principle is that the image is bent by the prism up into the viewer's eye. Since the eye observes in a straight line, the image appears to be below the prism on the copy paper.

CARBON PAPER

The most familiar carbon paper has a soft, greasy coating on one side and is used to produce duplicate copies in a typewriter or with a writing instrument. The marks produced by this carbon paper smudge easily, are nearly impossible to erase cleanly, and cannot be covered with paint. These conditions make regular carbon paper inadequate for commercial art use, and a number of special "carbon papers" are prepared primarily for the artist.

Graphite paper. This is prepared with the same graphite used to make lead pencils; the lines can be erased as easily as pencil after the work is finished. For this reason, graphite paper is used for any transferral of a drawing whose guide lines must be removed from the final rendering.

Sand paper. These transfer papers offer a graphite sheet and four colors as well: red, white, yellow, and blue. All of these papers are non-greasy and are available in rolls as well as sheets. The papers transfer satisfactorily on matte or glossy surfaces, and the lines may be erased or covered with paint.

Although all of these papers are excellent for tracing purposes, you can readily make your own in an emergency. Rub a 2B pencil on a sheet of tracing paper or visualizer paper. A softer pencil will produce too much graphite, which will smudge. A harder pencil may not produce a dark enough coating to leave a satisfactory tracing.

To make copying paper for dark surfaces, use white pastel chalk. Rub the chalk thoroughly into the paper and coat with a very, very light spray of fixative to cut down dust smudges. Pressure of the tracing pencil or stylus will break this flimsy coating and allow the chalk to make the transfer. Test this chalk paper first; there may be insufficient chalk or fixative on the paper to work well, and it may be necessary to add more of either.

Many artists prefer to make their own transfer papers, because they can control the color, intensity, and nature of the material used. Lines made thus are usually quite impermanent and are easily erased from the finished work. This is particularly true with silk-screened color stocks, such as Color-Aid, and printed papers like Pantone. Although these papers are quite durable, they are easily marked, and repeated erasure only exaggerates the original error. When working on such a surface after the tracing has been completed it is wise to use a slip sheet. Your hands can smudge the transfer lines and permanently mar the surface.

CARBON PENCIL

A name sometimes given to a form of charcoal pencil, the best known of which is the Wolff carbon pencil. (See *Charcoal.*)

CARBORUNDUM

The commercial name for an exclusive, artificial abrasive stone. It is harder and more durable than natural stone abrasives. Abrasives have many uses in industry, but artists are primarily concerned with oilstones and whetstones they can sharpen knives and drawing pens on. (See *Whetstones.*)

CARTOON COLORS

This is a brand name and a general category of paints used in the animation industry for painting on acetate cels. (See *Paints.*)

CASEIN

Casein, a water-based paint with a glue binder that is derived from milk curds, is almost exclusively a fine art medium. A traditional supplement to and substitute for oil paints, commercially prepared casein is available in tubes. Although it has many characteristics that resemble modern gouaches, casein never really took hold in the commercial field, where its place has largely been taken by acrylics.

Common Difficulties

Odor. The odor of the casein paints is quite pronounced and is offensive to many people. Additionally, some of the colors can curdle, or go sour. While this doesn't seem to affect the painting qualities, the paint does become grainy and the smell can become quite foul.

Drying. Although casein dries superficially in a matter of minutes, it does not really harden for a long time. But once it has hardened, it is waterproof and cannot be softened again. These two qualities cause problems. Commercial art, with its heavy use of lettering, often requires the addition of type over a painting. The most popular method of applying such lettering today is by the use of transfer type. But the slow hardening of casein prevents the proper adhesion of such materials, and they may not "take" on casein until it has dried for several days. In some instances, the paint may remain so soft that overpainting will dissolve the undercoat.

Conversely, once the paint is dry and hard, it cannot be removed. This makes it difficult to clean from tools and working surfaces. There is a casein brush and hand cleaner, but it is not too effective on delicate instruments that have been clogged with dried casein, and brushes are virtually ruined once the paint has been allowed to cake on them. The answer, again, is to keep the tools clean, even while you are working; and, of course, clean everything thoroughly once you are finished.

Dullness. Casein colors tend to lack the brilliance associated with other water paints. Coating the finished painting with a casein varnish will enhance the warmth of the painting and impart a glossy surface to the matte paint texture. The general effect of casein paints, however, is still rather subdued.

Muddy color. Casein colors do not intermix well. But they do blend with other water-based paints. When it is necessary to produce a blended color, it is wise to mix a tempera paint with the casein. The finished painting will still have all the properties of casein, but the colors will be purer.

CASEIN SHELLAC

A special, synthetic shellac prepared for use with casein paint. The shellac covers, protects, and imparts a finish that causes the casein painting to resemble an oil painting.

CEL

Designation derived from the abbreviation of celluloid that is applied to any clear plastic sheet. Used mainly in the animation field, where it originated, the term may be encountered in other applications. (See *Animation Cels.*)

CEL-GRIP

A brand name for a fluid that can be added to any liquid medium, such as watercolor paint, to prevent chipping and flaking from plastic and glossy surfaces. (See *Acetate Mediums.*)

CELLOPHANE TAPE

This is a transparent tape used by artists to repair torn art, reinforce fragile paper edges, join drawings or overlays, and similar binding jobs. (See *Scotch Tape.*)

CELLULOID

The first commercially successful plastic film, celluloid is brittle and flammable. For these reasons it has been largely replaced by cellulose acetate. Celluloid never attained a very wide use in commercial art except in the manufacture of movie film, but its abbreviated name—cel—is still applied to any plastic film, particularly the one used in the field of animation. (See *Plastic Films.*)

CENTER BOW COMPASS

A variation of the bow compass which has the control mechanism for setting the width of the leg opening located between the legs. This construction provides the most accurate and durable positioning of the legs. (See *Compasses.*)

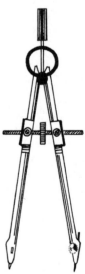

Center bow compass. Legs are positioned by turning the central screw.

CHALKS, LAYOUT

A selection of hard pastels prepared in shades of gray for use in creating halftone illustrations and tinted areas in black-

and-white layouts. Depending on the set purchased, there are usually three or four shades of gray in two tonal ranges—warm and cool in six or eight sticks—plus black and white. A more complete set includes colored pencils of matching values. The pencils are used for fine-line detail work and lettering and match the gray values of the pastels, which are used for large area coverage.

Although the warm and cool tones are designed to be used independently to duplicate the effects of different photographic or printing techniques, many artists prefer to intermix them. Pastels should not be rubbed or blended in most layout techniques, and the three or four values in these sets cannot produce renderings of any great complexity. Using both warm and cool tones in combination overcomes this limitation and creates visual effects of great variety.

The layout chalks and pencils are handled in the same way as pastels and colored pencils, and you should consult these sections for instructions on their use. (See *Pastels and Pencils, Colored.*)

CHALKS, OIL

These differ from other chalks and pastels in that they have an oil binder, rather than the normal gum arabic binder. This factor makes them perform somewhere between a pastel and a wax crayon. Their principal advantage is in producing a richer color, since the chalkiness normally associated with such a medium is reduced by the oil binder. They are also more durable once applied, having less tendency to rub off.

Oil chalks are essentially a fine art medium and there is little use for them in the commercial field. However, like any fine art medium, it will help you to experiment with many techniques, as each will broaden your understanding of the commercial techniques. In fine art the practice is not to spray the finished work but to frame under glass. In commercial art use a fixative, since the brilliancy of

the color and texture of the surface will be lost in photographic reproduction.

CHAMOIS

Chamois (pronounced *shammy*) is a cured animal skin. Chamois is extremely soft and durable, qualities that make it useful for spreading and smoothing charcoal, chalk, and pastel in large areas, much as the stomp does in small ones.

Chamois is also handy for wiping pens or for cleaning drawing instruments. It is quite absorbent and tough and will not tear during the cleaning, even with extreme use. Its softness prevents excessive wear to delicate instruments through continued rubbing. The thickness of the skin keeps ink from soaking through, so that your hands will stay clean while you work. Chamois is quite expensive, but art stores carry very small pieces sufficient for an artist's needs.

CHARCOAL

Used primarily for layout by the commercial artist, although it will always be a favorite rendering medium for the illustrator. Its intense black and its ability to be rubbed and blended make charcoal a valuable tool in many circumstances.

To meet the demands of the commercial artist, charcoal is manufactured in a number of different forms. Charcoal sticks, pressed sticks, and square sticks are all more or less similar forms of natural charcoal, which are preferred by the illustrator and the fine artist. Since these are a little soft and crumbly, they are a bit difficult to control when producing the detail needed for layout. Therefore, the pencil forms of charcoal are more frequently used by the commercial artist. There are a great many kinds of charcoal pencils—both wood-covered and paper-wrapped—produced by a large number of manufacturers. Essentially, the charcoal in these pencils contains a binder that makes the charcoal harder and therefore easier to control.

The differences between them are comparatively small, and only by experimenting with them can you choose favorites. Charcoal pencils are available at all art supply stores at varying prices and degrees of hardness. Typical of the best quality and the most popular form is the Wolff carbon pencil, which combines the convenience of the wood-covered pencil with the most uniform texture of fine charcoal.

Charcoal powder—another form in which charcoal can be purchased—can be used when a large amount of shading is desired. By dipping a stomp, a piece of chamois, or even your finger into the powder, you can produce subtle shading effects on your work without having to risk marking the surface with the point of a pencil or stick. (Even impurities in stick and pencil charcoal can scratch the paper.) The powder is also useful for tracing patterns. In this procedure, the pattern is prepared on paper and the outline punctured with a pounce wheel. The paper pattern is then placed in position and the charcoal powder is dusted over the surface so that it penetrates the small holes produced by the pounce wheel. The powder leaves small traces on the art surface which act as a guide for the final rendering technique. The powder may be dusted away quite easily when the art is finished.

Although charcoal is a medium that can be used on many surfaces, it performs best when applied to a paper that provides the maximum "tooth"; that is, a paper that has a rough, natural texture, not a hard, polished one. For this reason, try to work with charcoal on charcoal paper and visualizer paper. (See *Papers and Boards*.)

Whatever the advantages of charcoal— its black color and its easily obtained shaded effects—charcoal is a messy medium that gets both the artist and the artwork dirty unless handled with care and fixed immediately. Therefore, it has been largely superseded by the felt-tip dye markers. The two work well in combination, and you are urged to experiment with both.

Common Difficulties

Smudging. Charcoal is dusty. Almost any handling will smear the fine powder. When you are drawing with charcoal, always be sure that you place a sheet of paper under your hand to prevent smudging while you work. When you are finished, even with a small portion of the drawing, spray that portion with a workable fixative. Apply the fixative lightly, with repeated coats, allowing the fixative to dry between coats, or some of the powder may be washed away.

Dullness. Although charcoal is dark, excessive rubbing or reworking will tend to produce a drawing that is flat and dull. This is because the powder has been pressed too firmly into the paper, destroying the paper's reflective ability. Once this has occurred, there is no way to restore the brightness of the paper or the drawing. Prevent this problem by choosing a charcoal of the proper hardness (or softness) so that you can create effects with a minimum of handling. Like watercolor, charcoal is enormously enhanced by the contrast of the white paper against its brilliant blackness.

CHARCOAL PAPER

A soft, textured paper available in a limited range of muted colors, suitable for use with charcoal and pastel. The tooth of this paper has been prepared specifically to receive these soft, chalky pigments. Sold in sheets and pads, charcoal paper can be obtained in one color or in assortments. Good for drawing or sketching, charcoal paper is not used to any extent in the commercial field, even in illustration, since the soft, subtle effects are difficult to reproduce. (See *Papers and Boards*.)

CHINA MARKERS

A greasy, paper-bound pencil created for marking instructions, etc., on any surface. Occasionally, it is used as an art medium. (See *Pencils, Marking.*)

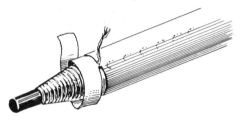

Typical marking pencil with its paper wrapping being removed to enlarge the point.

CHIP BOARD

A heavy, gray, uncoated cardboard used exclusively for construction and mounting. (See *Papers and Boards.*)

CHISEL-POINT PENCILS

An arbitrary name given to any pencil whose lead is broad enough to be sharpened into a flat, wedge-shaped point for use in sketching single stroke lettering or covering broad areas with a single, flat tone. (See *Pencils, Sketching.*)

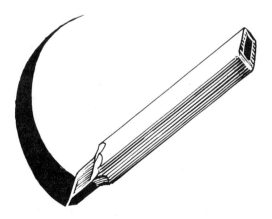

Chisel-point pencil. The point can draw wide or narrow lines.

CIRCLE CUTTER

A round steel rod, about as thick as heavy pencil lead, which has been sharpened to a long, beveled edge. The cutter is inserted into a compass and used in the way one normally draws a circle. The cutter blades may be purchased separately or already installed in a beam-type compass. The circle cutter is used to cut perfect circles in paper, light board, and plastic sheets.

Although simple to use, the circle cutter may present a number of difficulties and must be handled carefully. When you are using the cutter in your own compass, be sure to insert the blade so that the flat side of the bevel faces directly away from the center of the circle to be cut. This procedure will prevent the blade from dragging and cutting a ragged line.

The circle cutter should be cared for in the same manner as any other fine drafting tool. The point of the blade may be kept sharp with gentle honing on a whetstone.

Common Difficulties

Ragged or uneven cut. Even if the blade position is correct, do not try to cut when the legs of the compass are widely extended. The cutting edge will not meet the paper properly and will not cut well. Use a compass that has a beam or extension bar so that the cutting edge always meets the paper as close to a right angle as possible. (See *Compass.*)

Slipping. To prevent slipping, insert the point of the compass firmly into the paper to be cut, and apply steady pressure while turning. It may be advisable to use both hands. Try to make the cut in just one turn. The blade, even in the best compass, will rarely trace the same path twice, since the pressure needed to cut will force the compass point to shift slightly. If it is obvious that one turn will not penetrate the material, and more than one turn will be necessary to complete the cut, you must work in just the opposite manner. Use a very gentle pressure, and make the cut by turning the compass a number of times. The lighter pressure will keep the compass from slipping, and while it may take many more turns to complete the cut, the results will be more accurate.

Holes. Pressure on the compass will produce a pronounced hole in the center of the circle. If the cutout circle itself is to be used as art, it obviously should not have this hole in the center. You can protect the circle from the point with a piece of thick cardboard. Cut a piece of board smaller than the circle to be cut; tape or rubber cement the small board to the center of the circle. To keep track of the center (which is now covered by the small cardboard), be sure that you have guide marks outside the edges of the artwork. These marks will help you reestablish the center on the small cardboard. The cut may now be made without puncturing the art, and the board can be easily removed after the cut is made.

Dull blades. Protect the blade when not in use. Although the blade can be resharpened, the process rarely produces a cutting edge as effective as the original.

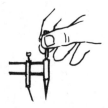

Circle cutter with double-beam construction.

COATED PAPERS

This term refers primarily to commercial printing papers that have been treated to make them more receptive to certain printing procedures. However, there are a limited number of art papers that have been coated, usually with clay, so that

they take certain dry media, like Conté lithographic crayons, etc., with better results than the more usual drawing papers. (See *Papers and Boards.*)

COLD TYPE

Term used to distinguish typographic proofs that are produced photographically from master negatives by machines that may or may not be controlled by computers. These processes are called cold type to differentiate them from traditional typesetting methods, which employ molten metal. (See *Hot Type* and *Type.*)

COLOR-AID

The brand name for a series of papers coated with an oil-based paint used extensively in the commercial art field for producing comprehensive layouts, designs, and presentations. There are over 200 colors, tints, and shades provided in the series, and the paint, which has been silk-screened on the paper, has a soft, smooth, matte surface. Designers colors, India ink, and transfer type, etc., take very well on this surface and produce a very finished effect, which in addition to the many colors, makes this paper so valuable to the commercial artist.

The sheets are sold individually in either the full size (24″ × 36″) which has a white edge (since the paint does not fully cover the surface) and in the more standard 18″ × 24″ sheet that has been trimmed so that the paint covers the full surface. (See *Papers and Boards.*)

COLORAMA

Brand name of a display paper produced by silk-screening oil-based paint on conventional paper stock. This paper is manufactured under a license from Color-Aid, the product's creator, and has largely replaced Color-Aid in many art supply stores. (See *Color-Aid.*)

COLOR CHARTS

A systematized presentation of the colors in the complete spectrum in terms of hue, value, and intensity. These charts are especially valuable for students who are studying color theory for design and to professionals who must describe colors accurately to others in the field, both in art and printing.

These systems provide comprehensive representation of the full range of colors in the artist's palette, how to mix these colors, and how they relate to one another. Each color in such a system can be identified by a code described in the system, which creates a standard of reference when you are discussing the colors. The full systems will come complete with instructions and theory study materials.

The professional charts are more concerned with the inks, paints, papers, etc., that artists employ. These may simply be collections of art materials, such as swatchbooks containing the actual samples. The more complex presentations are typified by a book prepared by Pantone, which prints examples of every possible variation of the four process inks—alone and in combination. Although such volumes are expensive they allow serious professionals to see beforehand the actual appearance of any combination, which they may then specify to the printer. Less expensive (and less complete) collections are available at printers or art supply stores.

COLOR KEYS (3M)

Color keys originated as a method of proofing color separation negatives before printing. (See *Progressive Proofs*.) But the color key process has a valuable function for commercial artists as well. By offering a wider range of colors than the original four-color proofs, color keys make it possible to create accurate overlays for comping layouts and dummy packages. The process involves assembling black-and-white art, making a Kodalith negative, and using this mask to expose the 3M sheet. Appropriate chemicals are used to soften and remove unwanted color, leaving a clear plastic sheet. Several 3Ms may be combined in a single layout, with the effect closely resembling finished printing. This is the quickest and most accurate way to comp small type and other fine detail. 3M color key sheets are available in opaque and transparent colors in either negative or positive acting format. These 3M sheets and the chemicals necessary to develop them are sold in many art supply stores. (See also *Imaging Systems*.)

COLOR WHEELS

Hand-held circular color guides with central pivots that permit artists to plan and preview color combinations in accord with traditional color theory. Similar in function to swatch books, color wheels are easier to use and contain printed references to conventional color schemes.

COMPASSES

Mechanical drawing instruments used to draw circles or arcs of circles. The compass contains two legs: one leg holds an interchangeable pencil, pen, or divider point and turns around the second, pivot leg, which is held stationary. Drawing a circle then is a simple action. There is an array of compasses offered wherever art and drafting supplies are sold. The differences in these instruments stem largely from the manner in which the two legs are joined together, and the distance the legs can be moved apart. There are three ways to join compass legs: conventional, bow, and beam.

Conventional compass. The legs are joined more or less directly with a screw or bolt, and the drawing position is maintained by the friction of the legs pressing against each other. With age, this friction

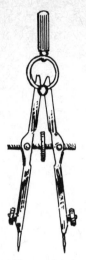

Typical compass with a center bow divider.

wears away the metal, causing the legs to become loose so that they are unable to retain any definite position. Naturally, such looseness causes errors in the circles being drawn. A number of variations in this joint have been designed to alleviate the friction while permitting the legs to hold a position firmly, so that the action of drawing does not spread them. As a rule of thumb, the more such a compass costs, the better the joint will be. However, any friction joint will eventually wear out, rendering the compass useless. This does not mean that these are bad compasses—only that they are less expensive. The better ones will give excellent service for several years, but they must be replaced eventually. You should be aware of this and be ready to make the change at the first sign of looseness. A certain amount of retightening is possible with some screw-joined models, but these wear out faster, anyway, nullifying their advantage.

Bow compass. Eliminates friction entirely and is a superior compass to the conventional one for the price. In this compass, the legs are not joined at all; they merely sit against each other and are held in position by a C-shaped clamp

of spring steel. Normal use will not impair this clamp, so the joint rarely wears out. The pressure of the clamp tries to force the legs open at the opposite end. This force, and the resulting width of the opening of the legs, is controlled by two different methods. In a simple bow compass, a bolt is passed through holes halfway down both legs. Tightening a nut on the bolt draws the legs together against the action of the clamp. Since the clamp will lose some of its strength over time, the control of the nut and bolt is not perfect. Pressure during the drawing—as well as a weakened clamp—will cause the legs to wobble, and create an imperfect circle. Therefore, the better bow compasses incorporate a more positive action. The leg holes, themselves, are threaded, acting as nuts. The bolt contains a turn screw at the middle, so that when the screw is turned, each leg is carried to a new position by the meshing threads. This is a very positive force, and the legs cannot get out of position, regardless of pressure, wear, or aging. Even a weakened C-clamp will not affect the accuracy. Such a compass, called "center bow," is by far better, even though it may cost more.

Beam compass. Has two independent legs that can be loosened, moved along a bar, and tightened firmly in a new position. There are no parts to wear out in this compass—no springs, joints, or delicate mechanisms that can be damaged. Therefore, the beam compass is the most durable compass. Another virtue of the beam construction is that no matter how far apart the legs are, their ends touch the paper vertically. In other compasses these ends approach the paper at ever-increasing angles. In some cases of inking large circles with a compass, you may reach a point where one tip of the inking nib of a compass cannot touch the paper at all; thus, no ink will flow. This problem is eased in many conventional compasses by having legs that can be bent, bringing the end of the leg into a more vertical position. This bending will reduce the maximum size of circle that can be drawn. The limitation of the beam compass is the accuracy of the settings. Even a very small adjustment cannot be made without loosening the leg completely. And yet, the very act of tightening the leg may force it slightly out of alignment.

The maximum and minimum openings of the legs determine the sizes of circles that can be made with any compass. Many compasses have an extension bar that fits into the drawing tool leg, making it longer, and increasing the size of the circle that can be drawn. All compasses have difficulty drawing very small circles. Even if the legs can be bent to get the ends very close together, it is difficult to turn the compass in this position, particularly while inking. For these very small circles, a variation of the bow compass has been produced. Called a "drop bow," this compass has a pivoting leg that is free to move up and down inside a metal sleeve. The pivot leg is placed lightly and carefully on the paper, the drawing leg is gently lowered until contact is made with the paper, and the top of the drawing leg is twirled with the fingers until the circle is completed. These actions, which are impossible with any other compass,

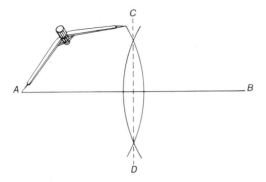

To divide line AB in half, use a compass to draw overlapping arcs from points A and B. Line CD, drawn through the intersection of the arcs, will be half way between A and B. Line CD will also be perpendicular to line AB.

are necessary for circles less than ¼" in diameter.

One last refinement is offered on a few expensive compasses: a vernier screw. This screw controls a very fine adjustment that can be made on the drawing leg only. The legs are first set to the approximate opening, then the vernier screw permits extremely small adjustments until the exact opening is reached.

All of these compasses can be purchased in a number of sizes, qualities, and prices. They come individually, in sets, or as parts of more complete drafting sets.

Common Difficulties

Slipping. The most common defect in working with the compass is the tendency to apply too much force to the pivot leg. The force digs a large hole in the paper, allowing the pivot leg to move a little, or else the force is transferred to the drawing leg, forcing apart both legs. This will cause the compass to produce a circle that is the wrong size or one that is irregular. Learn to hold the compass gently and use as little force as possible.

Cutting. Too much pressure on the drawing leg may force the compass to gouge the paper or force the drawing tool out of an accurate path. Again, use gentle pressure.

Ragged line. When inking with a compass, be sure that the nibs are operating perpendicular to the paper. If they do not, only one edge may make contact and cut the paper or make uneven deposits of ink on the paper. If the compass cannot be opened wide enough to prevent this angled contact, add an extension bar or use a larger compass.

Puncture. The hole made by the pivot leg is often disfiguring to the artwork. If you wish to avoid this hole, tape a small piece of cardboard at the spot the pivot point will rest. Make sure that you can determine the exact place for the compass point after the cardboard has been taped on. Use a T-square, etc., to establish reference points off the artwork, which can be lined up later, and make a mark accurately on the cardboard. Remove the tape carefully after drawing the circle, as tape may tear the surface of the artwork.

COMPASSES, TECHNICAL PEN OR MARKER

Similar in most respects to ordinary compasses, this compass features a large adjustable band which accommodates tools that are of greater diameter than conventional drafting equipment. The popularity of markers and technical pens among commercial artists makes this device valuable for drawing perfect arcs and circles.

COMPRESSORS

Machines that create air pressure for use with airbrushes and spray guns. These compressors are available in a wide range of prices and sizes. The best contain storage tanks that permit a steady flow of air at all pressures and condensation traps that remove the moisture accumulating in the compression process. All of them have gauges that allow you to regulate the amount of air released.

Any compressor is expensive. If you need one and are unfamiliar with their characteristics, be sure that you deal with a reputable supply house and get as much information as you can before making a selection. Since compressors have a wide range of uses in areas other than art, they are sold by many firms. Some of the finest compressors available are the ones made for dentists. They are quiet, dependable, and produce a steady air flow.

The two main considerations for the artist are the lack of water in the air flow and the pressure control. Different art needs require different pressures, and water suddenly ejecting from the line may cause an irreparable splotch on the art.

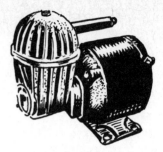

Small compressor used with airbrushes.

Common Difficulties

Failure. Compressors are fine pieces of machinery. The moving parts must be clean and well lubricated. All compressors provide explicit instructions for maintenance, and you should follow them to the letter. Since the compressor is not something an artist uses frequently, the tendency is to forget about maintenance. Make a visible record on the compressor each time you service it, and get into the habit of providing such service on a regular basis. Once the compressor has failed, expensive repair by the manufacturer is the only remedy.

Water. Even with moisture traps, it is possible for too much water to collect in the air line. Try not to use the compressor in a muggy environment. If you use the compressor for any length of time, empty the trap frequently and be sure that it is unclogged and operating properly. Should you have to work without a moisture trap, remove the spray device from the hose and allow the air to blow the moisture accumulation from the hose. Repeat this procedure frequently.

Pressure drop. Extended use of a compressor may cause the parts to wear, and disuse may cause them to deteriorate. Usually these parts are easily replaced and full operation is possible after only minor repair. However, discontinued models or undependable manufacturers may create a lack of these parts. Always purchase a compressor from a well-established organization and pick a model that is popular, so parts will be available as needed.

COMPUTER ANIMATION

Animation means movement, and computer graphics can be made to move. Animation movements can be divided into four general categories: shape, cycle, character, and special effects. The computer produces superior results in many of these categories, but there are significant limitatons. Traditional animation is still preferred where these limitations exist. Combinations of traditional and computer animation can be innovative and exciting. The following sections compare computer animation with traditional animation.

Shape Animation

Making a simple line or shape move is one of the easiest tasks in animation. A single piece of artwork or a cut-out is moved in small increments, and a picture is taken after each move. The computer can do this without the handwork—and in real time. Credit rolls are a perfect example. The computer creates the lettering, the speed of the roll is selected, and the computer produces the action. The result is fed directly to a video screen, recorded on tape, or converted to film. Each step is easier and quicker to perform and control than with traditional procedures. Replace type with other simple forms and regular motions, and the advantages remain. Even three-dimensional forms can be handled by the computer in this manner, as long as the shapes are composed of straight lines and simple curves. The process is called wire form or vectoring. Actually, only the points are plotted. These points are joined by simple, standard programs. Such constructions are easy for the computer, and usually take no more time than single, two-dimensional shapes.

As the motions multiply and become irregular, as the shapes increase in number and complexity, and as rendering is added, the computer's advantages fade rapidly. There soon reaches a point at which the time it takes to program the graphic construction, to plot the motions, and to generate the rendering takes longer than conventional animation. Sometimes it's easier to draw it than to try to figure it all out and explain it to the computer. Also the computer will be taking so long to complete an image that an animation camera will have to be used to record each frame separately. Now the only superiority of the computer will lie in its graphic abilities, and there it must compete with the aesthetic qualities of any other graphic method. Taken together, these factors make computer animation far more expensive than traditional animation. So this category is a standoff, with the decision resting on a balance of desired effect versus time and money budgets.

Cycle Animation

Cycles are repetitive actions. Wheels turning, rain falling, lights blinking are cycles, for example. A few simple pieces of art are photographed again and again, in sequence, to produce cycles. The computer's ability to repeat simple tasks rapidly and without error is a great advantage. An example is color, or palette, animation such as jet stream art on a television weather report. The lines seem to be made of little colored arrows that move along the path of the stream. That's a cycle, and it's done with a computer, albeit a rather special and expensive one. The arrows never actually move. A program merely shifts the color from one shape to the next, and creates the illusion of motion. The entire operation takes only minutes to construct and is very effective real-time animation. For many specialized cycles, used in isolation, the computer is exceptionally valuable.

Character Animation

This category includes human beings and all other living creatures. The movements of these real entities have intrigued and stymied animators from the beginning. The reason is the nature of the movements. They are rather slow and complicated. The difference between one frame (or drawing) and the next is often very slight. Attempting to keep the drawing accurate through these many small changes is very difficult. Comprised of the interrelated actions of many muscles, joints, and shifting centers of balance, these movements are hard to plan and execute with any semblance of realism. Live film also records a minute blur in the outline of any moving figure, however slow. To render this softness and accurately describe the shadows and textures involves an enormous amount of work with small chance of success. Such animation tends to wobble and flicker.

Through the years, animators have learned to avoid these problems. Coloring has been flattened, shadows simplified or eliminated, and movements stylized and exaggerated. In short, cartoon conventions have replaced realism. To compensate, concepts of squash and stretch, anticipation and reaction, and acceleration and deceleration have been formulated to make these simplifications more convincing. It takes much training and practice to work within these artificial limitations.

Can the computer help? A main impetus for computer graphics has been the desire to let the computer solve animation problems. The results have been mixed. The computer can do dull, routine tasks with unflagging virtuosity, but the outcome is mechanical and unnatural. To avoid this regularity requires abandoning the mathematical programs that make the computer so effective. Irregularities mean that human intervention is necessary, and the amount of work quickly surpasses conventional animation.

Where the computer excels is with geometric shapes (cubes, spheres, and cylinders), smoothly graded rendering (airbrush), and steady movements. The computer has difficulty with the same problems that plague conventional animation: complex and varying movements, blurred outlines, and realistic forms and rendering. A computer has to be told what to do. Realistic or stylistically convincing actions require constant instruction. Communicating these variations to the computer takes more time than drawing them. Writing programs doesn't help, since an infinite number of programs would be necessary for the infinite number of possible moves. That is true even with cartoon animation.

There are ways around some of these limitations. One is with rotoscoping, in which motion is filmed conventionally and the film is projected (a single frame at a time) through an animation camera's lens onto an animation table. The images are traced on paper that is punched with holes to match the pegs on the table. Modifications are made in the drawings, a rendered cel is produced (with identical peg holes), and filmed through the same camera and lens. Such a practice is nearly as old as animation, where it has been used to duplicate human actions and provide masks for combinations of live action and cartooning. Rotoscoping has been used with the computer, too, where it works as well, but not better, by itself. It tends to produce a flicker in any type of animation and works best when limited to short segments interspersed among other effects.

An ingenious system of creating character animation has been developed for the computer. Resembling rotoscoping, this system requires a human actor to wear an electrical harness that generates signals at key points on the body. The computer recognizes these signal points in much the same way it recognizes the position of the stylus on the bit pad. A construction vector program connects the points, creating a skeletal representation of the moving figure with very accurate actions. Solid forms can then be generated around the various vectors of the wire-frame skeleton and rendered with appropriate colors, lighting, shadows, and reflections.

Computer animation is neither an end nor an answer. It has not replaced the animator nor eliminated any of the animator's problems. But in combination with traditional methods, it has created some fascinating results. For instance, shadows and reflections caused by one or more light sources are an enrichment that was virtually impossible before. But the cost in time, money, and equipment far exceeds conventional animation. Character animation is a standoff, and may well remain that way. Probably, computer animation will create its own stylized conventions, just as early animation did. Improved software, declining costs, and more experience will help computer animation grow.

Special Effects Animation

This is perhaps the most dynamic area of growth in computer animation. It is difficult to find a movie or TV show that has not used computer-generated or controlled special effects. There are two reasons.

Control is one reason. The computer can make a camera duplicate any move exactly, so that multiple exposures with extremely accurate register are possible. Similarly, it can control the movements of both camera and model, so that small mock-ups can be made to appear larger and have realistic speeds and actions.

The second reason for animation's popularity in video media is because film and video are digital products. The visual images of a movie film or a videotape can be described in digital terms understood by a computer, which can then be programmed to distort or transfigure them. The effects of such distortions can then be recorded. Thus, desired effects can be achieved by reproducing the appropriate sequence of computer distortions. Such computer effects occur in real time. Similarly, a computer can be programmed to vary the electrical signals of a video transmission. This variation will also produce distortion effects.

Used singly, or in combination, these two factors permit images to be generated, flipped, twisted, distorted, colored, combined, masked, and edited in any way imaginable. All this can be done without disturbing the original quality of the film or video image, and will not leave telltale marks of the process.

To summarize, computer animation is an intriguing adjunct to conventional animation. Anyone entering the computer animation field should know that the requirements are stiff. There must be a knowledge of and familiarity with computer operation far greater than that needed for computer graphics. There must also be an understanding of handdrawn animation that is at least as thorough as any animator's. (See also *Computer Graphics* and *Animation*.)

COMPUTER GRAPHICS

Computer graphics may be considered to be any display that appears on a computer monitor, excluding the part that is communication between the operator and the computer. This display is composed of the overall patterns created by hundreds of thousands of individual pixels (short for "picture elements")—minute rectangular shapes into which the monitor screen is segmented.

Computer graphics images are generated in the following way. When the computer user activates a key, mouse button, or electronic stylus, a package of digits one or more bytes long is generated by the computer's operating system. Part of this information package is the "address" for the exact location of the particular pixel involved. The balance of the information package contains a code that activates a set of instructions included on the software disk (program) currently running in the computer. The computer's central processing unit examines the instruction, performs the required functions, and illuminates the pixel in the appropriate color. In this manner every pixel on the screen gets worked on until the composition is completed.

The power of the computer, the sophistication of the software, and the resolution fineness of the monitor screen determine the kind and quality of graphics that can be produced. Other factors are the number of colors possible, the availability of typographic alphabets, the ability to create images in two or three dimensions, and the nature of the rendering technique being imitated.

Computers are generally categorized as micro, mini, or mainframe, with mainframe being the most powerful. Personal computers are micros and are the smallest and least costly of computers. Fortunately, most commercial computer graphics systems can be operated by micros or small minicomputers. What does add to the cost of these systems are the so-called peripherals that are necessary for the successful completion of varying commercial computer graphics assignments. These include a color monitor, frame buffer, bit pad and stylus, copying device, and image grabber (or digitizing camera).

Color monitor. Most computer graphics systems will include a small, single-color monitor to display printed information concerning the status of such instructions as the program mode. To display graphics, a much larger color monitor is required. On television computer graphics systems there may be a further requirement for a monitor that accepts a specific RGB (red, green, blue) signal. On some computer graphics systems, the small monitor is eliminated. Menus, status reports, and like features can be displayed on the color monitor on command. These displays, which cover a portion of the graph-

ics field, can be removed when work on the graphics is resumed.

The frame buffer. The unique feature of computer graphics systems, the frame buffer, is absolutely essential for their operation. The buffer is a holding area for the finished output of the computer's actions. In other words, once the computer has generated the initial signal, identified the proper pixel, consulted the software instruction, and performed the required action, the output goes to the buffer—not to the monitor screen. The screen image is created by a continual monitoring of the buffer's contents. While the computer is acting on a signal for another pixel, the monitor is displaying the buffer's current contents. In short, the buffer saves time. While the computer must examine every pixel and act on instructions, the buffer reads out an uninterrupted sequence of final actions. Therefore, the computer can ignore the full screen and deal only with the new, incoming information. This is not too important when simple drawings are being started, but when painting the whole screen, it would take far too long to examine every pixel with each new instruction.

Bit pad and stylus. The bit pad is a small, free-standing drawing board that corresponds to the graphics field on the monitor. Drawing on the bit pad is accomplished with an electric stylus, or pen. Moving the stylus over the bit pad creates a signal recognized by the computer, which displays a cross-shaped cursor in the corresponding position on the monitor screen. Pressure on the stylus produces the same type of information as striking a key on the keyboard. This information is processed by the computer, which causes the pixel identified by the cursor to light up on the screen. The color of the illuminated pixel will have been chosen by placing the cursor over a color box on the palette menu and pressing the stylus down. As mentioned before, the palette menu can be called into view and removed as desired. On more advanced systems, increasing the pressure on the stylus increases the intensity of the color or widens the brush stroke.

Mouse. In addition to bit pads and pens, there are configurations that use a mouse with or without a pad. A mouse is a small, solid, lump-shaped device that resembles its namesake. The mouse is gripped in the palm of the hand and activated by pressing one or more buttons. While multiple buttons on the mouse allow for rapid color, brush, or function changes, many artists prefer the pen-shaped stylus, since it closely resembles more conventional drawing tools. Most bit pad-stylus-mouse systems use a sweeping action of the drawing instrument slightly above, but directly over, the pad area to invoke, reposition, or remove menu displays.

The copying device. A picture on a computer monitor can be viewed by a few people standing around the machine, sent by modem to another machine, or recorded on a disk in digital form to be brought up again on another identical computer. But the commercial art field deals with audiences that can number in the millions, and therefore the art must be reproduced in printed pieces, films, slides, or television. Consequently, an essential peripheral for a computer graphics system is the copying device, an interface that permits the capturing of images in one of these forms. Conventional printers and plotters normally associated with personal computers are not versatile enough to do this with the quality a graphic arts audience demands.

The simplest and least expensive way to obtain a copy of a computer graphic is to use a conventional camera and take a photograph of the screen. But to meet the strict requirements of professional art, special units have been designed to soften the hard-edged, step-shaped outlines of pixels, to guarantee proper positioning, and to eliminate external light and reflections. Other devices produce a television signal that is compatible with industry standards; single frames on 16 mm film stock to produce animation; or color separations for printing plates. Unfortunately, all are completely dissimilar, and different devices are necessary for each procedure.

The image grabber. An optional peripheral, the image grabber, is a video camera that records an image in an analog code that the computer can easily convert to a digital code. While complex systems can record a fully colored picture in such a manner, simpler black-and-white cameras can be effective in another way. The image is recorded in a range of grays. The palette is then changed, with a different color assigned to each gray. Instantly, the image on the screen assumes the colors so assigned. This method is excellent for producing posterized effects of photographs and for handling such line art as typography, lettering, and logos. These finished designs can often be recorded in such a manner that they can be recalled by a single keystroke. Larger designs may be recorded in sections, so that two keys will recall the complete design. Either way, the units may be inserted rapidly in other compositions. Similarly, some systems permit a full-color image to be captured by recording separate images with the three basic filters. When the computer combines them, they are blended in the same way color printing produces full color from the four-color printing ink process.

All of these hardware peripherals add to the size and cost of a computer graphics station. Color monitors, frame buffers, bit pads, copying devices, and image grabbers are not mass-produced items, because their applications are entirely for the professional world and the number of installations are limited. Creative individuals with a great deal of imagination and inventiveness have employed less sophisticated technology with considerable success. Desktop printing is an example of this. But such operations represent a very small proportion of the commercial computer graphics industry and the bulk of this work will be performed on the systems described here.

Computer graphics encompass three categories: Computer-Generated Graphics, Computer-Aided Design (CAD), and Computer-Assisted Procedures. Since the equipment used for all three is similar, if not identical, the main difference lies in the software. In fact, the software is the most important and often the most expensive aspect of computer graphics. It is the software that really determines what a graphics system can do and how it is accomplished.

Computer-Generated Graphics

The software for computer-generated graphics is of four basic kinds: character generation, paint programs, construction programs, and animation programs. In reality, no software program contains the instructions for one isolated group; there is always some overlap. Each software program concentrates on a specific area, and the method of operation emphasizes that particular approach. No attempt will be made to list every option of a program; they are extremely extensive. But the examples cited will give an overall idea of the functions offered.

Character generation. In computer language, typography is referred to as "characters." A program that produces word copy in a variety of typeface styles is called a character generation program. The specialization of these programs permits them to provide wider selections of typeface and finer quality of lettering. In addition, they may contain animation features for moving the lettering in various rolls and crawls, simple graphics capabilities for producing backgrounds, logos, and other flat designs, and limited paint-program functions for freehand drawing.

Paint programs. The purpose of paint programs is to provide the means for creating two-dimensional drawings, paintings, and compositions in a manner similar to conventional techniques. The paint programs do this by allowing a continuous line of color to appear as the cursor is moved. The quality and nature of this line will be determined by the following functions.

Brushes. All paint programs provide a number of brush or pen-point sizes, from a single pixel to extended groups of pixels, usually round or rectangular in shape. In addition, there will be random-shaped groups that will produce textured lines, such as would be produced by chalk, crayon, stipple, and airbrush. (On simple systems the stipple, or spatter, technique may be called airbrush, since a graded effect can be obtained with practice.) Most programs also permit the design of original brush shapes in single and multiple colors. These designs can be stored for future use. Therefore, any conventional technique can be imitated.

Colors. The color palette is a constant feature of any visible menu display in a paint program. Since most systems are capable of producing over 16 million colors, however, all colors cannot be shown at once. Even the total of available colors, which may number in the thousands, cannot be displayed conveniently. Subpalettes are called up to show this complete range. Any color in these palettes can be exchanged for any other color. All paint programs will provide a procedure for stepping through the entire range of possible colors by varying the hue, value, or intensity. The first step in any computer graphics operation should be the selection of a palette. These customized palettes may then be recorded for future use. Each color will also have a three-part, digital designation, based on its composition of red, green, and blue light. When a color is being used, its number will appear on the small, instruction monitor. Therefore, a color may also be acquired by entering this number on the keyboard. An additional feature permits placing the cursor on any pixel in the composition, and assigning the color of that pixel to the stylus. This simplifies the task of matching colors in a complex rendering.

Ramping. Even gradations between any two colors may be obtained by ramping. The selected colors are placed at opposite ends of a prescribed row of boxes in the palette menu. The ramping function fills the intervening boxes with a smooth gradation. These ramps can also be recorded, and any intermediate value selected for use with the stylus.

Primitives. Primitives are standard geometric forms, such as circles and rectangles, which can be created automatically by the computer. In this mode, a single pressure of the stylus anchors one point of the primitive. As the cursor is moved away from this anchor point by the stylus, a flashing outline of the primitive appears. This outline, called a rubber band, stretches or contracts to match the movements of the cursor. Once the desired form has been achieved, the stylus is pressed again. The rubber band disappears, and construction of the form is initiated. There is usually a choice over whether such forms are outline or solid. Any color may be selected, although the rubber banding will always be white.

Filling. Any enclosed form can be filled with any color by selecting the color and pressing the fill instruction on the menu. If there is a hole even one pixel in size, however, the color will "leak" out into the surrounding areas.

Magnification. Selected portions of the screen can be magnified for detailed work or for correction. For example, outlines of a form to be filled can be checked to ensure no holes exist.

Cut-and-paste. Any portion of the screen may be designated as a cutout. This segment can be moved to any other part of the screen with the stylus. When properly located, pressure on the stylus will permanently position that segment in place. There are several variations of this procedure: a single cut-and-move, which eliminates the image from its original position; multiple moves, which eliminate the original but permit many copies; and multiple moves, which do not eliminate the original but create step-and-repeat patterns with great accuracy.

Masks and friskets. Portions of the composition can be identified and protected from further actions. In effect, they are covered with a frisket. Depending on the program, the size, shape, and outline may be varied, with either hard or soft edges available.

Recording. A virtue of the computer is the ability to record a composition in varying stages of development. This permits artists to recall a previous stage, if subsequent work is unsatisfactory.

Construction programs. The purpose of construction programs is to provide the means for creating three-dimensional forms and objects in a three-dimensional space. The construction programs do this by describing each dimension in terms of an axis: X axis for vertical height; Y axis for horizontal width; and Z axis for depth. These forms will be determined by the following functions.

1. *Wire frame or vectors.* The first step of a construction is an outline drawing of every surface of an object—whether or not that surface is eventually hidden from view. This is accomplished by connecting points in space that define the limits of the object. Lines connecting the points are called vectors. The completed form, with every vector showing, is called a wire frame.

2. *Perspective.* The optical effect that makes the parts of an object that are farther away on the Z axis appear smaller than parts that are closer is perspective.

A number of factors contribute to this effect, and they must be entered into the computer. For artists without orthographic projection drafting or perspective training, the terminology may be confusing. All construction programs contain practice exercises that will clarify the situation.

3. Rotation. Once an object has been constructed, it can be viewed from any angle in space by rotating it around one or more of its axes. X-axis rotation permits the sides to be seen. Y-axis rotation reveals the top or bottom. Z-axis rotation turns the object like a cartwheel. An additional aspect of rotation that is possible with construction programs involves the development of three-dimensional forms from two-dimensional cross sections. Rotating the two-dimensional section around one of its sides produces a three-dimensional solid, much as a form is turned on a lathe.

4. Grouping. Most artistic compositions require more than one object to be created, and many complex objects are easier to construct by combining a number of simpler forms. Construction programs contain a function that permits these complex groups to be considered as single forms or groups of forms. This permits the groups to be moved or rendered as single units.

5. Rendering. A completed object can either be left in its wire form, have the hidden surfaces eliminated, or show the visible surfaces rendered. Any color available in the paint program palette can be applied flat (or graded as it moves further away from the light source). Such rendering is created automatically by construction programs and is extremely smooth and mechanical in appearance. However, many systems permit access to the paint program at this point, where modifications in the rendering can be made by hand. It is important to know that rendering cannot be accomplished if the computer does not recognize the object as a bona fide solid. Strict procedures are given for creating solids and must be followed exactly.

6. Light Source. How an object is rendered, and how its shadow is cast, is determined by the location of the light source: above, below, from one side or the other, from in front or behind. The light source must be described to the computer in mathematical terms. Similarly, the location of the object in space, whether near to the viewer or far away, will affect the lighting.

Animation programs. Animation programs permit the sequenced construction of a number of different positions for an object, which, when viewed in order, give the appearance of motion. In most animation programs, this is accomplished by establishing key frames—full drawings of the object as it appears at certain points along the path of action. The number of intermediate positions desired is input to the computer, which then constructs the necessary views. Once this has been executed, the entire sequence can be operated automatically, creating animation. This is easiest to accomplish in the wire frame mode, since the simple vector instructions take very little time to execute. Fully rendered drawings require much more power and buffering. Few systems provide real-time animation of fully rendered forms, so the art must be copied onto film or video one frame at a time. At best, only a few seconds of animation can be produced at a time.

Computer-Aided Design (CAD)
This term refers to the industrial, engineering, and architectural uses of computer graphics equipment. Basically, the hardware and software are identical to that employed by commercial art systems, with minor differences. Commonly used shapes, forms, and procedures are emphasized, while purely artistic rendering options are minimized. Terminology is much more specifically related to the appropriate industry. Copying devices tend

more to plotters which produce construction drawings, floor plans, and renderings rather than creative pictures. In addition, many of these systems can be connected directly to production machinery to produce the designed objects. Such a process is called Computer-Aided Manufacture (CAM); and the combination is known as CAD/CAM.

CAD procedures have little relation to the commercial artist beyond the similarity of terminology. Design to engineers means the definition of an object; one designs a car or an eggbeater. Design to artists means the creation of an artistic composition; one designs an ad or an illustration. But the equipment is often used interchangeably by both artists and engineers.

Computer-Assisted Procedures

The computer is used in a number of processes in the communications field. Most of these have to do with the production of color separations, the operation of printing facilities, the processing of film, and other graphics support operations. These have only limited interest to the artist—as they affect the presentation of his or her work.

Other computer systems are dedicated to very specific tasks that are of growing interest to creative individuals. While these systems do not create art, they manipulate or present it in ways that involve artistic taste and training. Artists should be aware of these systems, not only as a market for their creative output, but for the employment opportunities they offer. There may be difficulties in acquiring training, but the rewards are worth the effort.

Slide program control. Specialized hardware and software allows one or more computers to control any number of conventional slide projectors arranged in any imaginable configuration. A projector can only turn lights on or off and advance slides; the computer makes it possible to do these things quickly, accurately, and with a great variety of special effects. The lights may be brightened or dimmed over controlled periods of time to produce fade-ins and fade-outs, and overlapping projector images permit cross dissolves. With a sufficient number of projectors focusing on a single area, even full animation is possible. The use of soft-edged masks to prepare the slides and slightly overlapping projector images can produce a seamless, wall-sized image from the combined screening of thirty or more projectors. Used primarily for industrial conventions and meetings, these computers can handle an entire program, including recorded sound and auxiliary projection equipment, such as movie projectors, video monitors, and laser light displays. The effect of these performances is an experience like no other. Compared with similar projection media, slide shows are quite inexpensive, but the major advantage is revision. Slide shows can be altered for the cost of the slides, which can be exchanged instantly. For example, one organization took instant-slide pictures of delegates to a convention. These slides were inserted into the opening presentation of the convention, so that the delegates saw themselves entering within minutes of being seated. The design and presentation of these industrial shows has become a multibillion dollar industry employing many artists, designers, and programmers.

Special video effects. Images recorded on video tape can be altered and manipulated by distorting their electrical analog signals. Such effects as compression, expansion, flopping, twisting, contour mapping, and many others are produced this way. The computer assists these operations by providing accurate control and by recording specific sequences. Used extensively in television commercials and music videos, these techniques can be previewed and executed in real time. While the process does not create art in the conventional sense, it does employ the talents of art directors and designers. It is a promising technique for commercial artists.

Computer-controlled animation cameras. Computers have been linked to motors that not only move the animation camera, but control its shutter, focus, and exposure. Coupled with set-ups that control two-dimensional art and three-dimensional models, these cameras produce many of the special effects seen in commercials and movies. Without the computer, such accuracy and memory of movement for multiple exposures and fine matte work is virtually impossible.

Interactive video disks. An offshoot of conventional video disks, which record visual material in digital form, these recordlike disks are read by a beam of laser light—rather than by a needle—and can store hundreds of thousands of images on a single surface. The ability to present succeeding images thirty times per second creates the visual continuity of normal film or video. The special feature of the video disk is its ability to move instantly to any preselected spot on the disk. This permits a viewer to select alternate courses, and so is ideal for training and educational purposes. Given a question, the viewer's answer can either detour the program through additional explanatory material or skip to the next level of instruction. Thus the pace of instruction can be controlled without disrupting a class or embarrassing the learner. Similarly, stored library material can be viewed selectively and repeatedly. The potential is also great for home entertainment, where visual games can permit the player's actions to trigger alternate visual reactions. Creating and programming these packages promise to be a worthy occupation for the creative designer.

Common Difficulties

Resolution. Although a computer image contains over half a million pixels, a magazine illustration contains that many halftone dots in only a few square inches. While computer resolution can be enhanced during the copying process, it takes time and money. As far as the print media are concerned, computer art is still a rather costly alternative to conventional illustration.

Color. Computers are capable of producing more than sixteen million colors. This is embarrassing wealth, since the average eye can distinguish only among two thousand colors. Even a trained expert can separate a mere twenty thousand colors. Since the palette menu can only show a handful, most default palettes (the colors that appear when the computer is started up) contain mostly brilliant and intense hues. A good composition rarely involves such a combination, and the artist is expected to replace these initial colors with a more subdued selection. This requires good taste and a lot of training in color theory.

More difficult for many artists is the fact that computer color is based on light and the subtractive combinations of red, green, and blue. Pigments, the artist's normal medium, additively combine basic red, yellow, and blue. For example, if red and green pigments are mixed, a brownish purple is produced. If red and green light are mixed, pure yellow light is created. This makes mixing colors on some computer systems rather difficult. The computer's solution is to ramp the colors. But utilizing these intermediate values in a natural way is not easy, because the accidental effects created by blending pigments as they touch one another are difficult to imitate. It takes a keen eye and much practice.

Hard copy. Getting an image from a computer screen is the main problem confronting computer graphics. It's probably the one area that offers the greatest opportunity for improvement. Selecting the proper copying system requires as much thought and investigation as any other part of the system. Remember that the different requirements of print, video, film, and slides seem to prevent any universal system from being designed. Be cautious about off-hand claims and untested combinations. Understand that component interfaces can be more important than the components themselves.

Type quality. Most classic faces are available only by paying royalties, and all require extreme care when being transferred to a digital program. The programming of type requires an excellent type designer as well as a good computer technician. Because both are scarce, many typefaces on computers are unattractive, difficult to read, poorly designed. For much computer type, one must provide for plenty of "air," and not crowd the type with busy backgrounds or design elements.

Kerning. The moving of individual letters to correct uneven spacing is named for a practice employed with metal type. Since the kern, a round ball on the end of a swash, often spreads the letters too far apart, typographers undercut the metal so that the kern overlapped the metal of the next letter. With body copy, such spacing is not as important as in headlines and other display type. Since most computer graphics involving type are of the latter category, the ability to kern type is important. All computer graphics type systems provide automatic kerning for the obvious letter combinations such as an 'L' and a 'T,' but for good design a graphics system should permit independent kerning, and the operator should have a thorough knowledge of typographic design.

Animation. Just because a computer can make a few simple movements does not mean that it is a complete animation facility. Animation is an extremely complex field, and the computer's contribution to it is still evolving. Without a thorough comprehension of animation, the computer will be of limited help. Read some of the technical reference works on the subject before selecting a computer animation program. (See also *Computer Animation.*)

Creativity. The skills necessary to operate any computer graphics system are often technical, despite the user-friendly nature of most of them. Technical people have been the first to use them, and this has led to an excess of technical compositions, the so-called Gee Whiz graphics that quickly became the norm and dominate the popular conception of the medium.

It is important to realize that although there is much about the computer that is revolutionary, its artistic value is as a production tool.

Training. Commercial computer graphics facilities utilize equipment that is not available for the average student or new professional. Schools find that buying sufficient stations for a normal class is prohibitively expensive. Professional installations are economical only if they are used continually and they are rarely available for training practice. Similarly, the cost of paying an employee and a teacher during the training period is hard to justify. Manufacturers often provide classes, but these are expensive and rarely permit the extensive practice necessary to become truly proficient. Therefore, most organizations prefer operators with considerable experience, which makes it hard at the beginning. Become the best designer possible; computers need designers more than technicians. Get as much experience with computer graphic systems as possible. Try to get an internship or apprenticeship. Many schools offer such options to outstanding students and these individuals are usually the first ones hired.

COMPUTER TYPE

Computer type is produced in two ways: by one of the cold type methods and by character generation for inclusion in computer graphics. (See *Cold Type, Computer Graphics,* and *Type.*)

CONCENTRATED WATERCOLORS

Intensely brilliant, highly transparent water-soluble, dye-based paints sold in individual bottles or sets. The bottles are capped with eye-droppers for convenience in handling. Concentrated watercolors stain strongly and leave no residue, which makes them ideal for creating layouts and art that resembles the effects of printing inks. Similarly, concentrated watercolors are excellent for laying washes of color over black-and-white photostats and photographs without obliterating the details. They are also good for retouching color photographs, although the original color must be bleached away before changes can be made. These colors can be applied with almost any drawing tools, including pens, brushes, and airbrushes. And they can be wiped on with cotton swabs, bits of cloth, or sponges.

The drawbacks of concentrated watercolors are the reverse of the advantages. They are a "dirty" medium, impartially staining fingers and drawing equipment. These colors are difficult to make opaque; adding white paint to the watercolors creates a pale, chalky tint that has little resemblance to the original color and is invariably streaky. The tendency of the colors to bleed makes concentrated watercolors a "one shot" medium, discouraging overpainting. Mixed colors tend to muddy, and corrections are difficult. Tools must be cleaned thoroughly when changing color. Even a small trace is enough to affect the second color. (See also *Dyes.*)

CONSTRUCTION PAPER

The familiar, rough-textured, colored stock that is standard in grade schools throughout the country. Essentially, it is a heavier, slightly smoother, Manila paper, and it is suitable for few commercial jobs. The quality is too poor and the colors available are too few and dull for most sophisticated artwork. Only the black paper, which is durable and opaque enough for most jobs, finds general acceptance. (See *Papers and Boards.*)

COPY CASTERS

A collection of scales and charts that will determine the amount of space a given amount of copy in a given typeface will occupy.

Copy casting is probably the least popular and most misunderstood area of commercial art. Many artists consider this a function of the production department and do not learn anything about the process. This is unfortunate, since type makes up a large area of modern design work. Mastering the ability to specify type properly involves the ability to approximate the number of characters that will fill a given area. This simple mathematical problem is rendered even easier with the use of a copy caster. Practice with the copy caster will remove a great deal of ignorance and uncertainty concerning type and lead to a greater assurance on the part of the artist and, hence, a greater design ability.

Complete instructions are included with the casters, and a number of schools offer courses in type specification. Get as much knowledge as you can in this important area of commercial art.

COPYING MACHINES, COLOR

The appearance of the Xerox color copier provided the artist with another interesting tool and technique. This copier, and others similar to it, have made inexpensive color copies available for mechanicals and layouts. But the original Xerox copy has a certain graininess and color distortion that creates exciting modifications of photographs and art work. Artists have been quick to use these prints with or without additional drawing or painting. In fact, the better the copier, the less distortion, and some feel the less valuable to artists.

The vast majority of color copying is provided by more accurate photographic methods, with copying machines being valuable mostly for their creative possibilities.

COQUILLE BOARD

A heavy bristol board with a pebbled surface that produces a line technique when worked on with a dry medium such as crayon or pencil. This allows the artist to produce a half-tone drawing with full shading effects that can be reproduced directly and inexpensively as line art. Coquille board is available in several sizes and textural patterns. (See *Papers and Boards.*)

CORRECTION TAPE

Correction tape is white drafting tape used primarily to cover errors. (See *Tape, Correction.*)

CORRUGATED PAPER AND BOARD

This familiar packaging material with its open interior structure of undulating paper is used in displays because of its light weight, durability, and low cost. The dull brown color is always covered with colored paper or paint, etc., to create inexpensive props for signs and merchandise. (See *Papers and Boards.*)

COTTON

Plain, ordinary cotton is one of the artist's most valuable materials. It can be used for creating art effects, cleaning art surfaces, and for cleaning equipment and tools.

Purchase cotton at a drugstore, and be sure to get one of the better brands. The cheaper the cotton, the more impurities it contains. Cotton's greatest value is its softness; it doesn't scratch. The impurities in cheap cotton will scratch delicate surfaces and create unwanted streaks in art treatments. You may prefer any one or all of the various forms in which cotton comes; roll, puff, or swabs (Q-tips, for example).

Cotton can be used to wipe pigment directly onto a drawing or to color photographs or photostats with dyes or inks. In these cases, the cotton serves as a kind of brush without a handle. It is dipped into the medium (wet or dry) and wiped or smudged onto the drawing, creating loose, soft-edged areas of color. The cotton swabs are particularly helpful in handling color in small or finely defined areas.

Photo retouchers find cotton an absolute must. Cotton will not mar the delicate emulsion of the photograph. Use roll cotton and clean water in generous quantities and change them often when cleaning the photograph before starting to retouch. Use swabs or twist small amounts of roll cotton around the tip of a pointed stick (the sharpened end of an old paintbrush, for instance) for removing small impurities or making corrections during the retouching. This use of swabs is very effective for removing paint from an area that has been retouched with an airbrush. Consequently, it eliminates the need for a frisket when retouching such delicate and indefinite areas as hair and facial features. Be sure to change the cotton frequently while you work; the smallest amount of paint on the cotton will leave a smear that dries into a much more obvious stain than you might realize. Only the cleanest cotton moistened with the freshest water will prevent the development of this dusty residue.

Cotton is ideal for use with rubber cement thinner, water, or various solvents for removing stains from prepared surfaces like Color-aid and Color-Vu papers. Once again, cotton will not scratch or mar these sensitive materials, and can be changed frequently during the removal

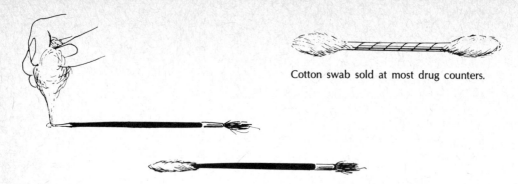

Cotton swab sold at most drug counters.

Method of making a swab with cotton and the sharpened end of an old paintbrush. Such swabs are easy to make and easy to replace.

process. The cotton should be *moistened* with the solvent (not soaked), the wiping action should be gentle and brief, and it should be repeated often with clean materials until the stain has been removed.

Drawing equipment like the airbrush, pens, and drafting equipment can be kept clean with cotton. Here again, a small amount of cotton twisted on the end of a pointed stick can reach into inaccessible areas of tools and equipment and can be changed frequently to ensure complete cleaning.

Common Difficulties

Lint. Avoid using cotton with rubber cement, oil paints, glues, or any other sticky medium. The small fragile fibers break or pull away easily and become embedded on the artwork. There may be no satisfactory way to pick off the lint once it has stuck to the art.

Lack of control. Too much cotton, particularly in a swab, may make it difficult to do fine detail work. The smaller the amount of cotton you use, the finer the control you have in both creative and corrective work. It is most practical to use a sharpened stick for such fine work. Make the point small and clean with sandpaper and add the smallest amount of cotton you can handle, twisting it back and away from the point. With a little practice, you will be able to make a swab

that is capable of producing a stroke as fine as a very fine paintbrush.

COVER PAPER

A term used by commercial paper establishments to describe a heavy stock suitable for the covers of booklets and folders. These stocks are produced in a wide range of colors and textures, with and without deckled edges, and usually there is a lighter, matching text stock for use within the booklet. A full sheet of these papers is roughly 24″ × 36″ in size, although different companies may have different basic sizes; and indeed, even the different papers within a given company may vary slightly. Commercial artists use single sheets of these papers to produce comprehensive layouts to look as much like the finished job as possible. For these purposes, many paper distributors furnish sample sheets at no cost, since they hope to acquire the business when the job is produced. Also, these papers are stocked, to a limited extent, by many art stores. There they may be purchased by the sheet to produce layouts, displays, and presentations. Cover stocks are also excellent as flap papers to protect and identify finished artwork. In this case it is more economical to order a large quantity directly from a paper distributor than to buy single sheets from an art store. (See *Papers and Boards.*)

CRAYONS, CONTE

Small, square-shaped drawing sticks with a consistency of very hard wax. These may be used on drawing papers, pastel papers, and watercolor papers. Use the crayons on the side to create broad effects, or on the edges for line details. Conté crayons come in black, sanguine, brown, and white, and are also available in pencil form.

More within the domain of the fine artist than the commercial artist, the fine quality and consistency of Conté crayons makes them highly prized as a drawing medium. For this reason, you might like to experiment with them both in layout and illustration.

CRAYONS, LITHOGRAPHIC

Lithographic crayons are especially prepared, black wax drawing sticks in paper wrappers, not unlike marking pencils. Although prepared for use in fine art on lithograph stones, they are extremely useful to the commercial artist as well. Lithographic crayons are of a very high quality and come in a range of hardnesses, factors which make them excellent for line art renderings on textured illustration boards and papers. The texture of these drawing surfaces causes the wax to adhere only to the high spots. The amount of pressure determines the amount of wax deposited on the surface and the size of the dot, or wax mark, made on the surface. Since the lithographic wax is intense black, the mark will always be black, no matter how small the dot is. And since the "valleys" in the textured surface will remain white, a finely detailed tonal rendering may be made that will be ready to photograph as line art for the platemaker's camera. In short, by using lithograph crayons, the artist may do a tonal rendering that may be reproduced as line art, a good method of controlling cost while creating expensive effects. This is especially good for newspaper advertising. (See *Illustration Board, Textured,* and *Lithographic Crayons.*)

Common Difficulties

In using these crayons, there is a tendency to make too dark a rendering. It is advisable to practice using a very light pressure, or touch, with the crayons. Remember that the "color" depends on the size of the wax dots. It is much better to build up the size of these dots with repeated strokes of the crayon, rather than trying to get the right pressure with one stroke. In the event that you do get a spot too dark, use the flat part of a clean razor blade and gently scrape off some of the wax. Be sure to dust these scrapings away very carefully so that future pressure does not press and blot them into the drawing.

Extensive use of a crayon or working in an extremely hot room may cause the wax to soften. This may cause too much of the wax to be deposited. To avoid this, try using a crayon of harder consistency or cool the crayon under a cold water tap.

CRAYONS, WAX

These are usually associated with grade school art, but they are also very useful for the commercial artist. Rather than use them in the normal techniques, try mixing them with other mediums. For instance, the wax repels water. Combining paint or ink washes over wax crayon drawings can produce some fascinating effects, since the wax will repel the other medium. Dyes, in particular, work very well with wax crayons in this manner. (See *Wax, Crayons.*)

Common Difficulties

The wax crayon is a soft and rather crumbly medium. Great care must be taken to remove excess wax before it is smeared into the drawing or gets onto other drawing materials and surfaces. Also the softness causes the tip to blunt very quickly. A simple sharpener is often provided with the larger crayon sets, or they can be pointed quite easily with a knife or razor blade. Avoid using your regular pencil sharpeners and pointers because the wax will clog them.

CROCUS CLOTH

A heavy cloth with a prepared surface of jeweler's rouge, crocus cloth is an extremely gentle abrasive. As jeweler's rouge can polish soft jewelry without damage or wear, crocus cloth is excellent for cleaning and polishing the metal surfaces in ruling pens, airbrush needles, and similar art tools. Crocus cloth may be purchased from your hardware store.

CROP MARKS

Simple straight lines inked on a finished mechanical as a guide to the printer, so

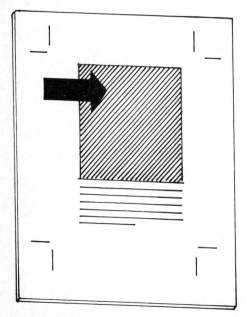

Simple mechanical with crop marks on the corners defining the shape and size of the final job. (Note that the end of the arrow will be trimmed away. This is called "bleeding" the art.)

that the final job can be trimmed to the proper size. Crop marks should always be applied in pairs (to determine a straight line) and should appear *outside* the printing area, so that the marks are eliminated by the final cutting. (See *Die Cut.*)

Crop marks are also used to indicate portions of photographs, etc., when such material is being used only in part. The marks are drawn in the same manner, but with a grease pencil (to prevent damage to the emulsion). The marks must still be drawn outside the area to be used, so that these instruction indications are not reproduced in the finished art. To avoid possible damage to photographs, etc., crop marks can be made on a tissue overlay.

CROSS SECTION PAPER

A ledger paper upon which has been printed a grid of light blue lines. The size of the grid may vary from ⅛" to ½". The 1" squares within the grid are printed in a heavier line. Cross section papers are used to construct graphs, act as a ruling guide for lining up pasted down material, and serve as a measuring guide for making drawings in a larger or smaller scale. Since the light blue lines will not be picked up by the reproduction camera, cross section paper can be used for finished art. (See *Papers and Boards.*)

CURVES, ADJUSTABLE

The adjustable curve is a ruling edge whose contour may be altered by bending. Unlike French curves, or irregular curves, which cannot be adapted to unusual shapes, adjustable curves can be twisted into any shape. Made of metal, spring coils, or plastic, these curves permit the artist to duplicate any shape and serve as a guide for finished penciling and accurate inking with drafting tools.

Since ruling pens are difficult to use because they must be twisted in the same direction as the curve while inking, India ink pens are the more popular tools to use with these or any other curved guides (templates, French curves, etc.).

The adjustable curve must first be twisted into the desired shape and placed in position on the artwork. While the curve is held firmly by one hand, the other hand guides a drawing tool along the edge to create a smooth and accurate line. Depending on the material from which they are made, adjustable curves are comparatively delicate. They must be kept clean and protected from undue stresses.

Common Difficulties

Kinks. Many of these adjustable curves are bent too much, producing a permanent kink in the contour. Such a kink makes the curve inaccurate and destroys its value. Twist the curve gently whenever you use it, trying to avoid unusually sharp shapes. Store the curve in as straight a position as possible to prevent any curve from "setting." Setting may be permanent and will interfere with the contour of any subsequent curve, causing it to be distorted and slightly angular. Such setting can sometimes be removed by running the edge of the curve over an edge of a table, for example, while exerting firm pressure. This action tends to equalize the distortion, so that a new curve may be produced with a higher degree of accuracy. But the best procedure is to avoid the kink in the first place.

Blotting. Many curves do not allow space to exist between the edge of the curve and the tip of an inking tool. Contact between these two areas will allow ink to flow under the edge, creating a blot. If the edge of the curve cannot be raised above the paper, the inking tool must be held in such a manner that the tip does not contact the edge. This is not easy to do and requires a great deal of practice. Before you attempt the finished inking, it is suggested that you practice a similar curve on separate paper. Do this a number of times until you feel confident that you can ink the curve without hesitation and yet keep the tip away from the edge.

Jagged lines. Holding the inking tool an even distance from the edge while following a curve is difficult, particularly if the edge of the curve is raised away from the paper; any variation in this distance will produce jagged or uneven lines. Even an India ink pen, which does not have to be turned during the inking, can waver in the execution of an involved curve. Unless the pen is held in a constant position, directly upright, an uneven line will result. Constant practice and familiarity with these curves are necessary to produce satisfactory results.

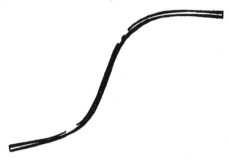

Simple flexible rule that can be adjusted into a great variety of curves.

CURVES, IRREGULAR

The proper name for prepared curves, more commonly known as French curves. (See *French Curves* and *Curves, Adjustable.*)

CURVES, PREPARED

Another name for French, or irregular, curves. You will find that many stores that carry mechanical drafting supplies will have items such as ship, aircraft, and loft curves. These are similar to the convenient irregular curves except that their shapes are solutions to common problems within their respective industries. Since these curves are expensive, they do not have much use in the commercial art field. Their functions can be easily duplicated by the other curves in general use. (See *French Curves* and *Curves, Adjustable.*)

CUTTER, DUAL

A knife containing two blades for making parallel cuts. The distance between the blades is adjustable, and the blades can be replaced independently.

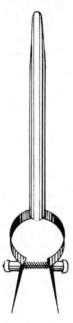

Common style dual cutter with adjustable blades to control the width of the cuts.

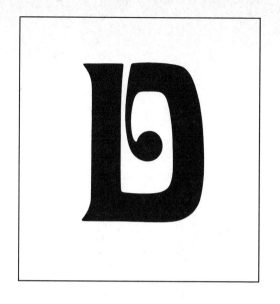

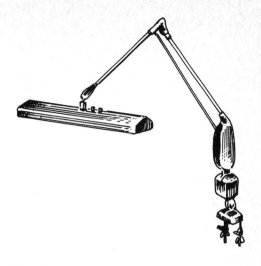

Dazor lamp.

D'ARCHES PAPER

This is an extremely fine, imported, French watercolor paper. It is hand-made, 100% rag paper and is available in three weights—72 pounds, 140 pounds and 300 pounds—and three surfaces—rough, fine (cold pressed), and smooth (hot pressed). These 22″ x 30″ sheets are some of the finest watercolor paper available in the world today. As such, they are better suited to the fine artist and the illustrator than the commercial artist. But if cost is no factor, and if you enjoy working with the best, this is it. These papers are also sold in watercolor blocks and mounted on cardboard, like illustration board. (See *Papers and Boards.*)

DAZOR

Brand name of the original artist's fluorescent lamp, the prominent feature of which is a goose neck that permits the lamp to be positioned without drift. Other manufacturers have subsequently incorporated variations on Dazor's design, and art stores now offer a wide range of such lamps. The Dazor is still available. (See *Lighting* and *Lamp, Fluorescent.*)

DESIGNER'S COLORS

A product classification given to very pure, water-based gouache paints used by commercial artists. (See *Paints.*)

DIRECT POSITIVES

The direct positive, or DP, is an inexpensive reproduction process that produces copies similar to photostats, while eliminating the negative-making step. The advantages are in the time saved in processing and in the cost. Although a DP is more expensive than a single photostat, it costs less than a negative/positive stat combination. Also, the DP process is entirely automatic. The operator sets the controls for paper size, enlargement or reduction, and activates the machine, whch contains sections for development, washing, and drying. DPs can be obtained as single-step negatives, and on transparent films.

The availability of this or other methods depends on your location. Ask your copy service firm whether it offers photostats, DPs, or other photographic copying processes. (See *Photostats.* See also *Enlarger-Reducers.*)

DISPLAY LETTERS

The alphabet constructed in wood, metal, plaster, plastic, or cardboard. They may vary in size, style, and depth and are meant to adhere to displays, doors, and windows, etc. Your art supply store will have samples and catalogs available.

Work with an accurate layout to establish the position of the letters positively before adhering. Use a good glue adhesive and apply it sparingly, using a flat stick or brush so that the adhesive can be placed accurately. Ideally, the adhesive should not be allowed to touch the edges of the letters. Excess adhesive may be squeezed beyond the letter area during the application and damage the final appearance. Nearly all the adequate adhesives require an extensive drying time. Make allowances by providing support for the letters during this time. Straight lines of letters may be both aligned and supported by a strip of wood held in place by clamps, etc. Or individual letters may be held in place by drafting tape. A stronger tape may damage the letter or the display surface when removed.

Common Difficulty

Poor adhesion. Most people underestimate the actions of temperature extremes on display materials. Displays that are exposed to the sun, indoors or outdoors, are subjected to tremendous pressures through expansion and contraction caused by the heat of the sun. Rubber cement, in particular, cannot hold display material for more than a few hours in direct sunlight. When in doubt about the location or duration of a display, use epoxy, a modern plastic adhesive, and the bond will be permanent. (See *Adhesives.*) Always be sure that both the letters and the display surface are scrupulously clean and dry before adhering, and avoid temperature extremes during the application. For example, a job begun in the early morning while it is still cool may become overheated when the sun rises, causing the letters to fall away before the glue has set. Shield the drying letters from sun, rain, etc., until the glue has had a chance to set and harden thoroughly.

DIVIDERS

A divider is a compass without a pencil or ink attachment. The divider is used for transferring dimensions from one source to another by direct comparison. The legs of the divider are extended until the sharp points on the ends of the legs match the source dimension exactly. The divider may then be placed on the new location and the dimension transferred by a slight pressure, which produces small punctures in the paper. Most drafting sets provide for the function of a divider by including a metal pin that may be placed in the lead holder of the compass. This will suffice in most cases, unless you must do considerable circle drawing at the same time you need the divider. Having to change the points frequently can be annoying, but quality drafting sets will include both compass and divider. One extremely handy version of the divider has a vernier screw on one of the legs for very fine adjustments. Choosing, working with, and caring for a divider requires the same attention afforded a compass or other drafting tools.

DRAFTING MACHINES

The drafting machine is an extremely accurate mechanical device for reading measurements and creating lines of any angle anywhere on a drawing board or table. The drafting machine combines the functions of a T-square, triangle, ruler, and protractor.

A drafting machine is composed of a pair of rulers (or scales) joined in a right angle. This unit, which serves the function of a triangle, is adjustable. A protractor dial on the machine may be set in any position and locked. Once this

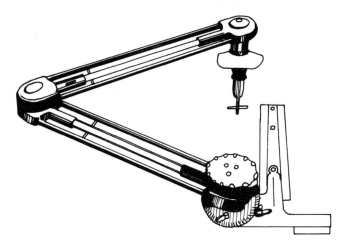

Typical drafting machine, less the horizontal rule. The vertical rule is shown attached in position.

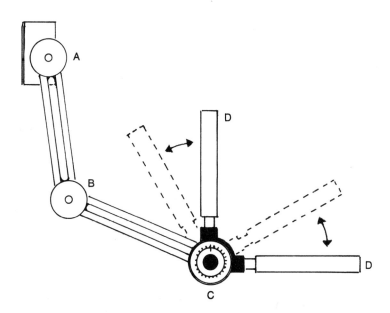

Simplified diagram of a drafting machine. A is mounted firmly to board or table. Both B and C are free to pivot. C also contains a protractor scale which can be set and locked at any angle. D shows removable scales which pivot with C. Once locked at C, the scales remain in the same position, wherever they are moved.

position has been established, the arms of the drafting machine allow the unit to be moved over the drawing surface without altering the relative position of the rules. In other words, a line drawn against the edge of one of the rules in one position will be parallel to any other line drawn against the same rule in any other position—as long as the dial is not changed.

The advantages of the drafting machine are its accuracy and convenience. The T-square may slip, if not held firmly or if the edge of the table is irregular. In both cases the resulting lines will not be parallel. The drafting machine is always accurate, as long as the end of the arms is mounted to the board.

The parallel ruling straight-edge covers the entire working surface when moved, meaning that ink bottles, etc. must be cleared from its way. The drafting machine is relatively small and can be moved around most obstructions on the drawing surface. When not in use, the machine fits compactly in one corner of the area, leaving the surface free and uncluttered.

With any mechanical drafting system other than the drafting machine, triangles, rulers, and protractors must be used. When not in use these items must be removed, or else they will get in the way, where they run the risk of being knocked around and damaged. With their inclusion in the drafting machine, there is no extraneous clutter.

Drafting machines are available at all drafting supply stores in a wide range of prices and models. Art supply stores may carry them, but a word of caution should be given. There are very inexpensive drafting machines, actually toys, that have few of the features that make the machine so valuable. These simple drafting machines will have poor arm mechanisms that wear out quickly, allowing the machine to slide all over the surface unless held firmly. They will also be fitted with permanent rulers, while the better machines will have a wide range of interchangeable rulers of many sizes and scale markings that will adapt to any job. But most important, the simple machines will have a very limited protractor; in most cases this protractor will be capable of assuming only a few standard positions, such as 30°, 45°, and 60°—the angles of the normal triangles. Such limitations make the cheaper drafting machines less helpful than the items they replace. A good drafting machine will cost more but will be worth it if you do a lot of mechanical drawing.

Common Difficulties

The only difficulties involved with the drafting machine are those caused by mechanical failure. The machine is a delicate mechanism that must be treated with care. Maintenance instructions will be included with the machine and should be followed. But the most important thing is attitude. Many artists are used to the comparative ruggedness of their simple tools, and the ease with which they are replaced. You cannot abuse the drafting machine and expect it to hold up. With normal care and attention, though, such a machine will last you for your entire career.

DRAFTING SETS

A collection of drawing instruments in a velvet-lined case. The number of tools and their quality vary considerably and so does the cost. For the commercial artist, the complex and expensive sets are unnecessary. However, all artists need some basic mechanical drafting tools. Since they provide sufficient tools, at moderate cost, in a convenient and protective case, the intermediate sets are recommended.

The simplest necessities for the artist are the ruling pen and the compass (with an extension bar for drawing larger circles). Although the simple drafting sets contain only one compass and/or one

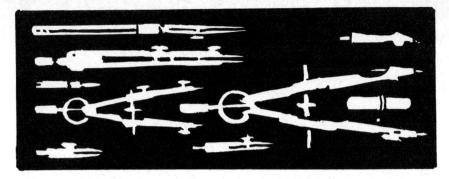

Contents of a typical, small drafting set suitable for commercial artists' basic needs.

bow compass, interchangeable pencil, ink, and divider tips are also provided. These tips have shanks that can be inserted into openings in one leg of the compass and are held by a set screw. To change the function of the compass, loosen the set screw, withdraw the tip, replace it with the desired tip, and retighten the set screw.

Sets which provide separate compasses for each function are more practical, since you do not need to interrupt your work in order to make the changes. It is false economy to purchase the cheapest set, since it will wear out quickly; a moderately expensive set may last you all your life. Moreover, the set will include a small tube which contains pencil leads, spare parts, and a small screwdriver to make simple repairs and adjustments.

The tools in a drafting set require constant care. This maintenance has been fully discussed in the sections on the individual tools, and you should read these sections carefully.

DRAFTING TABLES

A large drawing table with many features that are designed for the engineering draftsman or architect who must work with extreme accuracy on large blueprint drawings. These features are not very different from those in other large drawing tables. (See *Tables, Drawing.*)

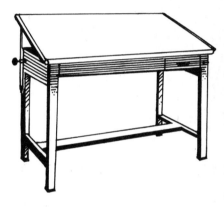

Common drafting table, suitable for many artistic functions.

DRAFTING TAPE

This is an opaque tape with gentle adhesion for holding drawings on work surfaces while they are being worked on. (See *Tape, Drafting.*)

DRAWING BOARD

The term drawing board can refer to either a rectangular shaped piece of wood used as a surface upon which drawings are secured during work or to a cardboard backed sheet of art drawing paper upon which actual art is created. (See *Drawing Boards* and *Papers and Boards.*)

DRAWING BOARDS

A portable, wooden working surface. Usually 1" thick, drawing boards come in a large choice of sizes and woods. The more expensive the board, the more durable the wood. Soft enough to take pushpins and thumbtacks, these boards provide an excellent working surface for any drawing paper. When new, each board has all its sides perfectly straight, at exact right angles to each other. This permits accurate use of T-squares and all other mechanical instruments. Since the relatively soft wood does wear and warp in time, more expensive boards have a metal edge attached to the left-hand side for permanent T-square accuracy. Work can be attached to the board with drafting tape, or with thumbtacks and pushpins.

Since any flat surface can provide an adequate work area, the drawing board is hardly an essential piece of equipment for the commercial artist. And even with normal use, it does tend to become scarred and warped rather quickly. But there are many uses for drawing boards, regardless of their condition.

The mobility of a drawing board is probably its greatest asset. You can tilt your artwork to any angle by propping the board up; you can turn your job sideways or upside down; you can take the job with you for research, discussion, or homework; and you can store the job away while you work on something else. Thus, you can keep several jobs going simultaneously, each on its own board. Having a board for each job will let you avoid repeated tacking or taping which can damage a piece of artwork as it is removed and replaced on a single board. Wrap a newspaper or other clean scrap paper around the board—covering the art—when you are not working on it.

Boards can serve as pad backing for drawing papers. These papers, normally sold in expensive pads, can be purchased quite cheaply in loose sheet bulk. Buying inexpensive paper and securing a number of sheets to a board with pins, tacks, or clamps gives you all the advantages of working with a pad, with none of the cost. For example, a ream (500 sheets) of full-size drawing paper may cost little more than ten dollars. These same sheets, cut to conventional sizes and padded, may cost well over one hundred dollars.

There is another bonus from this method of handling drawing paper. Pastel, charcoal, and pencil are mediums that work much better when there is a soft, thick cushion under the sheet on which you are rendering. Working with a pad, you eventually reach that last sheet or two, and the cushion is gone. This takes away the spring and "feel" of the paper; pastel, in particular, will now leave harsh, uncontrollable strokes. In addition, the unwanted texture of the cardboard backing of the pad will begin to show in your strokes. With a stack of paper pinned to a drawing board, you can always add or take away sheets until you have exactly the right "feel" for the job. You can even insert a selected piece of cardboard (or something similar) to create a texture when you wish.

Old drawing boards that have become too scarred and warped for fine detailed work can still be used with such materials as illustration board. The inaccurate edges can be overcome by attaching a metal straight-edge or a parallel ruling straight-edge. Boads that have become too damaged for any other use make perfect cutting boards. Using one board strictly as a cutting surface will keep your new equipment in good shape longer.

One last use: old drawing boards are ideal for stretching watercolor paper. (See *Papers and Boards.*)

DRAWING INK PENS

Used for illustration and other creative work—as opposed to ruling pens, which are used for drafting—to produce accurate lines on mechanicals. (See *Pens.*)

DRAWING INKS

These are thin, transparent liquids produced as an art medium for use primarily with pens. (See *Inks, Drawing.*)

DRAWING TABLES

These are tables with adjustable wooden tops, for artists and drafters. (See *Tables, Drawing.*)

DROP BOW COMPASS

This is a form of compass created for drawing very small circles in pencil or ink. (See *Compasses.*)

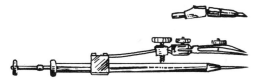

Drop bow compass with interchangeable legs, allowing the compass to be used to draw pencil or ink lines.

DRY CLEANING PAD

Small cloth bags filled with a finely powdered eraser. Such pads are not used to remove errors from drawings, but to protect the drawing surface and prevent it from becoming dirty while the drawing is being completed.

Shaking the pad, or striking it against the drawing surface, deposits a fine layer of powdered eraser over the entire drawing surface. This powder does not interfere with the drawing, but absorbs grease (from perspiring hands) and graphite (from drawing pencils) while the drawing is in progress. This fine film also cleans rulers, triangles, T-squares, etc., while they are being used and prevents them from smudging the graphite.

Once the drawing its finished, the powder is easily removed with a dusting brush. Such brushing does not disturb the drawing.

DRYERS, MECHANICAL

When ink or paint must be dried quickly, a small portable hair dryer is useful. These appliances provide heat that overcomes humid conditions. They usually have stands that free your hands for other tasks during the drying period. When you're doing overpainting, correcting, fixing, and similar operations in rapid succession, a dryer can save valuable time. For example, let us create a hypothetical layout. At every step, a dryer speeds up the work, insures complete drying, and prevents the smudges that come when you touch wet artwork. First we apply a background of pastel. We must protect it with fixative before further work can be accomplished on the chalky surface. The fixative will be slow to dry if too much is applied or if the weather is damp. Next, we draw a small illustration, also in pastel, on the background after it has dried. This, too, must be fixed before continuing. Now we wish to create a line of lettering over both the illustration and the bckground. We do this with paint. The paint may dry slowly since the fixative prevents absorption into the paper. After we finish the layout, an error is detected—a part of the illustration is in the wrong color. Using the method described in the section on pastel, we wipe off the fixative over the error and remove the incorrect pastel with lacquer thinner. Although volatile, the thinner becomes gummy when mixed with the fixative and may dry slowly. (See *Pastels.*)

After the job is finished, it must be covered with a protective plastic film and framed with a mat. But our final coat of fixative may not yet be dry and may be smudged by the protective overlay. Here is where our dryer is valuable.

Quicker drying can also help control difficult techniques such as wash applications. These watercolor washes are used to cover large areas evenly or with graduated tones. You must work quickly with large amounts of liquid to produce a satisfactory wash. Yet when the wash is finished, the wetness is a drawback, for the pigment will tend to continue to drift in the liquid, creating uneven areas of color. Here again, the dryer is valuable. (See *Watercolor.*) The faster the wash can be dried, the less tendency for the pigment to settle out at the bottom or the edges of the wash.

DRY MOUNT

Dry mounting is the process of bonding a photograph or other art to a mounting board by means of an adhesive sheet which is inserted between the two surfaces and subjected to heat and pressure in a dry-mount press. Thus the process is dry as compared to a bond made with rubber cement or other liquid adhesives.

The sheets of dry-mount tissue are sold in packages and are packed with slip sheets to facilitate handling. Rolls of tissue are also available for more extensive use. These dry-mount tissues may be bonded with an ordinary iron, or with hand welders—which resemble soldering irons with broad, flat ends. The welders are available in a number of sizes and are excellent for small-size jobs. However, the normal commercial procedure is to use a dry-mount press.

The dry-mount press, which resembles an outsize waffle iron with flat plates, is the most expensive part of the dry-mounting process. Even the smaller presses may cost several hundred dollars. However, dry mounting is far superior to any other method of mounting, and should be considered necesasary when photographs are to be mounted. Photographs are difficult to mount without buckling. Any distortion in the photo caused during the drying of the developed print will prevent it from lying flat. When adhering the warped photo to a flat surface, pressure must be applied evenly or the photo will buckle and crack the emulsion, destroying the photo. The heat and pressure of the dry-mount press stretch the photo back to its true shape automatically and prevent damage to the photo during the adhesion.

With a hand welder, tack a sheet of dry-mount tissue to the back of the photo or other piece of art to be mounted. This tacking prevents the sheet from slipping out of position when it is inserted in the dry-mount press. Be sure the dry-mount tissue covers all areas of the surface to be adhered, and trim off any excess tissue extending beyond the edge of the art. If it is necessary to use more than one sheet of tissue to cover the area, be sure that there is no overlap. Any overlap in the tissue will produce a ridge in the final presentation. Accurately place the art and tacked-on tissue onto the mounting board, again to prevent slippage. The three pieces, now lightly tacked together, are then placed in the dry-mount press, which has been set to the proper pressure and warmed to the recommended temperature. Close the press for the period of time necessary to affect the bond, and then release the press. Remove the art promptly and allow it to cool in a flat position to prevent warping. (See *Welders, Hand.*)

The instructions concerning the proper temperature, pressure, and time are provided with the press, some of which operate automatically. Follow the instructions carefully; any variation will result in an improper bond.

Common Difficulties

Tissue overhang. The dry-mount tissue expands under the heat and pressure of the press. This may leave a slight outline of tissue around the finished mount. This tissue cannot be removed. You can pre-

Small hand welder for tacking large jobs to be inserted in a dry-mount press, or for completely handling smaller jobs.

vent this from happening by trimming the tissue slightly under the size of the finished art. This expansion is slight and the undertrimming should never exceed 1/32″.

Bubbles. Old tissue or improper temperatures may cause the mounting to be incomplete. Use only fresh tissue that has been stored in a cool, dry place. If a bubble occurs, allow the piece to cool and then repeat the press procedure, varying the press temperature and pressure slightly. Remember that too hot a press may prevent the bond as much as too cool a press.

Damaged surface. Under some conditions, the plate of the press may adhere to the art and damage it when removed. Be sure that photographs are clean before mounting. Chemicals or paint on the surface are liable to adhere or discolor with the action of the press. When mounting artwork, place a slip sheet over the art before pressing. Avoid high temperatures and pressures. In fact, it is wiser to leave the art in the press for a slightly longer time rather than to run too high a temperature or too great a pressure.

Insufficient size. Regardless of the size of the press, there are always pieces of art that are bigger than the sheets of tissue and the press. In this case, use several pieces of tissue, being careful not to overlap them. Tack each piece separately. Place the artwork in the press a section at a time. In this manner, working on one corner at at time, most presses may accommodate art many times the size of the press. To avoid ridges at the limits of the press, work with a slightly lower pressure and increase the time in the press to compensate.

Tilted art. Improper tacking procedure may cause the art to twist slightly in the press. You cannot correct such a mistake, since the bond is permanent. Be sure that the tissue is tacked properly before inserting the art in the press.

DUSTING BRUSHES

These have soft bristles, about 2½″ long, set in a wooden holder. Some brushes curve up at the tip like the runner of a sled. These brushes (which are flat and about 8″ or 9″ long, excluding the handle) are recommended for keeping working surfaces clean. The curved tip allows the brush to be used in small, hard-to-reach places, and the soft bristles will not damage any artwork that is in progress.

The brush is the most effective method of cleaning away loose dirt, and is practically essential in urban areas where dust or soot settles quickly on exposed surfaces. Rubbing or wiping this type of dirt—instead of brushing it—can produce smudges on your artwork which are then difficult to remove.

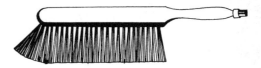

Dusting brush.

DYE MARKERS

(See *Markers.*)

DYES

The term dye usually refers to a synthetic chemical substance of extreme brilliance, clarity, and staining ability. However, some natural pigments with these characteristics are also called dyes. The common quality of all dye colors is their lack of residue in liquid form. Left standing, there is no solid precipitate. These features make dyes excellent components for many paints and markers. Diluted with water, they have found great favor as concentrated watercolors, available at most art stores in individual, eye-dropper capped bottles or sets. (See also *Concentrated Watercolors.*)

Common Difficulties

Stains. Concentrated watercolors will stain anything they contact: paper, hands, tools, etc. To clean up or correct dye mistakes, use a dilute solution of chlorine bleach. Any of the household bleaches sold in grocery stores is adequate. These bleaches are already diluted, but additional water should be added to them for use with these colors. How much you dilute them will depend on the colors. Blue disappears with only a trace of bleach, while yellow resists the longest. Experiment with a duplicate set-up first. In any event, do not allow the bleach to remain for more than a few seconds. Flush with clear water immediately. (On artwork, where excess water is harmful, just keep wiping small amounts of water until the bleach is gone.) Bleach is destructive to paper, brushes, and even metal. Do not use bleach with a sable blush; it will destroy the hairs. Use a cotton swab.

Clear the color from an airbrush by spraying dilute bleach through the brush, and immediately spraying clear water in the same manner. Clean your hands and working surfaces with bleach, and rinse them with water. The offensive odor and slightly oily feeling caused by the bleach can be removed by washing with regular soap and water.

Bleeding. Concentrated watercolors are going to bleed. Various non-bleed white paints are marketed that profess to cover, but they do not. Some of the more powerful colors (yellows, greens, and pinks) will bleed through anything. If you do have to cover a dye-rendered area for any reason (lettering, corrections, additional art, etc.), try spraying the art with fixative before overpainting. Be careful. Use the fix sparingly. The dye will bleed into the fix itself if it is too wet. Use several very light coats and allow plenty of drying time in between.

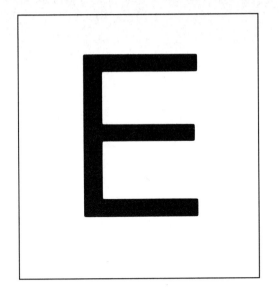

EASEL, DISPLAY

To permit artwork and displays to stand erect, a small cardboard bracing unit may be adhered to the back of the piece at the base. This brace, called a display easel, is held in position by a fold-out flap, which can be locked into place while standing or folded flat for storage. These braces, with or without the cardboard display areas, are sold in most art stores and stationers. You can also construct them from cardboard. The illustration shows how these units look and serves as a guide for you to copy when making one.

Larger, more elaborate units, complete in themselves, are also available. These presentation units usually contain loose-leaf binders so that several sheets may be punched and inserted to produce a flip chart presentation. Flip chart stands are available that open either vertically or horizontally. The range is wide in both style and size In addition to your art store, check binders and stationers for a wider selection.

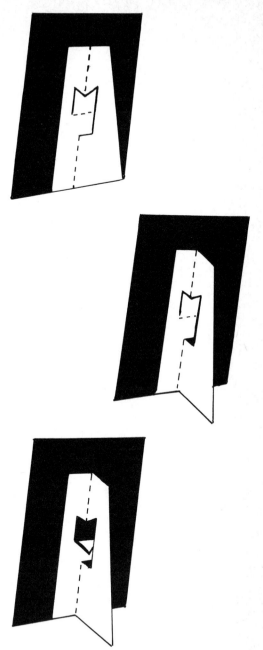

Simple, easy-to-make display easel mounted flat on a piece of art. Dotted lines show folds, heavy lines show cuts. Glue only those parts of the easel to the left and below the dotted lines. Easel wing has been folded away from the art so that the unit can stand. The locking flap has been folded down to prevent the wing from moving.

EASEL, PAINTING

This is neither required nor preferred by the vast majority of commercial artists. Even illustrators who spend most of their working hours painting or drawing seem to find drawing tables more conducive to their work. There are many styles of easels, and if you like working with them, a selection will be available at your art supply store.

EGG CRATES

These make extremely satisfactory paint-holders. Made of plastic, with twelve cups originally designed to hold eggs, the egg crate is easily cleaned and holds just the right amount of paint for all normal purposes. Many housewares sections in dime stores and department stores carry them, but you must usually buy both the top and bottom units. Some art supply stores also carry them and you may buy only one if you wish.

Be careful about what you use in the egg crate. Some paints and solvents will quickly melt the plastic. Rubber cement thinner will dissolve the plastic, but more slowly. If you wish, the egg crate can be kept clean by using disposable palette cups. These cups fit into the egg crate very neatly and may be thrown away when finished, without dirtying the egg crate at all.

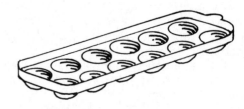

Egg crate, suitable for mixing paint.

ELECTRIC ERASER

A small, hand-held, electrical tool containing an eraser-tipped point. The spinning eraser permits a vigorous action in

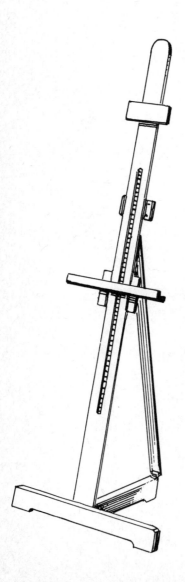

Typical studio easel, sturdily constructed of wood.

small areas, a procedure that is difficult if not impossible with hand strokes and a conventional eraser. (See *Erasers* and *Eraser, Electric.*)

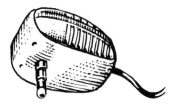

Small, hand-held electric eraser.

ELLIPSE MACHINES

These machines—also referred to as ellipse compasses or graphs—include a variety of devices that help artists construct ellipses of many sizes and degrees. Ingenious in design and construction, their operation is actually simpler to execute than to describe. Essentially, the size of the major and minor axes of the desired ellipse are set on adjustable arms of the device. The method of determining these dimensions and setting the machine vary with each instrument and are explained in the accompanying directions. Once the machine has been set and placed in the proper position on the drawing, a handle of the apparatus is moved by hand in a circular manner until a complete ellipse is formed. Capable of use with either pen or pencil, the ellipse machines can draw ovals of a wider range of size and degree than are possible with ellipse guides or templates. Check with your art supply store; they will be able to provide a demonstration of the machines they carry, and assist you in your choice.

Common Difficulties

Although the operation of these machines is simple, the actual execution requires practice. The primary requisite is a constant speed in moving the device. However, the moving parts are of such a nature that the device moves easily at times and

with difficulty at others—all within one ellipse. For this reason, you must practice quite a bit to be able to anticipate the changes in speed and to vary the pressure you are exerting on the handle as you work. In all cases, the change of speed will affect the quality of the line, although the result is more noticeable with ink. In short, the ellipse machines are no panacea. Used properly with skill and practice, they will produce beautiful ellipses with none of the limitations inherent in the ellipse guides. In careless hands, they are merely an expensive toy that produces indifferent results.

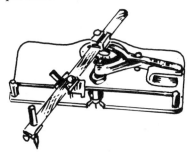

One of several ellipse machines used for creating ovals of all sizes and shapes.

ELLIPSE TEMPLATES AND GUIDES

Sturdy plastic sheets containing openings to guide the drawing of ellipses in either pencil or ink. These templates, which are also referred to as guides, come in two forms: complete and partial ellipses.

Partial ellipse templates are less expensive, since more sizes can be contained on a single template. However, the template must be reversed during the drawing process, which makes it difficult to construct an entire shape smoothly. This is especially true when trying to ink a form.

Complete ellipse templates contain the entire shape and also the major and minor axis lines, which help in setting up the template properly and consistently. A single template will produce only ellipses of one shape, identified by the number

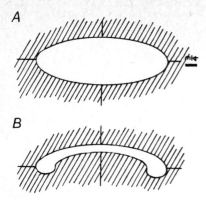

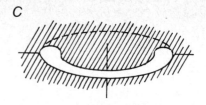

(A) illustrates a portion of a full ellipse template with its major and minor axis lines. (B) shows a partial template example that must be flopped to complete the drawing (C). While the partial template contains two ellipse sizes and can contain more shapes on a single template, the full template form is easier to use with inking tools.

of degrees. There are fifteen degree sizes in a complete set. Two sets are available. The first has major axis measurements of ⅛ inch to 2 inches. The second set measures 2⅛ inches to 4 inches. Increments are ⅛ inch in the smaller sizes, and ¼ inch in the very largest. Variations and combinations of these two forms are manufactured, and are offered by art stores along with other templates.

Although ellipse templates are for use with either pen or pencil, the normal ruling pen is difficult to use, since it must be turned in a complete circle as the ellipse is drawn. As with any template or stencil, a technical pen works best. (See *Pens.*)

Common Difficulties

Blotting. Even with an India ink pen, it is difficult to prevent the edge of the pen from getting too close to the bottom edge of the guide. Ink will usually seep under the edge of the guide in these cases. To prevent this, do not use ellipse guides while inking without placing something underneath the guide to lift it off the paper. An easy method is to place a triangle on the artwork, under the ellipse. The opening in the triangle is usually sufficient to accommodate the oval being drawn. In this manner, the tip of the pen will be well below the edge of the guide and seepage will not occur. When working in this manner, however, keep the pen exactly vertical, or the ellipse will

be uneven. This is another reason to use the India ink type of pen, since such pens work best when held vertically.

Irregular ellipses. If the shape of the ellipse seems to wobble, or if the line does not rejoin itself precisely, the drawing tool has been allowed to slant during the drawing. Practice drawing with the tool held exactly vertical.

Smudging. Like all drawing guides, the ellipse guide will become dirty and must be cleaned. Use warm water and mild soap, since they will not harm the plastic material. Dry the guide thoroughly after cleaning.

Nicks. The plastic of the guide is soft and easily marred. Do not use the guide for cutting. It is much easier to draw an ellipse and cut the shape freehand, so that you will not risk harming the surface of the guide.

ENAMELS

Any paints that dry to a smooth, glossy finish, whether they are oil- or water-based. The most familiar of these are the paints that are sold in hardware, paint, and wallpaper outlets. These paints are used in display work. (See *Paints.*)

In addition, several brands of enamel are carried in smaller quantities by art supply stores. Typical of these is Flo-Paque, which is particularly valuable for painting on glass, ceramics, and metal.

The use of these paints is very limited in the commercial art field.

ENGINEER'S SCALE

A prism-shaped rule containing several scales used for translating dimensions in preparing scale drawings, an engineer's scale differs from other scales in that the inch has been divided decimally. (See *Rulers.*)

ENLARGER-REDUCERS

This is a rather arbitrary designation for a wide range of machines that permit you to project an image of an object or a picture so that it is larger or smaller than the original. Such a practice allows you to obtain reference material the exact size of your layout or drawing. You can trace such an image, eliminating any errors in detail and saving considerable time.

It would be convenient if these machines were referred to by the common designation "enlarger-reducer," but they are not. And, since their construction and operation also vary considerably, you will find them listed separately in this book.

Luci. Pronounced like the woman's name, Luci was coined by the Lacey organization to market its highly popular machine. Like many traditional art supplies, the Lacey Luci has been discontinued. However, both the brand name and the nickname have proved to be so euphonious and descriptive that they are often mentioned when referring to any machine of this type. (See Viewer, below.)

Projector. Designation confusingly applied to both viewers and opaque projectors. The latter reflect light from an object or picture and project it on an independent screen. (See *Opaque Projector,* and *Viewers.*)

Viewer. Most frequently means the Goodkin Viewer, which closely resembles the discontinued Lacey Luci. Specifically, these are self-contained, outsize cameras without film holders, but with clear glass backing, attached lighting, and calibrated controls.

Camera lucida. Optical prisms that do not project an image, but refract the view of an object so that it appears on the drawing paper. The term *lucida* is the basis of the abbreviation *Luci.*

Photostat, direct positive. Photographic processes that produce copies of the desired image to a specified size. Relatively expensive machines can be purchased by individual artists for this purpose but are only economical for those who do a large volume of such work. Most artists use photostat houses and other copy services, which maintain standard fee schedules.

EPOXY

A modern, extremely strong adhesive composed of two thick fluids which must be mixed before activating the bonding characteristics. Neither fluid alone will adhere anything. Once mixed they produce a chemical reaction that hardens the mixture in a few hours regardless of any external factors, such as moisture. (See *Adhesives.*)

ERASER, ELECTRIC

This is a small, hand-operated electric motor, the shaft of which is fitted to hold a small eraser, usually a pink pearl or ink eraser. When the motor is running, the erasing head rotates. Gentle hand pressure combined with the rotation is sufficient to produce an excellent erasing action. Since the erasing is accomplished by the rotation of the eraser, lateral movement—or scrubbing—is eliminated and extremely fine control is possible. The erasing head may be replaced when it is worn out.

The electric eraser is used where an extensive amount of erasing and fine control is essential. Since these conditions are met more frequently in drafting than in commercial art, and since the artist uses a larger variety of erasers than those that adapt to the electric eraser, this excellent tool is an option rather than a necessity for work in the commercial field. (See *Erasers*.)

ERASERS

Any one of a number of materials and devices for removing unwanted marks from a working surface. Although this is a simple enough operation, there are quite a few erasers available on the market. Which one you choose will depend, to a great extent, upon the materials you are using.

Any art medium or surface is capable of being erased. The most common eraser is made of rubber and is intended to remove pencil marks and smudges. But the artists' use of paints, inks, and dyes, as well as different papers and boards, has created the need for a wide range of erasing materials. These include various chemicals and abrasives. The various types of erasers are described below in relation to their functions.

The eraser is used to remove extraneous marks from a piece of finished art, or to correct a mistake. Although the function of an eraser is rather obvious, it should be made equally clear that an eraser is effective only if it accomplishes its purpose without leaving a result that is worse than the original error. For this reason, the choice of the eraser is just as important as its manner of use. This choice must be governed by the nature of the medium and the surface to be erased.

Erasing pencil lines. There are five basic erasers for pencil lines and smudges. The most common is the ordinary pink, soft rubber eraser; the most familiar is the

Pink Pearl. It is effective on all normal graphite pencil marks and smudges. This soft rubber comes in varying degrees of hardness. The harder the eraser, the deeper it will dig into the paper and the more effective it will be in removing deeply imbedded marks. It is important to select the proper degree of hardness, for any eraser tends to destroy the surface of the paper and can make further work difficult. Pick the softest eraser that is effective. The fewer strokes you use, the better you will preserve the condition of the drawing surface.

The next two types of erasers are more specialized, having been developed for artists and drafters. They are the *kneaded eraser* and the *art gum eraser.* Both are so soft that they leave the surface of the paper virtually untouched. They will remove a pencil line if used intensively, but they are primarily for cleaning. For instance, if you are working very lightly with a pencil and have created a number of lines, only one of which is desired, you will probably strengthen the correct line by drawing over it again, using greater pressure. The application of a kneaded or art gum eraser will remove the incorrect lines, but will leave most of the desired line. A pink eraser would remove them all impartially. (See *Pink Pearl.*)

The kneaded eraser has a further advantage in that it can be kneaded and thus formed into any shape you wish. By shaping it properly, you can work in very small areas and make extremely fine corrections. The kneading process also absorbs any dirt that has accumulated on the eraser, leaving the rubber perfectly clean for the next stroke.

The art gum eraser leaves a fine, crumbly residue as you work. This residue is excellent for removing smudges. Rub it lightly over the surface and it will pick up all smudges without removing any drawn lines. When you have finished, brush the crumbs from the surface with a brush or a clean rag. Because of this cleaning action, the crumbs, already pre-

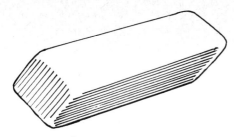

Common pencil eraser.

pared, are commercially available in a cloth bag that is made of coarse mesh. Called a dry-clean pad, it can be tapped sharply over a drawing surface, producing a light film of these crumbs. This film may be left on the surface while you are working. The crumbs are too small to interfere with the drawing, but their presence continually absorbs the excess graphite, not only from the paper, but from T-squares and triangles as well. When the drawing is finished, the film is brushed off, leaving a clean surface ready for any further work. Perhaps more important, your drawing tools are also clean and will not cause smudges when used next time.

An eraser of synthetic material has been developed that has none of the general characteristics of natural or artificial rubber. Most erasers are either so gentle that they cannot totally remove a heavy pencil line, so abrasive that they destroy the paper surface, or so rubbery that they smudge loose graphite. The "plastic" erasers absorb graphite like a kneaded eraser, but have sufficient body to withstand heavy pressure. Because they contain no abrasive, paper fibers are not ripped with repeated applications.

The last eraser for pencil work is the *ink eraser.* Like a pencil eraser, it is made of rubber, but has abrasives added to the rubber. Made for ink corrections, it is used when a hard pencil (or a heavy stroke with a regular pencil) has created a mark too deeply imbedded in the paper for a softer eraser to remove. (See *Eraser, Electric.*)

Erasing ink lines. The ink eraser just described is the primary tool for removing ink from paper. In all cases, ink will penetrate deeply into the paper fibers; no surface cleaner will completely remove these marks. Thus a rubber eraser may be inadequate. Liquid ink eradicator, a common stationer's product, may be effective with delicate inks and will not harm the paper surface.

However, India ink is usually a different matter. In this case, the drawing surface must be disrupted; the only question is the degree to which you must damage the paper fibers. If a large mark is to be removed, the abrasive rubber ink eraser may not work well. The rubbing action tends to drive tiny pieces of dried ink more deeply into the paper and thus make the job more difficult. The more you clean, the dirtier the surface becomes. The same will be true if the ink has soaked too deeply into the paper.

In cases like these, a pure abrasive should be used first. One of the best is the *fiberglass eraser.* The tiny filaments of glass scratch the ink off; but since the filaments break off as you rub, they do not dig too deeply into the paper or force the ink further down into the fibers. After you have removed the major portion of the error in this manner, a rubber ink eraser may be used to finish up and remove any final traces.

An effective tool, always available to artists, is the razor blade. If the stock upon which you are working is of sufficient high quality, it will take a remarkable amount of abrasion without permanent damage. Therefore, you may use the flat edge (not the corner) of the razor blade to scrape off the surface of the paper where the mistake appears. The value of these abrasive actions is that they remove the paper fibers uniformly. Repeated strokes with a rubber ink eraser will dig a trough into the paper. The edges of this trough will be rough and will collect dirt easily; these rough edges will cast shadows that are visible and destroy the smooth character of the paper, so that further work in the area will blot and appear ragged. The pure abrasives (fiberglass, razor blade, etc.) take the paper down evenly. They cut quickly and do not tear the fibers. Thus, the surface remains relatively smooth and can be worked over again without difficulty. If, after a reasonable amount of work, there is still a stain on the paper, cover the area with a fine layer of white watercolor paint.

Erasing dyes. Dye errors may be removed in the same manner as ink, but dyes are much easier to handle. Regular household chlorine bleach will remove all the dye color. Chlorine is, however, a rather strong chemical; used to excess, it will destroy the paper. The household bleaches are already diluted, but it is best to dilute them still further.

Some dye colors—the blues for instance—can be bleached with only a slight amount of chlorine. Some, like the reds and yellows, require stronger action. There is no way to predict how each color will react.

The varying reactions mean that you must practice before applying bleach. The amount of bleach, the amount of water used to dilute the bleach, and the method of application will be altered by each case.

As a rule, a small swab of cotton is the best tool for applying bleach. Brush bristles are destroyed by chlorine, and other materials may not provide fine enough points for delicate control. Cotton is cheap, easily replaced, can be shaped into any point, and resists the corrosive action of the bleach. First of all, wet the cotton with water. Gradually add bleach by dipping the wet cotton into pure bleach. The longer the cotton is held in the bleach, the stronger the concentration of bleach will be. Start with fresh cotton for each trial. The best results are obtained with the least amount of bleach that removes the color. Excess bleach will brown the paper. In stubborn cases, pure bleach with no water may be necessary. In fact, there are times that several washes of pure bleach will be required. Also be sure to blot up the bleach solution as soon as the color has faded. The longer the bleach sits, the more damage it can do. When you have finished your correction, rinse the area with clear water to remove any chlorine; if any trace remains, new colors will be bleached out as soon as they are added.

Erasing paints. Paints will respond to a combination of treatments. Use a razor blade to scrape away as much of the surface paint as you can. Then an ink or hard pencil eraser will remove the remainder. Be careful to keep the surface as smooth as you can, so that new paint will not be blotchy or ragged. A kneaded eraser will pick up the fragments of paint which you have scraped off, so they will not be accidentally smudged into the surrounding colors. This method will work equally well with water- or oil-based paints.

Water or turpentine (or a more powerful petroleum solvent) will, of course, dissolve the paints and allow them to be wiped off, provided that the surface is hard and nonabsorbent enough so that the colors don't soak in further. The scratching technique works particularly well when the error is near a finished part of the rendering, which you do not wish to disturb. It may be very hard to *wipe* any solvent next to this finished area without damaging the paint.

Erasing prepared surfaces. There are a number of papers like Color-Aid, Colorama, and Pantone that come with a prepared surface. They tend to be extremely sensitive and will mark easily. Erasers and solvents (even those recommended for these materials) of all types leave stains that are extremely obvious and impossible to remove. However, since these are almost all prepared with oil-based colors, a wash of clean water, repeated rapidly, but very gently, will remove most water-based paints if the wash is applied before the paint has had time to set and dry. The key is to use cotton or some other very soft material and avoid any pressure that will force the paint into the surface or leave a scar. Do not make more than one stroke before exchanging the cotton for a new, clean piece. Work from outside the correction area into the middle of the error. This will prevent the pigment from spreading.

Color-Aid and Colorama are made by silkscreening thick oil paint onto paper. The thickness of the surface helps when you must correct small errors. A razor blade will scrape off the error—and some of the surface paint as well. But the thickness of the surface paint will leave enough color so that a minor correction will not show.

Pencil line erasures and rubber cement stains will always show on these papers and cannot be removed. Rubber cement stains can be equalized, however, by brushing a coat of cement over the entire surface and then removing all the cement at one time. Now the entire sheet is stained evenly and will appear perfectly clean. If these stains are not even, spray the entire sheet with fixative; this has a darkening effect and will neutralize the stains.

There is no special care for erasers. The rubbing variety must be kept as clean as possible, of course, and must be thrown out when they become too dirty. Kneaded erasers eventually pick up too much dirt and lose their cleaning and kneading properties. Here again, get rid of the eraser and get a new one.

Common Difficulties

The only common complaint about an eraser is that it does not work because it is being used for the wrong purpose. If you are having problems, make sure that you are following the instructions above; make sure that you are using the right eraser in the right way for the particular job.

The only reason for failure, then, will be that the eraser is dirty. Material imbedded in kneaded erasers will leave streaks. Dirt on rubber erasers will smudge. Weak bleach, dirty water, or soiled cotton will leave stains. If all of these conditions have been met and you are still having excessive problems, try using a better grade of paper or board. Strathmore rag stock papers, for example, are of such high quality that many destructive erasing techniques are actually used as creative drawing methods.

ERASING SHIELDS

Small rectangular pieces of metal into which have been cut various sized and shaped holes. These openings will conform to just about any area that must be corrected by erasing. The virtue of the shield is that it allows you to erase with great vigor and with harsh erasers without damaging the art in adjacent areas.

The shields are handy and inexpensive, and you will find them at any store that sells drafting equipment.

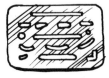

Erasing shield. Made of metal with various openings to mask erasures.

ETCHING PAPER

These papers are prepared especially to absorb ink in the engraving method of printing, of which etching is the primary example. Like a fine drawing paper, they produce the best results in an etching press. In the etching process, lines are gouged in a metal plate. Ink is wiped into these lines and the rest of the plate is wiped clean. Paper is laid over the plate and pressure is applied. The ink is drawn up out of the lines by the pressure of the press and the absorbency of the paper. The thickness of the ink and the slight ridges in the paper caused by the pressure forcing the paper into the lines creates an embossed effect that is distinctive with etching. Naturally, these subtle characteristics and the slow hand-produced reproductions have little use in the commercial art field. Yet the process is increasingly popular as a hobby, a professional sideline, and as a means of experimentation, and growth, for an artist. For these reasons, etching papers are now carried by many art supply stores, as are the other implements of this fascinating procedure. (See *Papers and Boards*.)

ETCHING PRESS

A sturdy device for exerting vertical pressure used to produce copies from etching plates, wood blocks, and linoleum cuts. The presses vary in size, are quite expensive, and are limited to the slow reproduction of limited editions of fine art quality. These presses have no use in commercial art, other than as a hobby or a means of experimentation, and development, for an artist. The information necessary, should you wish to pursue this fascinating field, can be acquired from specific books dealing with the etching process or from your printing press dealer. If your local art store does not carry them, they will usually be able to obtain the necessary information from the manufacturers for you.

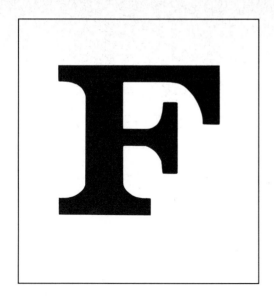

FIBERGLASS ERASER

This is a bundle of very fine strands of glass fibers held together in pencil form, used for scratching or abrading ink stains to remove them from paper surfaces. (See *Erasers.*)

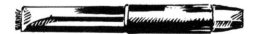

Fiberglass eraser shown in a plastic handle case.

FILING CABINETS, FLAT

The flat filing cabinet is a piece of furniture designed for the drafter for use in storing blueprints. However, these sturdy, spacious cabinets are excellent for storing all manner of art supplies. Since the weight of some art materials is considerable, these steel cabinets are much more satisfactory than wood cabinets, which will warp and sag. However, since steel cabinets are expensive, you should keep your eyes open at the secondhand office equipment stores, where you might find occasional bargains.

The dimensions of the drawers are also important. Many blueprint files are larger than necessary for most commercial art papers; thus you will pay more for the larger drawer size and not be able to utilize all the space. 20″ × 30″ is the largest common size of illustration board; 25″ × 33″ is a standard full sheet of printing paper; 18″ × 24″ is the common sheet size of special art papers, such as Color-Aid and Colorama, etc. Keep these figures in mind when choosing a cabinet, and check the dimensions of any other stock you wish to store before selecting a cabinet.

Filing cabinets come in many different sizes and numbers of drawers. Some types nest one on top of the other to permit maximum use of vertical space. The best cabinets have ball-bearing drawer slides, which perform best under heavy loads and constant use. Most of the other varieties, though cheaper, will become bent in time and difficult to open and close.

FIXATIVE

A liquid applied to a drawing or painting to set the pigment and prevent damage through smudging. Fixatives are waterproof and durable, and can protect artwork from most normal wear and tear.

Fixatives are made of plastic, varnish, shellac, or lacquers in highly volatile solvents that allow the fixative to be painted or sprayed onto a surface. The simplest form of sprayer is the mouth-type atomizer. However, the atomizer method of spraying fixative is awkward and difficult to control and should not be considered by the modern commercial artist, except as an emergency measure.

The main reason for using fixatives is to protect the finished piece of art from any external damage. A drawing or painting that has been "fixed" cannot be smudged or soiled. Fixatives are available for all art mediums and now come in aerosol cans that are convenient, accurate, and uniform in the quantity and nature of the spray. The labels on the cans fully describe the uses of each particular fixative. Practice and experimentation will allow you to find the one that suits your use best. It is even possible to avoid one of the most objectionable features of fixatives: the odor. Certain odorless brands are now marketed, although their other characteristics may be somewhat altered by this change. Try them and see.

The wide range of fixatives or varnishes have many uses in every stage of art. There are even workable fixatives. These leave a surface that is not much different from the original. In other words, further work can be done on the fixed drawing or painting in the same technique as if no fixative had been used; the work that has already been fixed will not be distorted. Also, fixatives are perfect for combinations of mediums. For instance, paint will "bead" or refuse to take on pastel, unless the surface has been fixed.

Many paints bleed, becoming tinged with the underlying color. Even casein, which is waterproof when dry, remains soluble for at least a day. Fixatives, applied between layers of color, help to prevent bleeding.

Fixatives can be used to prevent glare caused by the reflection of photographic lights. Special matte fixatives are made to reduce the shine of the finished art surface; this shine can cause washed-out photocopies or imperfect printing plates.

Fixatives can be used in the manner of fine artists who varnish or shellac their finished painting. These finishes, sold in spray cans, impart a matte or glossy surface to the final picture as they protect it.

Most fixatives tend to discolor the pigment slightly. This is not necessarily a disadvantage. The fixative (with its matte, glossy, or tinted finish) often enhances the work, giving it a quality that can be acquired in no other way. These fixatives act as toners that pull the final painting together. The only difference between these fixatives and the varnish of fine artists is that they are sprayed on. By using the aerosol spray, you can control the amount with great accuracy.

One special use for fixatives should be mentioned. Type proofs, as they come from the typographer, are rarely completely dry. Although typographers use special, quick drying inks, and many organizations use infrared dryers, the ink may be smudged as the proofs are handled. This is particularly true when you are doing paste-up mechanicals. Rubber cement thinner, used to move pasted-down type, and the rubber cement itself, dissolve the freshly printed ink. When the rubber cement pick-up is pulled over the surface to clean off excess cement, the pick-up will smudge the type. For this reason, it is good to get into the habit of spraying all type proofs with fixative before handling them. Properly sprayed proofs will never smudge. But be careful; too much fixative *also* dissolves the ink and causes a faint bluish halo to bleed around the type. Almost invisible, this bleeding destroys the hard edge of the type so that it is impossible to get a clean reproduction.

Whatever the use of the fixative or the type involved, proceed with care. Always try to have the artwork in a vertical position and spray at right angles to it from about 12″ away. This will prevent the occasional large drop from causing a puddle. Cover the surface quickly with a light coat. If more fixative is needed, apply a second coat. Fixatives are very volatile and will dry fast. If the fixative is allowed to soak the artwork, the pigments will float and bleed. *All* fixatives will create a hard, glassy surface if they are applied too heavily. Such a surface is difficult to work on. But most important, read the label thoroughly. Fixatives are volatile, flammable, and *toxic* if used improperly. Follow the instructions on the can or bottle. Avoid high temperatures, flame, and poorly ventilated working spaces. Never puncture a spray can or place it in an incinerator.

Common Difficulties

No spray. With the push-button spray cans, fixative may collect, harden, and clog the small spray opening. A scratch with your fingernail will usually dislodge this blockage. If not, try scraping the opening gently with a knife or razor blade. In extreme cases, try to puncture the opening with a fine pinpoint. Puncturing is not too desirable a procedure, since the pin may force the hardened material more deeply into the nozzle, where it cannot be removed. Puncturing may also damage the nozzle so that the can will not work without a new nozzle.

When clearing the nozzle, keep the can pointed away from you. The blockage is only in the tip of the nozzle and pressure will have built up in the tube; when the block is removed, this pressure will force the spray out and into your face, if you are not careful.

If the nozzle is rendered useless for any reason, do not throw the can away. The small plastic nozzles lift off easily and are interchangeable. Take the nozzle off a good can and use it in place of the damaged one. In fact, it is a good idea to keep the nozzle from empty cans near at hand in case of emergency.

Glassy surface. If the nature of the fixative (or the amount used) causes the surface to become so hard and glassy that you find it difficult to work, try sanding the surface lightly with very fine sandpaper. If this sanding is done gently, the surface may be roughened enough to take any medium. Of course, if the sandpaper is too coarse, or if you rub too hard, you may destroy the artwork.

If you are trying to use paint, add some acetate medium. If none is available, run your wet paintbrush lightly over a cake of soap before loading it with paint. Do not use detergents; it is the glycerine in the soap that does the trick. Do not use too much soap or you will get suds.

Corrections. Once most fixatives have been applied, it is impossible to correct any mistakes in the work. The only way to make a change is to remove the fixative. However, this is extremely difficult and not too successful at best.

If it is imperative to make a correction, use lacquer thinner. All fixatives are dissolved by lacquer thinner, but so are most art mediums. Dampen, do not soak, a clean piece of cotton with lacquer thinner, and gently blot the area of the correction. This will soften, remove, and absorb the fixative. Allow the area to dry completely, and attempt to remove the error with a good quality ink eraser or with the flat edge of a razor blade.

If this does not work, repeat the blotting with the cotton dampened with lacquer thinner. Be sure that this cotton is clean. Do not use a piece of cotton more than once; it wil have picked up some fixative or pigment, however slight. Let the surface dry again and repeat the erasure. You may have to repeat this process several times if the fixative has been applied too heavily. If you have no lacquer thinner, try acetone or nail polish remover. If you work carefully, never rubbing, it is possible to remove enough of the fixative without damaging the surrounding artwork, so that corrections can be made. When you finish, apply a new coat of fixative, blending it in well.

FLAP PAPER

Any piece of commercial art—rendering, photograph, mechanical, or layout—should be mounted firmly and covered with a flap. The flap protects the art and presents a professional appearance. For these reasons, some care should be used in choosing the stock (paper) involved. Most large agencies and studios even go to the trouble of printing or embossing their names on their flaps, while most others at least affix an identifying label. Thus, the flap becomes an advertisement

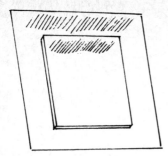

Step 1: To attach flap paper, place art face down on paper and apply cement on top.

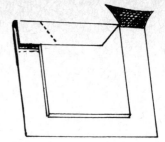

Step 2: Fold over flap paper and cut top corners diagonally.

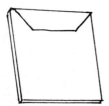

Step 3: Trim away excess on three sides.

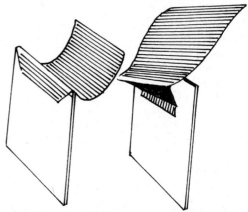

Proper flap (left) opens easily, stays neat, closes properly. Improper flap opening (right) lets the paper fall away at the top making it difficult to hold and close.

in its own right, and makes it easy to recognize the origin of the art when changes, corrections, or new work are being considered.

This doesn not mean that the stock must be expensive; common wrapping paper is often used. The main considerations are neatness and consistency. Familiarize yourself with the papers available, and try several of them before you make a decision.

To attach the flap, simply tape the flap paper to the top of the board holding the art. Alternatively, fold the top of the flap paper over the top of the art and adhere it to the back with rubber cement. The important point is to adhere the flap at the extreme top, front, or back. If the flap is taped to the back, most of the paper will not be adhered to the art; it will fall away from the art when lifted, creating an awkward, untidy, and unattractive presentation.

Trim away any excess paper or tape with a razor blade, keeping the blade as straight as possible to prevent cutting into the art. This trimming is more easily accomplished if the whole unit is turned over with the flap paper on the bottom. In this position, the sides of the board will act as a guide for the razor blade, and your flap will be the exact size of your board.

The job is now done and ready for your identification and delivery to the client. Just as a picture is enhanced by a frame, so a piece of art is enhanced when properly flapped.

FLEX-OPAQUE

This is a brand name for a fluid that converts any liquid medium into one that will adhere to plastic and glossy surfaces. (See *Acetate Mediums.*)

FLINT PAPER

A thin paper coated on one side with very rich, shiny colors. Unlike other background papers, flint papers come in just a few basic colors; but they are so shiny and bend so easily without cracking, that they are highly valued for producing comprehensive layouts that resemble finished printing that has been varnished. This is particularly advantageous in producing packaging dummies. Flint papers are sold in 20″ × 26″ sheets. (See *Papers and Boards.*)

FLIP CHARTS

This is a descriptive name given to a collection of presentation sheets, usually bound to a self-standing unit which permits one sheet to be viewed, then flipped out of the way, exposing the next sheet. (See *Easel Display.*)

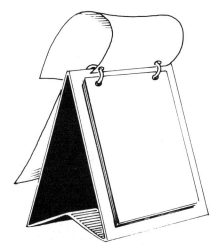

A flip chart is typically used for presentation. It folds flat for carrying.

FLOCK

Refers to a fine, velvety residue of cloth fibers (usually rayon). Colored and adhered to paper or board, flock produces a pile effect like a suede or velour. Flocking is done by a few industries primarily producing wall or display coverings. It may be possible to find flock, adhesives, and spray guns at some art stores so that you can cover your own surfaces, but usually the only form of flock available in most art supply stores is in the form of flock paper and board. A limited number of colors is available, and the only use for the material is in the field of display. (See *Papers and Boards.*)

FLO-PAQUE

This is the brand name of a popular general-purpose enamel used to cover all surfaces. Available in most art supply stores in one- and two-ounce jars, Flo-Paque is offered in forty-eight colors. These pigments adhere to glass and ceramics without heat treatment or other processing. Flo-Paque is thinned or removed with Dio-Sol thinner and can be protected with a glossy, waterproof glaze or with an alcohol-proof coating called A1 Pro-Cote. (See *Paints.*)

FLUORESCENT LIGHT

This is any lamp that contains a fluorescent tube in place of the conventional electric light bulb. In art circles, the light from the fluorescent tube is considered to create conditions more similar to daylight, thus allowing more accurate color matching than the electric bulb. Usually the best results come with a combination of both lights. (See *Lamp, Fluorescent.*)

FOAMCORE

A sandwich of two sheets of shiny, heavy paper enclosing a Styrofoam center. The

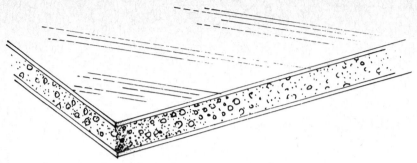

Cross section of a foamcore sheet showing the sandwich of bristol board and Styrofoam.

result of this union is a very light board, much lighter than illustration board or mounting board, but with several times the structural strength. A full sheet of foamcore is 40″ × 60″, larger than any other boards, since the lack of weight makes such a size easy to handle. At present, the only color available is white, but other papers may be adhered to the board without causing it to sag. Foamcore is also easy to cut; a razor blade will slice through it with ease, whereas a heavy mat knife can hardly penetrate the heavier boards in one pass. As might be expected, foamcore is rather expensive—though well worth the price. (See *Papers and Boards.*)

FORMATT

Brand name of a pressure graphics product. Formatt is the only transfer type that requires the cutting of the backing sheet in order to transfer characters to the art surface. (See *Transfer Type.*)

FOUNT INK

The name of an India ink variation produced specially for use in certain drawing pens. (See *India Ink* and *Pens.*)

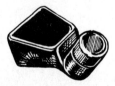

Goose-necked fount ink bottle.

FRENCH CURVE

A mechanical drafting tool that has proved to be very valuable to the commercial artist. Constructed of a single piece of plastic, it contains a variety of curved edges that may guide a pencil or pen. These curves are expressons of mathematical formulas and have precise meanings to the mechanical engineer. However, the artist does not need a knowledge of math to use them. A virtually unlimited variety of French-curve patterns is available in art and drafting supply stores. Usually artists will buy a few that will serve all their purposes adequately.

The French curve can be used with either pencil or ruling pen. Since the latter is difficult to control around the curves, it is much more satisfactory to use an India ink pen. Naturally, when you use a French curve with any inking tool, the quality of the paper must be good enough so that the ink will not run or blot. The smoother the paper, the more easily the pen will follow the curve.

The French curve is used only when the artist must draw an exact line that is irregular in contour. Ovals, S-shapes, and the like are often encountered in commercial artwork and there is no better way to create them than with the French curve.

Always do a free-hand pencil sketch of any curved line that will eventually be finished with a French curve. This will allow you to create a smooth, flowing line that will act as a guide when you

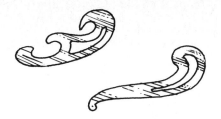

Two representative irregular (French) curves. Many other sizes and shapes are available.

begin the more difficult, detailed work. Still working lightly in pencil, place the French curve on the paper and attempt to position it so that the largest possible segment of the line coincides with the edge of the French curve. Do not be disappointed if you are unable to construct the line in one step. Although there are many French curves available, it is improbable that you will find one that solves your problem in one stroke. Ovals, in particular, require at least four steps in drawing. Working in small arcs, the beginner will tend to use too much curve in any one step; this will make the finished curve angular and ugly. A preliminary pencil sketch will help to minimize this problem.

When you have drawn one segment lightly in pencil, repeat the operation, trying another part of the French curve. Draw in such a manner that the arc will overlap the previous line. This will help the continuity of the curve and prevent angularity. When you have repeated this operation a sufficient number of times to have completed your drawing, repeat the entire drawing with a sharp, hard pencil. If the preliminary work has been done lightly, you may erase the surface with a kneaded eraser, leaving only the finished, accurate line. (See *Erasers*.) It is now possible to check your work accurately and make sure that the curve has been properly drawn. You have also removed any distracting marks that might cause errors during the inking.

If you intend to ink the same line with a pen when you have finished the pencil drawing, you may find it difficult to remember the many parts of the French curve you have used. Mark the parts of the plastic curve with a red grease pencil. (See *Marking Pencils*.) These marks are easily removed with a rag after you are done. If it is necessary to turn the curve over while you are working, mark the plastic with a graphite pencil. The mark will be harder to see, but will not stain the paper.

For those who will always have trouble working with a pen, the line may be finished with a brush. The indentation caused by the hard pencil will act as a guide for the brush, making your job easier.

Common Difficulties

Blotting. When inking with the French curve, make sure that the pen point is never brought into contact with the edge of the curve where it meets the paper. The ink will run under the edge and smear. To prevent this, place a triangle under the French curve; or you can tape coins to the underside to raise the curve above the paper.

Smudging. Keep the French curve clean. Wipe it frequently as you use it. Wash the curve when it gets dirty enough to smudge the paper; use regular hand soap and lukewarm water. Dry the curve quickly and thoroughly when it is clean; hot water—or leaving the curve undried—will cause the plastic to warp.

Nicks. Never try to use the French curve as a guide for cutting with a knife. It is almost impossible to avoid nicking the plastic with the knife blade. Needless to say, this will destroy the usefulness of the curve.

FRISKET KNIFE

A light, very sharp knife suitable for cutting clean, accurate shapes in a variety of frisket materials. (See *Knife, Frisket*.)

FRISKET PAPER

Light, transparent (or slightly translucent) paper used for preparing friskets. The paper is sold at all art supply stores, comes in sheets or rolls of many different sizes, and may be plain or coated with a gentle adhesive.

In use, frisket paper is peeled from the protective backing sheet, adhered to the artwork, a portion cut out with a frisket knife, and removed. The surface opening is cleaned to remove any traces of the adhesive or guide markings, and the color applied. After the color has dried, the remaining frisket is peeled gently from the surface and discarded. The procedure is repeated as often as necessary.

Common Difficulties

Bleeding. Paint will seep under the edges of a frisket that does not adhere sufficiently. There are several strengths of adhesive in frisket paper, and you should be sure that you have obtained one that has enough strength to resist the stretching caused by wetting during the application of paint. Storing the paper over long periods of time may also cause the adhesive to weaken, particularly if there are temperature extremes. This damage will manifest itself in bubbles or creases between the paper and the backing sheet. A paper so damaged will not offer a proper bond and should be replaced.

Tearing. At times the frisket paper will make too tight a bond even when the lighter adhesives are being used. When the frisket is removed, the surface of the artwork will come away with it, destroying the artwork in most cases. Any frisket paper will do this if left on too long. Try to work with friskets only when the rendering can be finished in one day. Leaving frisket paper on the artwork overnight is often sufficient to create this powerful bond. If you must work with a frisket for extended periods, cover the portions of the art not being worked on with paper

first so that only the edges of the frisketed area are covered with the frisket adhesive. Even if the bond becomes very strong, these small areas will peel away easily.

FRISKETS

A frisket is any device that protects part of the surface of a material so that color can be applied to the other parts of the surface not protected by the frisket. A frisket is, in effect, a stencil.

Friskets can be made of any material that can be cut into the desired shapes. The kind of material used to make a

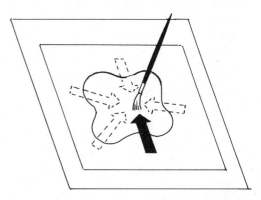

To prevent build-up or seepage at the edges of the frisket, draw the paint into the opening of the frisket from outside.

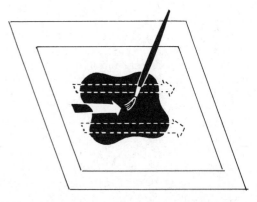

Once the area has been covered with paint, and before the paint dries, stroke marks can be eliminated by drawing the brush across the area in one direction. Do not add paint in this step, and use as few strokes as possible; a larger brush may help.

frisket will depend on personal preference, the medium being used, and the effects desired. It is possible to make friskets adhere to the surface while working or to allow the frisket to rest freely to prevent damage to that surface. There are so many variables that it will be possible to suggest only the main categories of frisketing; the reader may improvise and extend the range of materials and techniques.

All art stores carry some form of frisket paper. This is essentially a thin, transparent sheet of plastic with or without an adhesive coating. Because the frisket paper is thin and transparent, you can place it on the working surface and cut it out to the desired shape with great accuracy.

Coated sheets are available in several degrees of "stickiness," which poses a problem of choice. The lightly sticky adhesives do not damage a working surface, but they tend to pull off too easily and will barely adhere to a painted area. The heavily sticky adhesives hold extremely well under all conditions, but may become too stuck to the surface. When these firmly adhered frisket papers are removed, they may tear the paper, damage a painted surface, or leave an annoying residue that is difficult to clean away.

The uncoated papers must be made adhesive with rubber cement; they are too light to be used dry. To apply the rubber cement, line a cardboard box with wax paper and place a sheet of frisket paper perfectly flat in the box. Pour a thinned mixture of rubber cement over the paper and tilt the box in all directions to spread the cement evenly over the entire surface. Finally, drain the excess cement back into the rubber cement container and allow the coated paper to dry.

If the cement has been thinned properly (about 50% cement and 50% thinner), it will remain tacky on the frisket paper, even though dry, and will serve perfectly as a temporary adhesive. This process produces a very satisfactory frisket paper,

but few artists are willing to spend the time or to endure the trouble and mess involved.

There is also a liquid rubber frisket, sold in bottles, which may be applied with a brush or pen. This liquid dries into a solid sheet that may be peeled off easily once the job is finished. The difficulty is that the liquid dries too quickly, clogging pens and ruining brushes so that they are worthless even before the job is finished. The liquid frisket is water-soluble before it hardens, and ammonia will slow the drying time, dissolving the lumps that tend to form during application. However, if the liquid frisket is too diluted, it will not fully protect the paper beneath, requiring a second coat before it is thoroughly effective. Work quickly and carefully, use small amounts of the liquid frisket and keep the rest covered; clean your tools continually while you work and avoid going over an area until it has dried completely so that you will not pick up lumps.

When using a brush, do not dip it too deeply into the liquid frisket, so that the heel of the brush remains clean. This will prevent the brush from expanding and splitting. Even so, the chemicals tend to destroy the pointing qualities of a brush so that fine, detailed work becomes impossible. Therefore, try to outline the frisket area first while the brush is still accurate, and fill the area last when broader, cruder strokes are sufficient.

Liquid friskets are extremely valuable because you are able to work with intricate shapes, unusual edges, and small confined areas; but you must be prepared to lose a few brushes in the process.

Another frisket material is stencil paper. This is a glossy card (like oaktag) that cuts easily and produces a clean edge. It is not meant to adhere to the work surface. As the name implies, it is made for cruder, stencil-like techniques.

In addition to these commercially prepared frisket materials, you have limitless sources around you. Any piece of paper:

any straight edge, guide, or template; any kind of tape is a potential frisket—and these materials may be used in many variations. Edges may be torn instead of cut, openings may be shifted during color application, and the color may be applied with different techniques. For instance, try airbrushing paint through a loose weave cloth or a piece of window screen. The only limits are your imagination and your technical ability.

With so many variables, it is impossible to establish rules for using friskets. But general guidelines do exist; let's discuss them in terms of the art mediums:

Airbrush. Most airbrushing requires some form of adhesive frisket. The force of the air blows the paint under the edges of a dry frisket unless it can be held down firmly. Old linotype slugs, which you can obtain from your typographer, are excellent for holding down the edges of dry friskets. Photo-retouching requires a transparent frisket, so that you may cut the frisket after the frisket paper has been applied to the photo. This is the only way to insure complete accuracy. Photo-retouching also requires a light paper that cuts easily, so that the knife blade does not dig into the photo and damage it. Use a frisket knife for such cutting. (See *Knife, Frisket.*)

Use liquid frisket when working with portraits and similar subjects that do not lend themselves to hard, mechanical lines. This will avoid that crude, retouched look. When the frisket has been prepared and adhered, use the airbrush in the normal manner, stopping often to let the paint dry. Airbrush paint is necessarily thin and watery; the frisket will get extremely wet and eventually will curl away from the paper if the paint is not allowed to dry.

To create soft, but regular, edges, use a straight-edge or a similar prepared form and hold it ¼" away from the paper. Operate the airbrush a fair distance from the work and be sure that the spraying motion is regular and even. With practice,

you will produce a pronounced edge that tapers off quite softly, as some of the paint will drift back under the edge of the frisket.

Paints. Any paint that is applied with a brush works well with any type of frisket. Indeed, such textures as stippling, sponging, blotting, etc., are most easily controlled with a frisket.

Regardless of what frisket you use, be careful to work from the outside edge of the frisket toward the middle of the opening. Once the entire surface has been covered in this manner, it is possible to smooth out the paint by running a few strokes in the same direction over the entire area. This final stroking should be done very lightly, so that paint is not forced under the edge of the frisket.

Concentrated colors. These colors require adhesive friskets. Their consistency is much too thin for any other kind. Even then, these watercolors must be applied with the greatest care, as they will tend to bleed under the edges of the frisket. If possible, you should spray all watercolors. Otherwise, work as dryly as you can and avoid the edge of the frisket as much as possible.

Inks. Like dyes, inks are difficult to apply with friskets. Since they build up color with each stroke, they cannot be applied evenly unless they are sprayed on.

Pastels. The soft, chalky dust from pastels will inevitably creep under the edges of a dry frisket; but the adhesives on any of the prepared papers mar the surface just enough to discolor subsequent rendering. Try to use a prepared frisket paper only when there is just one frisketing to be done; whenever possible, cut out the frisket shape before applying it to the work surface. If you must cut the frisket on the artwork, use a kneaded eraser to clean the surface thoroughly before applying pastel. This cleaning tends to even out any irregularities in the surface so the pastel will lie smoothly and evenly.

When several frisketing jobs are necessary, use only a dry frisket. Work carefully from the edge of the frisket into the center of the opening. Use a stomp, a clean piece of cloth or tissue, or even your finger (if it is clean and dry). Rather than stroke the pastel stick directly onto the paper, shake some pastel dust from a sandpaper pad, then rub gently; this will prevent streaking.

When the color has been applied, remove the frisket carefully. Some pastel dust will be on the paper outside the desired area. Remove this dust with a clean kneaded eraser, being careful not to destroy the edge of the rendering. If the shape of the color area is complex, be sure to keep the part of the frisket that you cut away in the beginning. Place this piece over the rendered area and clean around the frisket with the kneaded eraser, always working from the center of the frisket outward toward the paper. Before proceeding to the next frisket area, fix the previous rendering with fixative. Since too much fixative will seal the paper and make it unreceptive to pastel, put the original frisket back on the paper when you apply the fixative; thus, only the previously rendered areas will be fixed.

Pencils, crayons, etc. Any of these are extremely easy to apply and will work equally well with any frisket material. No special instructions are necessary.

Rubber cement. On certain papers like Color-Aid and Colorama, rubber cement can leave a pronounced stain. Thus pasting up art on these materials can be a problem. The simplest procedure is to retain the paper from which you have cut the shape to be pasted and use it as a frisket. This will allow you to apply cement only where it is needed. Since the dry cement is visible on the colored paper, the shape of the cemented area acts as a guide for position when you are pasting the art down.

There are many ways of creating novel friskets and techniques. Beautiful effects can be achieved with the deckled edges of handmade papers, with the edges of newspapers, and with torn construction paper. You can smudge pigments with your fingers, with erasers, and with nearly any substance you can name. Other tricks will produce an endless variety of results. The main thing to remember is that practice and experimentation will be necessary to get the full value of the frisket process.

All prepared frisket papers must be protected from high temperature and high humidity. These conditions will affect the adhesives and destroy their usefulness. Keep all friskets clean. If you use a triangle as a frisket, for instance, clean it thoroughly first.

Common Difficulties

Bleeding. Pastel, as well as all liquid mediums, will bleed under even the best friskets. Avoid excessive amounts of such mediums and stay away from the edges of the frisket as much as possible. If any frisket gets too wet, it will curl, expand, and pull away from the paper. Keep the frisket dry while working. If it gets wet, stop and let it dry.

Drafting tape, while a good frisket, has a pebbled texture to prevent too firm a bond and to permit easy removal. When using tape, do not move the pigment toward the tape, but always over the tape into the middle of the frisketed area. If this does not work, try pressing the tape down more firmly at the extreme edge with something hard like a ruler.

Ragged edges. If the frisket is removed while the pigment is still wet, the edge of the frisket will drag some paint along and create a ragged edge. Always wait until the paint is dry. If too much paint has been applied, some of it will stick to the frisket and will be pulled away when the frisket is removed. Avoid using too thick a paint mixture or applying too much or too many coats as it will pile up at the edges. This high edge of pigment will crumble easily and will smear. Always work toward the middle.

Poor adhesion. If you are using a prepared paper with a proper degree of adhesion, but the frisket will not hold, it is probably the fault of the frisket paper. Heat and humidity destroy the effectiveness of the best adhesives. Even if the paper was just purchased, it may have been stored in the art store for some time. Always attempt to get the freshest stock you can, and protect it in your own storage. Any adhesive will dry out with age and become useless. Do not attempt to work on paper that is several years old.

If the frisket is new and it will not hold, the paper on which you are working is at fault. Grease from perspiration will destroy any effective bond. Many paints and fixatives will also prevent proper adhesion. In these cases it may not be possible to remove the grease, paint, or fixative; you may have to work with a dry frisket.

Torn paper. If the frisket adhesive is too strong, it will pull up part of the paper surface when removed. Try using a less sticky adhesive. Poor quality papers and boards will also be easily damaged regardless of the adhesive. Use only a good paper or board. Any adhesive, if left adhered too long, will tend to make a permanent bond. Try to do any frisketing job within one working day. The longer the frisket remains on the paper, the more difficult it will be to remove.

Many kinds of tape will damage the paper when removed. To prevent the tape from sticking too firmly, cover most of the area to be protected with paper first, leaving about $\frac{1}{16}''$ open. Then apply the tape to this final small area, overlapping the protective paper. This not only prevents the tape from sticking, but saves on tape.

Discolored paint. Friskets applied over a freshly painted area will often pick up some paint or leave a stain. Cover most of the area with paper first, before applying the frisket.

Residue. Many prepared frisket papers will leave a residue of adhesive when they are removed. This residue is not easily cleaned off and can damage further work or dirty a finished job. Usually this can be remedied by using a frisket with less adhesive strength. If some residue still occurs, try cutting with less pressure, and do not press the frisket down as hard.

If residue still remains, try removing it with a rubber cement pick-up or a kneaded eraser. Don't rub. Blot at the residue. If it will still not come off, use a piece of cotton wetted with rubber cement thinner. This will dissolve the residue. However, keep blotting and do not rub. Change the cotton several times. Rubber cement thinner will not dissolve any water-based or dry art pigment, and if the process is done gently, will not stain the art.

Knife marks. If the frisket paper is too thick, if the knife is too dull or heavy, or if your pressure is too hard, you may produce damaging cut marks on the finished art or photograph. Always use the thinnest frisket you can; use the sharpest, finest frisket knife or blade; and cut as gently as possible. With practice, you will discover that the feel of the knife is different when you are cutting only the frisket and when you are cutting beyond into the paper.

Bubbles. Frisket paper that has begun to deteriorate will develop spots that have lost adhesiveness. These spots will cause uneven adhesion or bubbles. As long as these bubbles do not occur at a cutting line, they will not affect the job. Such defective spots will show clearly on the frisket paper while it is still attached to its backing sheet. Any difference in color will be a signal that the frisket paper is not adhering to the backing sheet and that it will probably not adhere to the work surface.

Cutting problems. All cases of difficulty with cutting—cut marks, residue, paint discoloration, etc.—can be avoided by cutting the frisket before applying it to the work surface. This is possible with all but the most complex shapes. Since both the frisket paper and the backing sheet are somewhat transparent, the cutting may be done before you remove the frisket paper from its backing by placing *both* over the artwork. As you cut, the backing sheet will protect the artwork while permitting an accurate cut.

FRISKETS, LIQUID

Fluids that dry into rubbery sheets, creating temporary marks on drawings. Like frisket paper, these sheets protect the covered portions of a drawing while other areas are being rendered. Unlike frisket paper, liquid friskets can be applied with pens or brushes, eliminating the difficulty of maneuvering a knife blade around small or unusual shapes, and thus the danger of cutting into the drawing, itself.

Once the rendering has been finished, the dried liquid frisket is removed by peeling it from the surface like a rubber sheet. (See *Friskets.*)

Common Difficulties

Incomplete coverage. Liquid frisket must be applied in a fairly thick and uniform layer. If any portion is too thin, paint will seep through. It may be necessary to apply more than one coat.

Clogging. Liquid friskets dry quickly, creating a gummy residue on pens and brushes that destroys their effectiveness. Ammonia will help keep the liquid from drying so fast, but it thins the frisket, causing incomplete coverage. However, rinsing your tools in ammonia will help keep them clean while you are working.

Stickiness. The drying liquid frisket acts much the same as rubber cement—it sticks to itself. The drying liquid frisket on your tool will stick to the dried portions already applied, which will come away with your tool. Make sure that you keep the tools clean.

Drying. Since the liquid frisket dries quickly, pour a little into a cup for immediate use. As this thickens, remove it and pour in a fresh amount. At the same time clean your tools thoroughly.

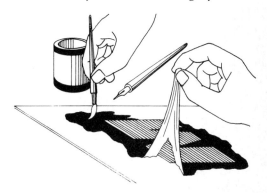

Liquid frisket is applied by brush or pen. The frisket is easily stripped from the rendering when dry.

FROSTED ACETATE

Pencil, ink, paint, dyes, rubber cement, etc., do not adhere well on transparent plastic films. Thus, when preparing an overlay—usually for a separation mechanical—a matte surface is provided on some of these films which facilitates their application. The least expensive and most common of these is frosted acetate. (The procedure for using frosted acetate, and similar materials, is described in *Plastic Films.* See also *Acetate.*)

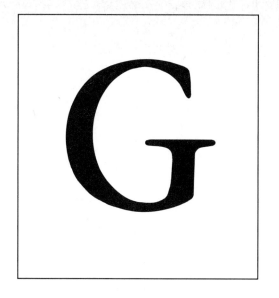

to prepare a surface for illustration painting. Acrylic gesso differs from conventional gesso only in the plastic binder, which creates a surface with a slightly rubbery feel. Like conventional gesso, acrylic gesso may be used with any paint, but its main advantage is the superior surface it provides for acrylic paints. Art supply stores will usually carry both ready-mixed or dry forms of gesso, which, when mixed with water, can be applied in any manner or technique to provide texture or "tooth" to a painting surface. For example, gesso thinned with water can be brushed on with any kind of brush, so that the basic surface texture is relatively unchanged. Thick gesso can be spread with a palette knife. Cloths and sponges, even your fingers, can be used to create unusual textures without limit.

GELS

Sheets of colored plastic. This plastic is thicker and more brittle than the conventional plastic sheets (acetate) used by the commercial artist. The primary purpose of gels is to color light. That is, a gel placed in front of a light bulb will produce colored light. As such, gels are used extensively in the theater and in display. But the choice of colors available in gels is so wide, the hues so intense and transparent, that many commercial artists like to use them to create art collages and to indicate color panels on artwork. Unfortunately, gels do not come with an adhesive backing, and any adhesive tends to mottle the color. It is usually necessary to tape the gel to the surface and hide the tape with a mat. Since this is not always possible many artists prefer to use Bourges and similar plastic sheet products. (See *Plastic Sheets.*)

GESSO

A plaster-like substance, made of chalk, white pigment, and a binder; it is used

GLITTER

A powdered preparation of highly reflective material available in various colors. Although glitter is more easily identified with arts and crafts, it does have a certain application in sign writing and display.

Glitter must be applied with an adhesive, preferably one that dries rather slowly. To obtain the maximum brilliance of glitter, always apply the adhesive first and then dust the glitter over the wet surface. Before starting, make provision for collecting the excess flakes that do not adhere. Do not press the glitter into the adhesive. This will cause the surface to become clouded with adhesive, destroying the sparkle effect.

Common Difficulty

Shedding. The flakes of glitter are brittle and the adhesive does not afford a firm hold. Therefore, a surface treated with glitter tends to "shed." Since this is unavoidable don't handle the finished work and prevent any other piece of art or display from touching the glitter also.

GLUE

This is a term that applies to a wide range of liquids that are used for adhering all kinds of materials. (See *Adhesives.*)

GOUACHE

General name given to a group of opaque, water-soluble paints that includes designer and poster colors and the technique of painting with them. Traditionally, gouache paints were opaque watercolors that were thinned, on the painting, with Chinese white. Consequently, any watercolor that was combined with white was termed *gouache.* In fact, the technique often included other mediums such as pastel.

The distinguishing feature of gouaches is the binder, a water-soluble glue such as gum arabic. Modern gouaches range from full opacity to near watercolor transparency. The addition of white paint is optional. Available in tubes, jars, and pans, these paints are usually referred to by names other than *gouache.* By whatever name, they are the mainstay of the commercial artist. This is because they are comparatively inexpensive, offer a variety of techniques, can be used in virtually all commercial art tools, and are soluble with water even when dry—a special advantage because commercials artists do not use paint with the same frequency as illustrators or fine artists. Paint often sits on palettes for weeks and months. But a few drops of water will return the paint to its original consistency. This also facilitates corrections and revisions. Gouache works well with sable brushes, whose fine points and springiness are most suitable to commercial artists' requirements. Gouache dries to a soft, matte finish, and is rarely combined with mediums or varnishes.

On occasion it may be desirable to slow the drying or to permit the paint to adhere to glossy surfaces. But adding anything to the paint will tend to diminish its covering ability and create streaks. It is more practical to select paints with these characteristics if such work is extensive. For instance, Pelikan designer colors contain additives that retard drying, and acrylic paints are superior on glossy surfaces such as acetate.

There are no set procedures for applying gouache. Airbrushes, stipple sponges, ruling pens, lettering brushes, and virtually any other tools can produce interesting and satisfactory results. But as with any other watercolor paint, the best effects are obtained with the minimum of strokes. This means that much planning and practice should precede the actual work. Don't go back into an area once it has dried. The gouache will dissolve, but the results will look streaky and muddy. Overpainting is possible if the strokes are quick and definite. Too much brush work will dissolve the paint underneath and destroy the effect. (See also *Paint.*)

Common Difficulties

Hardening. Gouache paints dry fast, even in the tube. Once a tube has been opened, the drying process begins. Before very long, the entire tube will have hardened beyond use. In an emergency, a tube can be torn open, the chunks of paint placed in a cup, and water added. But succeeding repetitions of this practice will wash out the glue binder, and the paint will become dusty and not adhere well. A word of caution: The finer the quality of these paints, the more susceptible they are to drying in the tube. If your art store does not have a rapid turnover, some products may dry before they have been opened. A gentle squeeze is a test of whether the pigment inside has become too stiff for convenient use.

Streaking. Although tempera paints are opaque, they will not cover with uniformity. It requires a great deal of practice to apply them smoothly. As with watercolor, it is necessary to work rhythmically, keeping the area to be covered uniformly wet. Once the paint has dried, it is impossible to paint into that area again without leaving streak marks.

If the paint has been diluted unevenly, streaks will also occur. To prevent this, work in a manner similar to the way you would work in watercolor. Wet the paper beforehand and try to float the paint in large enough amounts so that each stroke picks up the excess of the stroke before it. If the area to be covered has hard edges, use a fine brush and outline the area before spreading the full amount of paint. This will save you the time it might take to work slowly and carefully up to that edge. If the color must be absolutely flat, prepare a frisket and apply the paint with the largest brush you have. Keep the strokes going in the same direction, and continue to smooth the paint until it begins to dry. Occasionally, switch the direction of the stroke, moving at right angles to the previous direction. This will prevent too much paint from piling up in any spot. Work in from the edges of the frisket to prevent the paint from building up at the edges. Don't try to remove the frisket until the paint is dry. To correct a streaked area, first remove as much paint as possible. While tempera is opaque and will cover with a second coat, the irregularities of the paint beneath will cause uneven drying and thus will repeat the streaks. With cotton swabs or with a clean brush, wet the incorrect area and wipe away the paint. Wait until the area is thoroughly dry before making the correction. Then reapply water if necessary. This may seem like a waste of time, but it is the only way to be sure that the area has been wetted evenly. Then begin to paint as before. For extremely smooth areas, try using an airbrush. Tempera works well in the airbrush, if the paint is of good quality and has been thinned properly.

Bleeding. You will find that certain colors have a greater intensity than others, and will come through when overpainted. Although this occurs infrequently, it can be annoying. To prevent bleeding, try to use the more intense colors last, or spray the painting during its progress with a workable, matte fixative. This will not affect the painting procedures, but will tend to darken the colors.

Shine. Particularly with the jar temperas, you will discover certain parts of your painting seem to take on a gloss, like an enamel or a shellac. This is caused by an excess of the binding medium, which tends to separate out at the top of the jar when it has been left standing. If you do not stir the entire contents of the jar thoroughly, your brush will pick up more binder than pigment and gloss results.

Always stir the jar well before using, and take some paint out on a palette. This will prevent undue separation, and will allow you to close the jar, which will prevent the rest of the paint from drying out too fast. To a lesser degree, this kind of trouble will be found in tube paints as well. There will be less separation, but it will occur if all the paint squeezed from the tube is not mixed thoroughly before using.

Dustiness. Conversely, some areas of your painting may seem unusually chalky or velvety, and may produce discoloring dust when brushed. This is caused by the reverse of excessive binder. When you get to the bottom of the jar, all the binder may have been used up or may have dried up. This means that you are now painting with pure pigment, which is essentially chalky. Once again stir the jar well before using. To protect such a dusty spot, spray with fixative.

Spots. Once you have created a spot, it cannot be obliterated in tempera. The discoloration, usually caused by a drop of water, merely bleeds through each succeeding layer of paint. The only remedy is to remove all the paint and start over.

Erasure marks. All erasers, even kneaded erasers, leave strong marks if used with tempera. They tend to polish the painted surface, causing areas of high gloss. Once again, these spots will not be covered. Try to make all corrections with paint. If some pencil lines remain in unpainted areas, remove them carefully without touching the paint. If this cannot be done, erase the entire painting, keeping the pressure on the eraser constant and avoiding excess erasing in any particular spot. This will at least keep the discoloration even. Any final unevenness may be hidden by spraying the entire painting with fixative. Remember, this coating will darken the colors. If the paint has been applied with any thickness, a limited amount of correction can be accomplished with a few gentle scraping strokes by the side of a razor blade. Once again, any variation in the surface can be evened with a coat of fixative.

GRAPH PAPER

Ledger paper with a printed grid of light blue lines that acts as a guide when constructing charts and graphs. Also referred to as cross section paper. (See *Papers and Boards.*)

GRAPHITE PAPER

A form of transfer paper prepared with the same graphite used to produce lead pencils. A drawing transferred with this paper may be erased with the same ease as a pencil drawing. (See *Carbon Paper.*)

GRAPHITE STICKS

Composed of the same material found in ordinary lead pencils, but without the wooden casings. These flat, rectangular-shaped sticks are available in the softer grades (2B–6B) with which you are fa-miliar in the regular line of drawing pencils. (See *Pencils, Lead.*)

The large, uncovered surfaces of the graphite stick are very useful for creating broad effects in pencil renderings, and the square ends can be used for lettering. The exact width needed for any alphabet can be readily obtained by shaving the sides with a razor blade and a sandpaper pad.

Be sure that you use a graphite stick of the proper hardness for each job, and remember that the graphite will soil your hands. Clean your hands frequently, or you may smudge your drawing.

GRAPHOS

The brand name of an India ink drawing pen. Unlike conventional drawing pens, the Graphos pens' interchangeable nibs have swiveling covers that facilitate cleaning. (See *Pens.*)

Graphos drawing ink pen. The nibs of the pen are interchangeable.

GUIDE LINES

Lines that serve to determine the shape or position of any graphic symbol or representation. These lines act as a border or margin for the finished drawing, rendering, or mounting of such graphics, and are usually removed when the art has been finished. For this reason, guide lines are drawn lightly with a soft pencil, whose mark can be removed easily with a gentle erasing that does not damage the working surface or the art. (See *Erasers.*)

If the work is not for presentation, but is being prepared for reproduction, these lines may be drawn in light blue (which does not photograph).

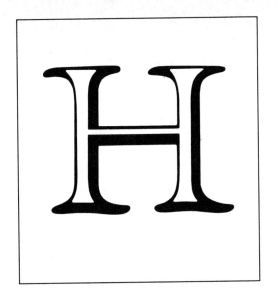

HABERULE

The brand name of a special ruler, or type gauge, used for copyfitting type. Also a copy-casting book that contains instructions for specifying type for copy being prepared for a typographer. (See *Copy Caster.*)

HANDLETTERING

The practice of producing finished lettering for reproduction through a built-up method as opposed to single-stroke calligraphy or sign writing.

In this procedure, lettering is first laid out roughly with a chisel pencil, modified and corrected with conventional pencil, traced onto bristol board, outlined carefully with a fine pen or brush, filled in with a heavier brush, and cleaned up or refined with a fine brush and white paint.

Handlettering is used to produce lettering with modified characteristics, to experiment with unusual designs and spacing, and to create new alphabets. Despite the existence of thousands of type faces, there is a continuing need for lettering that fits unusual spaces, suggests moods, or follows unique layouts (for example, curved shapes). This is particularly true of scripts, both formal and informal.

It is strongly recommended that any serious commercial artist acquire as much instruction as possible from a professionally qualified handletterer. The knowledge gained about type forms and aesthetics is most valuable.

To supplement classroom training, there are several good books on this subject, particularly *Lettering for Reproduction* by David Gates (Watson-Guptill, 1969).

HALFTONE SCREEN

A sheet of glass containing very fine lines etched into the glass with acid. The glass screen is placed behind the lens of a copy camera used to make negatives for printing plates. Light passing through the screen is broken into a pattern of solid dots of varying sizes (determined by the amount of light passing through), which transforms a continuous tone subject into a line negative used to produce a printing plate. In other words, a photograph, etc., which contains grays, is converted into black dots and white paper which visually appears to be gray. Since a printing press cannot print anything except a solid color, continuous tone material must be converted into such solid dots before it can be printed.

Similar, but even toned, effects can be created in the art by using benday, top sheet shading film, and single or double tone drawing boards.

HAND CLEANERS

Pastes that contain solvents for removing the common stains that may be acquired by an artist while working. Originally produced for industrial workers to remove grease, and office workers to remove ink and typewriter stains, these cleaners are now available in art stores and work well for the artist.

To remove certain *dyes* and *paints,* you may need to clean first with turpentine, lacquer thinner, or chlorine bleach, but the hand cleaner is excellent for removing remaining traces of dirt and for nullifying the prominent odors these solvents may have produced. Hand cleaners are sold in jars or cans and are used with water, like soap.

HAND RESTS

The original artists' hand rest, used to steady the hand when painting critical areas, is the mahlstick. This stick, with its small ball of soft chamois on the end, is a standby for fine artists and sign writers alike. However, the commercial artist, unless he works at an easel, has little need for such a device. His problem is merely to keep his hand from touching wet mediums already applied or from smudging a clean working surface. For this purpose, a scrap of paper or cardboard is often as effective as anything else. If the surface is wet, the rest can be built up from the surface by using books or triangles or whatever else is on hand. Certainly, the artist must keep the working surface clean, and the use of such a method is absolutely essential and should be practiced by the beginning artist.

For those who prefer a manufactured aid, a wooden hand rest is available that provides a steady bridge over the working area and allows the artist to proceed with a minimum of discomfort and chance of error.

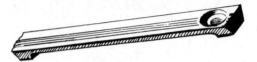

Typical hand rest with an opening for a jar of ink or paint. Scoring holds pencils, brushes, etc.

HOT TYPE

Typographic proofs produced from printed impressions made by metal slugs cast in traditional (and largely abandoned) typesetting machines such as the Linotype. Because these slugs were formed by pouring molten lead into special molds, the process came to be called hot metal or hot type, to distinguish it from newer computer and photographic typesetting methods. Similarly, the term is applied to hand-set type, which was made of molten metal. (See *Cold Type* and *Type.*)

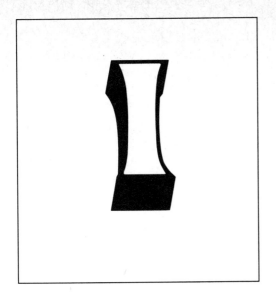

ILLUMINATING

The practice of embellishing hand-lettered manuscripts with color. Limited today to the decoration of such one-of-a-kind presentations as testimonials, illuminating is an extension of calligraphy.

ILLUSTRATION BOARD

This term covers a wide range of bristols of varying quality backed with cardboard that are used in the majority of cases where finished art is being prepared by the commercial artist. Illustration boards come in two surfaces: hot press—a smooth, highly polished surface—and cold press—a natural, matte texture. These boards are also sold in two weights, single and double ply. This refers to the weight of the backing cardboard and does not affect the weight of the bristol. A full sheet of illustration board is 40″ x 60″, but boards of many different sizes are carried by all art supply stores. (See *Papers and Boards*.)

IMAGING SYSTEMS

There are a number of product systems that permit artists to create original pres-

sure graphics. Although they vary in chemistry and composition, their preparation follows similar procedures. Black-and-white artwork is assembled on opaque or transparent backgrounds, depending on the system. A product sheet is placed in contact with the art and exposed to light (either ordinary or ultraviolet). The exposed material is treated with a developing fluid, which activates the adhesive backing and allows unwanted portions to be wiped away. The finished sheet is washed and dried and stored with a protective backing. The range of colors, the opacity or transparency of the image, and the kind of supportive equipment necessary varies with product and manufacturer. (See *Color Keys (3M)*.)

Common Difficulties

Chemical reactions. Most of the difficulties with these systems involve the use of particular chemicals and papers. The sensitivity of these materials requires absolute adherence to the instructions. Variations in time and temperature may inhibit proper results. Similarly, shelf life times may affect successful chemical actions. Be sure to follow the instructions exactly, and consult with qualified salespersons to determine how long such items can be stored and under what conditions.

INCH RULERS

This is the common ruler—each foot is divided into twelve inches, each inch is divided into quarters, each quarter-inch is divided into eighths, etc. (See *Rulers*.)

INDIA INK

India ink is the basic drawing medium for all line artwork and mechanicals that are to be reproduced by commercial printing processes. India ink is quite black, opaque, and waterproof; it is sold in small, pen-filler topped bottles containing ¾ oz., which can be refilled from larger, bulk storage bottles. In addition, a limited range of transparent colors are available in India ink product lines, but the black ink is the most frequently used in commercial art.

There are several brands of India ink on the market, and all are acceptable. But there are differences between these brands; the type of art you are doing may help you decide which brand to use.

Higgins India Ink. One of the popular American brands, tends to be thinner than the others—a feature that helps to prevent the ink from drying too rapidly and from clogging the drawing instrument. This thinness, however, does mean that it may take two coats to achieve an intense, opaque black. Inks of this type are best for use with drafting tools and are least successful with large area coverage.

Pelikan India Ink. Very popular German product, which covers better than the thinner inks; but it will dry, thicken, and clog much more quickly. Inks of this nature are best for all-around use, since they have some characteristics of each of the extremes.

Artone Extra Dense India Ink. Another American product, which is the most opaque. Its thickness almost makes it impossible to use with fine-opening drafting tools. It will clog and dry even during use. Inks of this type should be reserved for the occasions when fast, opaque coverage is imperative.

All the inks mentioned here are of excellent quality and enjoy complete commercial acceptance. The descriptions given above are intended only as general guidelines; many artists use one product for all their work and the choice of products is yours. In fact, most companies will produce several products in the overall India ink category, so that their alternative brands will duplicate one of the categories mentioned above. You should note that these differences do exist, so that you can experiment with several types before selecting any of them.

In addition, there are a number of specialized India inks, some of which may even be water soluble. Offered by all the ink manufacturers, these products are specifically prepared for particular tools and jobs. For example, several brands of fountain pen ink are sold. In general, it is wise to buy the brand of ink recommended by the manufacturer of a specific India ink fountain pen. Similarly, manuscript fount inks are designed for use with certain types of drawing and lettering pens, and you should try them for a number of nib pen uses. (See *Pens.*)

For working on very glossy surfaces, you may have greater success with acetate inks, although many India inks are sold for the purpose.

Since India ink in any form is usually indelible and quite durable it is difficult to erase. Artone produces an E-Z-Rase ink that helps reduce this problem.

Common Difficulties

Clogging. Nearly all India inks will thicken or dry out while in use or in storage. This may increase their tendency to clog the small openings in pens and drawing instruments. Do not buy more ink than you can use in a relatively short time—several months, for example. If the ink does clog in use, add a very small drop of ammonia to the ink in the pen; or dip the pen in ammonia before filling. Always shake the large ink bottles before using in order to correct any settling.

Smudging. India ink does not erase easily and it will leave a pronounced dark smudge when you attempt to remove it. Blot away as much of ink as you can from the surface before it dries. If the ink has dried, scrape the ink gently with the side of a razor blade. Brush off this scraped ink and gently erase the area with the finest, clean ink eraser. If any stain or smudge remains, cover it with a good quality opaque white paint.

Caking. Regardless of how much attention you pay to cleaning your drawing instruments, India ink will eventually leave a caked-up residue in hard-to-reach places on your drawing tools. Try cleaning these tools with ammonia. If the ink has become too thick or has hardened too long, ammonia may not work. Soak the tools in pen cleaner. *Do not scrape.* Scraping can damage the surfaces and destroy the effectiveness of any drawing instrument.

Blueing. If diluted, most India inks tend to become blue-gray. Since blue does not photograph in the copy camera, this can result in poor reproduction of wash drawings. When using India ink wash, add a small amount of yellow ochre watercolor paint to warm up the color.

INDIA INK DISPENSERS

These bottles are usually small and squat with narrow necks. The bottles were designed this way to prevent them from tipping over and spilling ink on a drawing. The narrow neck also limits the evaporation of these inks, which tend to dry quickly when exposed to air. Removing the cap from these bottles and filling an inking tool is a two-handed task. Even with pen points and pen holders, which need only one hand when being dipped into ink for refilling, the ink bottle can cause problems. The level of the ink may fall well below the narrow neck. Trying to dip the pen into the bottle to the right depth without touching the inky sides is difficult. If the ink is too low, you may have to use your other hand to tip the bottle to create a deep enough pool. And yet, if the inking tool runs dry in the middle of a job, it may be necessary to hold the work steady, leaving only one hand free for reloading the inking tool. Two types of dispensers make it possible to reload with one hand.

The fount ink bottle. Looks as though it is lying on its side and is excellent for pen points that must be dipped into the ink frequently. The design of this bottle creates a pool of ink that is much wider than the conventional bottle, which means its level remains constant longer. Even when full, this level is not much higher than a pen point. Therefore, when dipping a pen point into the ink, less caution is necessary to prevent overloading the pen or soiling your fingers. The neck of this bottle, which is angled slightly, is also larger than the conventional bottles; a pen holder is less apt to hit the sides of the neck and get inky when being dipped. Fount ink is similar to India ink and can be used as an alternative, and an empty fount ink bottle can be filled with any other drawing fluid you wish, so that you can enjoy its features, regardless of the medium you are using.

The pen-filling ink stand. Has a lever that removes the cap of the ink bottle when pressed by the heel of the hand. This permits you to use your fingers to place the pen nib under the quill or dropper of the cap, while the heel of the same hand holds the cap steady. Once pressure is released, the cap returns.

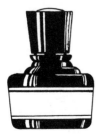

Representative India ink bottle with its dropper dispenser cap.

Hand-operated ink bottle stand. The cap is lifted when the hand depresses the lever.

With either dispenser, or even the conventional bottle, you are advised to buy the larger bottle of bulk ink. This is a more economical way to buy ink, and you can continually refill the smaller bottles from the larger one, keeping their level and consistency constant.

INDIA INK PENS

India ink pens, like drawing pens, is a general term for a large selection of drawing tools that may or may not use India ink. (See *Pens.*)

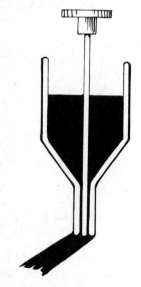

Hollow-point scriber. In all hollow-point pens, the central needle starts the ink, controls the flow, and cleans the tube of old, dried ink.

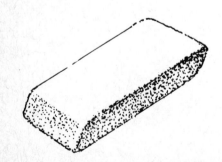

Ink eraser.

INK ERASERS

A hard, abrasive substance used to scratch ink off a paper surface; or a liquid which will dissolve or bleach away ink. (See *Erasers.*)

INK, MANUSCRIPT

The name of an India ink variation designed for use with certain lettering pen points. (See *India Ink* and *Pen Points.*)

INKS, ACETATE

Specially prepared inks for use on plastic sheets and other glossy surfaces that tend to reject conventional drawing inks. An excellent example of the opportunities for using acetate ink is on overlays.

Acetate inks are sold in bottles similar to those containing drawing inks and are handled in a similar manner, with either pen or brush, and require no preparation of either the ink or the drawing surface. Acetate inks may be either transparent or opaque, removable or permanent. A limited range of primary colors is offered. A thinner and a cleaner are also sold, for use when the rather quick thickening pigments make the inks difficult to apply or remove from drawing tools.

Common Difficulties

Settling. The pigments in these inks separate quite rapidly, even during use. It is necessary to stir and shake the bottles vigorously to insure complete mixing. Even unopened bottles will tend to settle, creating a hard residue on the bottom. You must get used to the idea of continual stirring to make sure that the ink is usable at all times. If this is not done, the inks will be either too thick or too thin, making drawing difficult or clogging the drawing tools. Use of the thinner or cleaner will help avoid some of these problems, but it will also dilute the ink to the point of poor coverage. It is better to observe normal cleaning and handling with water, which can be done if the ink is fresh and well mixed.

Streaking. Not only the settling, but the very nature of the medium causes the ink to lie unevenly. If you wish to create flat areas of color, it is preferable to use a frisket with some spraying device or with careful brushstrokes, as illustrated in *Friskets*.

INKS, DRAWING

Liquid mediums prepared for use with pens. While pens are limited to producing lines, drawing inks can also be used to create many other effects with other tools. With any paintbrushes, drawing inks can be handled like watercolors, producing washes and shaded rendering techniques. These thin fluids can also be used with airbrushes and other sprayers, although extra care must be taken to clean these tools after ink has been used in them. Like India ink, drawing inks are waterproof and come in a limited range of transparent colors.

Common Difficulties

Thinness. The pigment of colored inks can separate easily in some of the colors, producing a heavy sediment in the bottom of the bottle. If not dissolved, this sediment may also produce clogging in pens and airbrushes. This separation is particularly true of the lighter colors, such as white and yellow. Be sure that the ink has been thoroughly stirred or shaken to dissolve the sediment before using.

Bleeding. Like dyes, drawing inks are brilliant in color and bleed through any paint that has been used to cover them, either for corrections or overpainting. Allow the ink to dry thoroughly before overpainting and do the covering with an opaque white that is bleedproof.

Streaking. Inks build up color with each application, so that brushstrokes are almost impossible to eliminate. To avoid streaking, apply the inks in thin, diluted washes, repeating the procedure until the desired intensity is reached. Alternatively, apply the inks with an airbrush.

Errors. Inks stain papers and boards and are difficult to remove. On fine, heavy stocks a certain amount of erasing is possible with an ink eraser, but the results will vary with the color involved. Similarly, high quality illustration board will permit some correction by scraping with a razor blade or bleaching with a chlorine bleach. Here again, the different colors will afford varying success, and in all cases the surface of the board will be damaged to the extent that new color will not "take" in the same manner over the corrected area. The only practical way to make a revision of an ink rendering is to cover the ink with an opaque paint. Since the paint will not have the same effect as the brilliantly transparent ink, areas of correction must be quite small and a good deal of experimentation is necessary to get the proper results.

INKS, PRINTING

These inks are designed for printing presses. In this case, we are discussing the inks that are prepared for commercial printers as opposed to inks that are made for fine art and hobby printing. The latter are sold in art stores, are meant for handmade plates, and are more in the realm of practice covered in the introduction. Printing inks are important to commercial artists since they represent their actual medium. Regardless of how commercial artists produce their work, it is only when the piece is finally printed that it is complete. Therefore, it is impossible to be a really accomplished commercial artist without some knowledge of the printing processes and the inks and paper used.

Printing inks come in a complete range of colors. There is virtually no color that is not manufactured or cannot be blended with existing inks. Nevertheless, there are strong restrictions. First of all, what we call full color is, in reality, only four colors. To produce the full-color photographs that we have become accustomed to seeing, the printing industry has devised a process that uses four-color presses and plates that have been made by a filter system of photography that reduces these pictures into the four basic colors. These colors, cyan, magenta, yellow, and black, are standard throughout the industry and are referred to as process colors. Since they are standard, they are available throughout the country. In addition, there are a few colors that are used continually. If you will look closely at the bulk of the printed material around you, you will quickly see the repetition. There are actually only a handful in continual use. In many print shops there are presses devoted to each color, and they run steadily without change, job after job. The reason for this should be obvious. Cleaning the press, applying a new color, proofing that color for accuracy, and recleaning the press after the run may take longer than the actual job run, particularly with today's high-speed presses. Since the cost of the job is based mainly on the paper and the time on press, the cost of a new color can double the price of a job. Many clients faced with this economic truth will settle for one of the "standard" colors rather than pay the additional costs.

Other inks and colors react in unpredictable ways on different materials. Plastic papers and films require special inks. The Day-Glo colors, those vivid, fluorescent colors, are different for each printing process. On some presses these inks must be printed twice to achieve the proper effect. There are many black inks, each producing a different "color" and meant for different papers and printing methods. Varnishes and plastic coating can be added

by the printers. The point of all this information is to convince you that the field of inks and printing is large—much larger than can be covered by a book of this nature. And yet this information is vital. There are books that discuss much of this material, but they are scattered and quickly become out-of-date. The best teachers are your printers. Learn to work with them, ask their advice, and don't be afraid to ask questions before you start designing a job.

INSTANT LETTERING

This a brand name for a form of transfer type. (See *Transfer Type.*)

INT (Image 'N' Transfer)

A 3M process for producing original pressure graphics in white, black, and a limited number of colors. Black and white art is assembled and a Kodalith negative (or orange 3M color key) is made. This negative is used as a mask when exposing the INT sheet to light. INT chemicals are then wiped over the surface to eliminate unwanted color and to activate an adhesive on the remaining areas. The adhesive is protected by a backing sheet while the image area is allowed to dry thoroughly and harden. The finished sheet is then handled like any rubdown pressure graphic.

Common Difficulty

Sensitivity. The INT process is quite sensitive, and extreme care must be exercised when using it. The instructions leave little room for error. Shelf life is critical, and so is temperature and time of exposure. It is wise to practice on a small piece each time you work. Conditions will vary from day to day, and must be compensated for.

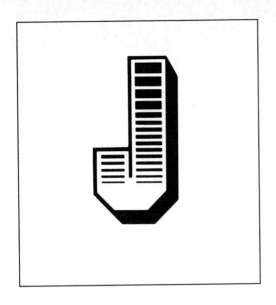

JAPAN COLORS

This is a name given to thick, pasty paints used for sign writing. These paints, which are sold in tubes and cans in stores carrying sign writers' supplies, are soluble in turpentine and are very quick drying. They are used for the bulk of inexpensive signs that must be placed out-of-doors and must be waterproof. An amount of paint is removed from the container and placed on any kind of palette or in any container. Sufficient turpentine is added to make the paint flow freely. The paint is then applied with a lettering brush. Naturally, the turpentine causes the paint to bleed badly on a paper surface. For this reason, Japan colors are used only on metal, plastic, or wood signs, or on sign cloth. All these materials are fine for outdoor use since none is harmed by weather. Once dry, the Japan colors are still easily dissolved by turpentine. This permits rapid correction and easy clean-up of tools and working surfaces.

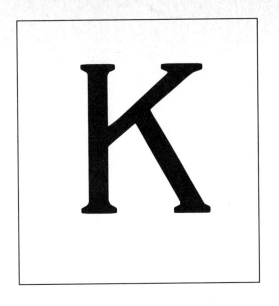

K

with your printers before you prepare the art. In this way you can learn the questions they will want answered and agree upon the proper method of imparting these answers. For example, different colors have different meanings when used for key lines: black means the line stays in the printing, red indicates a color panel or a photograph where the outline is removed before printing, and blue usually calls for a benday tone. All printers work differently, and it is wise to be sure that your printers are using a code that you understand so that there will be no mix-up in the final printing.

Key line drawing is sometimes used as an alternative name for a mechanical, due to its prevalent use in mechanicals preparation. (See *Mechanicals.*)

KERNING

Term, used largely in computer-generated typography, that refers to increasing or decreasing the space between letters. The word derives from hand-set metal type.

A kern is the rounded ball on such swash characters as *J.* In hot type these characters were difficult to space properly because of the wide sweep of the swash. Typographers, therefore, undercut the kern so that it would overlap the metal of the next character. In computer or photographic type (cold type), there is no metal, and characters can be moved (kerned) in either direction. (See *Cold Type, Computer Graphics,* and *Hot Type.*)

KEY LINE

Name given to the process of outlining the areas on a mechanical that are to be filled with photographic copy, tints, or other art prepared separately from the mechanical. Instructions for the treatment of these key lined areas must be included on instruction overlays attached to the mechanical and coded (keyed) to the accompanying art.

For this reason, it is advisable to confer

KNEADED ERASERS

This is a soft, malleable substance that absorbs, rather than abrades, discolorations on paper. As the surface of the eraser becomes soiled, the substance can be kneaded, presenting a clean surface for further use. (See *Erasers.*)

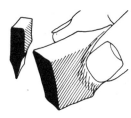

The kneaded eraser is easily molded to permit corrections in tight areas.

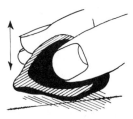

Blotting with a kneaded eraser removes excess graphite for cleaner results when using other erasers.

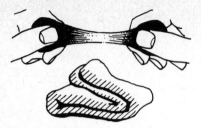

Stretching and folding the kneaded eraser absorbs dirt and provides a clean working surface.

KNIFE, FRISKET

Distinguished by the long, very sharp blade that comes to a fine point, frisket knives may be purchased complete or with replaceable blades. A fine example of the latter is the X-Acto knife. Used with the 11 blade, the X-Acto knife serves as an excellent tool for cutting all stencils and friskets. The very fine point is necessary for making a clean cut without exerting too much pressure. Bearing down too heavily while cutting could damage artwork. (See *Friskets.*)

Common Difficulties

Breakage. The very fine points on frisket knife blades ae extremely fragile. Any lateral pressure applied when cutting will snap off the tip of the blade. Avoid using the frisket knife when heavy pressure is needed to make a cut. Once the blade has been broken, a limited amount of resharpening with a whetstone is possible before the blade becomes too blunt for frisket work.

Tearing. The point of the blade is very delicate and dulls easily. If a blade begins to drag, tearing the paper instead of cutting smoothly, hone the blade gently several times on a fine whetstone. If tearing still occurs, the fault may lie in your technique. A frisket knife should be held vertically, between the tips of the fingers, like a lettering brush. In this manner, the knife can be twirled so that the blade always faces the direction of the cut. This

grip also lessens the pressure that can be applied, making it easier to maintain a steady cut at the proper depth. For this reason, use a frisket knife that is light and has a slender handle. (See *Knife, Swivel.*)

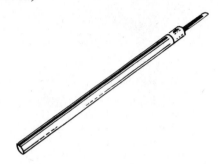

Frisket knife, shown with a replaceable blade.

KNIFE, MAT

A name given to a rather wide range of heavy-duty cutting blades designed primarily for cutting and trimming drawing and mat boards. Some of these knives hold a standard industrial razor blade, but most have a wedge-shaped blade that is considerably heavier and, therefore, more durable. The X-Acto knives, with their wide selection of blades, are also used for mat cutting.

The important feature of the mat knife is its blade, which can be reversed or changed quickly and easily, providing a sharp cutting edge at all times. This prevents tearing or ripping the fragile artist's boards.

The heavy-duty knives are usually composed of two metal pieces secured by a single screw. The blade, which is notched on its upper edge, can be placed in several positions, exposing more or less of the cutting edge, as desired. When the blade is properly set, the two pieces are joined and the screw tightened. When the cutting edge becomes dull, the screw is loosened, the metal pieces separated, and the blade reversed or changed. The

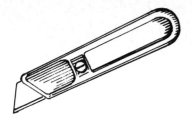

Mat knife. One of many available styles.

hollow space between the two metal pieces of the handle is a storage place for extra blades.

The razor-blade mat knives work in much the same manner as the heavy duty knife described above. They differ only in using razor blades, which are slimmer and sharper than the cutting knife, although the razor blade is less rigid and more apt to break.

The X-Acto knives come in a wide range of handle shapes and weights. Primarily designed as hobby tools, they are very satisfactory for a number of art uses, including those of the mat knife. Their blades are not reversible; one end is inserted into a slot in the handle. A sleeve is turned down tight on the handle, locking the blade in a chuck. The main virtue of the X-Acto is the range of handles and blades available, permitting the choice of any combination that suits your preference or the needs of the job.

The art materials store may offer additional variations on the mat knife. A recent innovation, for example, is a Japanese model that provides a long, slim blade that has been scored along the side. As the cutting point or edge becomes dull, that section is snapped off, and the remainder of the blade is advanced in the handle.

Once you are sure that your mat knife is sharp and ready for use, place the board to be cut on a firm surface. Masonite board or an old drawing board offers an excellent surface. Use a mat cutter guide or a metal ruler or triangle so that any knife slip will not damage the art. Try to position your work so that any cutting error will occur in the unwanted portion of the board. For instance, if you are cutting a mat, place the cutting guide on that part of the board which will form the mat. Place the knife blade on the side toward the middle of the board. In this way, if you should slip and drag the knife away from the cutting guide, you will destroy only the part of the board you were going to throw away later anyway.

Try to make your cuts with one stroke. The more times the knife is drawn over the surface of the board, the greater the chance for error. It is nearly impossible to duplicate the exact angle of the knife each time you cut, which means you will not get a clean cut and the edges will appear quite ragged. If the board is too thick, or if you are not strong enough, make one very light stroke to set the path of succeeding strokes. Then repeat this stroke, continuing to work with relatively light pressure. If you press lightly, the knife tends to follow the previous cut and will produce a clean edge. Continue cutting in this manner, until the knife has completely penetrated the board. Do not try to pull or break the pieces apart, because they will fray. If corners have not been completely cut, work on them separately with the point of the knife, pressing straight down instead of drawing the knife. This will insure clean, neat junctures.

Common Difficulties

Breaking. Any knife blade may break if the cutting angle is too sharp or if the pressure is too extreme. Razor blades are particularly brittle, and the fine cutting edge will break quite easily. To avoid breaking, expose as little of the blade as you possibly can. Also keep the knife as perpendicular to the board as possible. If you want an angled cut, use a mat cutter guide whenever possible. But always keep the pressure on the knife

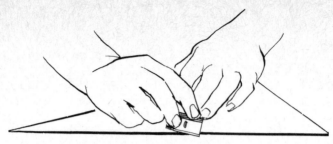

The proper way to cut using a straight-edge. The angle of the blade is low and the blade is drawn easily along.

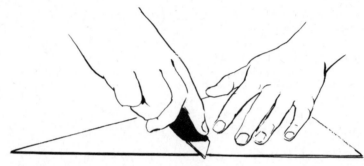

An improper way to cut. The high angle of the cutting blade permits the blade to wobble, gouging the straight-edge and causing the paper to be dragged and torn.

straight, so that you are pushing directly toward the point not down on the side.

Ragged edges. Repeated cuts, dull blades, and cutting errors will produce ragged edges. Proper procedures will prevent this, but they require considerable practice. If you do get a ragged cut, try to trim the edge with a razor blade. Do this free hand, and try to shave away just a little at a time until you have removed all evidence of the error. If there still remains some unevenness, use a clean piece of sandpaper and gently smooth down the cut edge.

Dull points. Even with a new blade, you may find that the knife is not cutting sharply. This usually means that the extreme tip of the cutting edge has been broken off. Particularly with razor blades, this tip is much more fragile than any other part of the blade and it can snap off even in normal usage. In most cases,

it pays to insert a new blade. However, since the lost portion is small, it may be possible to save the blade by stropping it carefully on a whetstone. Do this gently. As a rule, it will be impossible for the artist to sharpen a blade in this manner so that it will cut as good as new. However, with practice, you may become proficient enough to save a good many lightly damaged blades.

A word of caution: When you are throwing old blades away, place them in a container of some kind. Most studios keep an old coffee can with a slot in the lid. Remember that the people who handle the trash may be cut by any loose blades.

KNIFE, STENCIL

The stencil knife is quite similar to the mat and frisket knife, differing only in the sturdiness of the construction. Both the handle and the blade of the stencil knife are much heavier. The blade, though usually not replaceable, can withstand repeated sharpening with a whetstone.

A stencil, a mask or shield produced by creating a shaped opening in heavy stock through which pigment may be sprayed or dabbed, receives rather prolonged abuse, and it should be made of a durable material so that it will hold up during its use. The rugged characteristics of the stencil knife are designed to permit it to cut cleanly and easily through the heaviest materials. The same characteristics prevent the knife from performing as well when intricate detail is required. A frisket knife is better for such detail.

KNIFE, SWIVEL

A frisket knife with a freely turning blade mount. The purpose of the swivel is to permit you to cut intricate shapes without having to adjust the direction of the cut with your fingers. To further facilitate this action, the blade itself is L-shaped and angled from the holder and tends to trail the direction of cutting automatically. A locking sleeve on the neck of the holder may be tightened to hold the blade stationary for normal cutting. Blades are replaceable and they may be purchased separately.

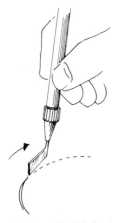

Swivel knife. The movable blade is used to cut circular shapes.

Common Difficulty

The only difficulty with the swivel knife is getting used to the action, which takes a great deal of practice. The angle of the blade, which helps prevent digging into the paper while cutting, puts the point of the blade a short distance away from the center of the holder. This distance is difficult to judge and is rarely equal to the radius of the cut. Therefore, the handle must be turned in a curve larger or smaller than the actual cut, or the blade will not follow properly. Allowing for this difference in turn radius and maintaining a steady pressure, which is a vastly dissimilar action, make the swivel knife difficult to use until you are thoroughly familiar with its handling. Be sure that you always hold the handle vertically, like a lettering brush, and let the knife blade trail by itself. Attempting to force the blade will produce a ragged or inaccurate cut. (See *Knife, Frisket.*)

KNIFE, X-ACTO

The X-Acto knife consists of two parts: a handle with a metal chuck, and a knife blade that is inserted into and held firmly by the chuck. The simple chuck action, the choice of handles, and the wide range of blades and tools that interchange in the handle make this knife the standard of the hobby trade. Although most of the blades and tools are made specifically for wood carving and for other hobby crafts, they are widely used by commercial artists. X-Acto knives are excellent alternatives for mat knives, frisket knives, and razor blades.

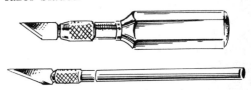

(Above) Heavy-handled X-Acto knife with a #24 blade, a typical combination for mat and board cutting. (Below) Slim X-Acto handle with a #11 blade, a typical combination for cutting delicate friskets.

KODALITH

Brand name for a film that produces a heavy, opaque film negative (or positive). Available from many photostat or photographic services, Kodaliths are used whenever a dense, lightproof mask is necessary. In conventional black-and-white film negatives, the dark areas are actually translucent. While printing papers are not affected by this, 3Ms and INTs require fully opaque masks. So does backlit photography for film animation and slides. In these cases, Kodaliths, or opaque film negatives, are essential.

Common Difficulties

Pinholes. Kodalith film is extremely high contrast, and the finished film contains many pinholes. Most Kodalith services will cover most of these holes with a rust-colored film opaquing paint. The rust color does not affect the masking quality, since only light transmission is involved. However, even such touching up is, at best, only partially effective. It is necessary to place the Kodalith over a very strong light source and fill in the holes that inevitably remain. Few of these will be visible in normal light, so be very careful. Many animation and slide presentation firms have entry-level jobs for simple art, paste-up, and Kodalith repair.

KRAFT PAPER

The familiar, brown wrapping paper that is used for the majority of bagging and wrapping chores in commerce. In commercial art, it serves about the same function. Occasionally it will be used as a printing stock to achieve an unusual effect, and many artists use it as a flap paper to protect their finished artwork. (See *Papers and Boards.*)

KROY LETTERING MACHINE

An alternate system to transfer type and photolettering, the Kroy lettering machine is a comparatively simple and inexpensive device for producing finished lettering. The machine contains two rolls of material: one of plain white paper, the other of opaque plastic. The operator selects a character and adjusts the spacing; the machine stamps the form from the plastic film and bonds it to the white paper. A number of different typefaces and sizes are available. (See also *Photolettering; Transfer Type.*)

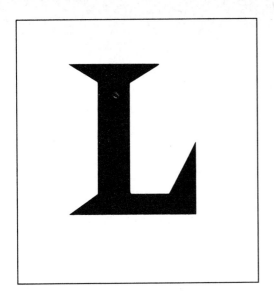

LACEY LUCI

This is the former brand name (pronounced *lace-ee loose-ee*) of a series of camera-like machines used for enlarging or reducing the image of a subject and projecting it on a glass plate, at which point the image can be traced on a sheet of translucent paper. The name survived the product and has become generic for all sorts of devices which are used for the same purpose. (See *Enlarger-Reducers*).

One of the main virtues of these machines is their ability to transform three-dimensional objects into flat images. Bottles and cans, boxes in perspective, and any complex object that will fit on the table can be traced directly—eliminating hours of sketching and possible inaccuracies. Similarly, lettering can be curved or placed in perspective by bending or tilting the original on the table. (This may be difficult on some models in which the table is mounted on a slant or vertically. However, you can construct a simple platform to hold the object with scraps of cardboard held by pushpins or tape.)

The instructions that accompany the machine describe these and other variations that can be produced with the different machine models.

LACQUER THINNER

The product designation for a group of solvents that can dilute or dissolve lacquers, varnishes, and shellacs. The most common forms of these solvents are composed mainly of acetone or mineral spirits. (See *Solvents*.)

LAMP, DAYLIGHT

The leading alternative to the fluorescent lamp in the commercial art field. Like the fluorescent, it has a floating arm and clamps to the desk. The primary difference is the bulb—a 100 watt, incandescent bulb—instead of the fluorescent tubes.

The colors of art prepared under artificial light will not look the same when viewed in the daylight. To reduce this problem, the daylight lamp features a color corrected lens, which makes the light similar to daylight.

Unlike the large, rectangular shade of the fluorescent, the circular shade of the daylight lamp tends to focus the light in a smaller area. This sharp focus is excellent for fine detail work, but does not light a large working area. Scientists have established that the combination of intense shadow and brilliant spotlighting is extremely tiresome and causes eye strain. If you work with a daylight lamp, have sufficient room lighting to prevent this strain.

LAMP, FLUORESCENT

This lamp is available in large and small, with one or more tubes, and in combination with conventional bulbs. There are several manufacturers of such equipment and each offers a number of models. The most important quality to artists is the lamp's ability to be set in position without having it drift. Several mechanisms per-

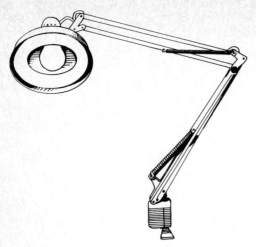

A combination lamp with both conventional and fluorescent bulbs.

form this function, but with varying degrees of success. As a rule, the more expensive models work best and last the longest. Some have screw-type locks to ensure position. If they do not, be sure the floating action is well balanced so that continued use will not weaken the joints. Many models will also permit the lamp to be mounted on inclined drawng boards. In such an installation, be sure that the lamp base is fully upright. Tilted bases disturb the floating-arm action, and can also cause the mechanism to produce an irritating hum. Most fluorescent lamps have an annoying ability to create a flicker or strobe effect when hands or objects are moved quickly beneath them. For the most part, this will not disturb the artist. However, older tubes may accentuate this strobe effect to the point where it is actively annoying. Replace such tubes at the first sign of deterioration. Prolonged exposure to flickering and strobe causes eye strain, fatigue, and headaches, and distorts true color.

LAYOUTS

The term *layout* applies to any preliminary sketch prepared for any number of situations, many of them having nothing to do with art, thereby causing more confusion than any other art term. Art layouts include thumbnail roughs, rough roughs, clean roughs, rough comps, and finished comps, among others. Probably no two people have a common understanding about any one form of layout and because of this countless hours are misused preparing work that is inadequate or overdone.

There are five basic layout groups of importance to commercial artists. The names for each of these groups, though relatively familiar, are essentially arbitrary and not universally agreed on. The following grouping is meant only as a frame of reference. Whatever your client calls it, its purpose will be found in one of these five sections.

Thumbnails. As the name implies, most thumbnails are small, quick sketches. The artist uses them as a shorthand to jot down ideas and to experiment with designs and colors. Their actual size is unimportant; so is their degree of finish. They are for one person only—the artist. On occasion, one artist may communicate with another by means of this thumbnail shorthand, as when an art director gives instructions to an assistant. Obviously, such a simple layout should take only seconds, although the thought process may take a while.

Rough. The rough is an expanded thumbnail. Still reserved mainly for the artist alone, it should be done as close to full size as is practical. Size has a powerful effect on a design, and the sooner the work is seen at full size, the better. Besides size, another function of the rough is to explore the viability of a design idea, and to ensure that all the pertinent material is included. Such a layout may be shown to other artists and art directors to check comprehension of the instructions and to elicit initial criticisms. A rough layout should only take ten minutes. Spending more than this per layout is probably a waste of time.

Visuals. This completely arbitrary term defines a layout group that has far too many names, including clean rough, finished rough, rough comp, and quick comp. Artists receiving instructions with such compound qualifiers may easily misunderstand its function and spend too much or too little effort on its execution. Confusion can be eliminated if artists comprehend the layout's intended use. A visual has the purpose of presenting initial ideas to nonartists who are part of your team: copy writers, account executives, creative directors, and the like all need to be informed of your progress and be able to offer advice and criticism. They are often misled by the sketchy nature of rough layouts and offer ill-advised misinformation. Verbal explanations and layout revisions are time consuming and can often lead to costly misunderstandings, hence the visual.

Visuals cannot be billed to the client directly, so no one wants to spend too much time preparing them. What you really do is another rough—with just a little more care spent making sure that the details are recognizable. A visual is neater and more accurate than a rough, but not more "finished." A typical visual should not take more than fifteen minutes to do. Naturally, the size, color, headlines, and other main features should be correct and indicative of the final appearance, but should not be labored or over-rendered.

A crisp visual with lots of snap and sparkle may even be shown to understanding clients. But be careful. Many clients find a visual just as hard to comprehend as others do a rough. It may take quite a while for a client to become accustomed to evaluating a visual, but it will be rewarding if you can work this way. Such clients may be able to give final approval without any further presentations, which can save you considerable time and money, since the final bill will be the same whether or not you do more work.

Comps. There is only one reason for doing a comp (or comprehensive, to give it its full title), and that is to show it to the client for final approval. You (your agency) pay for any changes made without approval. Any changes made after client approval the client pays for. It's that simple. For this reason the comp is as complete as it is possible to make it. Actual type can be set and finished illustrations and photography used—any amount of time and money it takes to make the comp look like a printed piece.

Most beginning commercial artists misunderstand the functions of layouts and approach every assignment as if it were a comp. But this is a waste of time, effort, and money. Don't do a comp unless you have to. Most large agencies have highly skilled specialists that only produce comps. They are highly gifted and highly paid. Only extremely competent and experienced artists are considered for such work, even though it is tedious and not truly creative. If you are a good designer and artist, you may never need to do a comp in your professional career.

Mechanicals. Most art students are surprised to find mechanicals included in the list of layouts. But check the original definition of layout. Contrary to most students' conceptions, commercial artists do not produce finishes in the true sense of the word. Even illustrators and photographers do not. They produce elements that are included in the only true final, the printed piece. The printer produces that, and from printing plates on a printing press. Therefore, the only "final" an artist handles is the mechanical, which shows the proper size, position, and color of every item in the piece. The platemaker takes all these elements and, following the instructions on the mechanical, makes the plate that prints the finish. How that finish looks is determined by the mechanical. The same is true for film, slide, and video productions, where the camera operator replaces the platemaker. Most artists regard doing mechanicals as boring and noncreative work, but it is really the most important layout of all. True, the excitingly creative decisions have largely been made, but the subtle design decisions, the spacing refinements, the choice of color tints and combinations all require the most expert eye and judgment. You cannot call yourself a true commercial artist until you can prepare an accurate and visually pleasing mechanical. You must prove that you can do a good mechanical before you can be trusted to take on wider creative responsibilities. This is the main reason entry-level artists usually begin with mechanicals.

Two important remarks about layouts. Layout technique has passed through many fashions, including watercolors and pastel. Today they are produced with markers and little else. Clients expect marker layouts, and agencies use them exclusively.

Finally, when you receive a layout assignment, find out what it is for, who will see it, and how much time and/or money is allocated. Try to ascertain whether a simpler form will be satisfactory; you could save everyone a lot of expense.

LAYOUT CHALKS

A commercial euphemism for a set of hard pastels containing black, white, and gray only. Used for preparing black and white layouts. (See *Chalks, Layout.*)

LAYOUT PAPER

A light, semitransparent, bond or onionskin drawing paper used in the creation of layouts. Also referred to as visualizer paper, although the term layout paper usually refers to the heavier, more opaque bond. Available in pads of many different sizes. (See *Papers and Boards.*)

LEAD HOLDERS

Lead holders, for use with drawing leads, are simply metal or plastic tubes containing spring-activated chucks which hold a piece of lead. Unlike a mechanical pencil, they do *not* release the led at a slow, measured rate by means of a twisting action. Once the chuck has been opened by depressing the plunger on the end of the holder, the lead is free to slide out of the chuck. This feature permits you to instantly select the degree of protrusion you wish, or to replace or exchange the lead without difficulty. Since the exchange of leads is accomplished so quickly, you may work with only one or two holders and any number of leads.

Perhaps the prime advantage of the lead holder is the constancy of its size and weight. There are never any awkward pencil stubs or ungainly lengths of long, new pencils to disturb the "feel" while drawing or lettering. And, this way, the lead may be used to the final fraction of an inch.

The lead holder is available in a number of styles and sizes to accommodate varying lead thicknesses. Some of these holders may also include identification devices that enable you to set the particular number of the lead currently in the holder or different colored holders may serve the same purpose. A few holders are equipped with pocket clips. If this is important to you, a simple metal clip may be attached to the holder. These clips may be purchased at stationery counters, if they are not available at your art store.

Representative lead holder.

In short, the lead holder is a clean, comfortable, economical replacement for the pencil.

LEAD POINTERS

Lead pointers, for sharpening points on drawing leads, are circular, weighted devices that contain sandpaper. The pointer has a revolving top with an opening through which the lead holder is inserted. This opening firmly seats the lead holder; the protruding holder is then gripped like a handle and used to turn the top. This action brings the point of the lead against the cone of sandpaper inside and gently shapes the lead into an extremely sharp, accurately formed point.

By varying the length of lead extending from the holder, you may control the shape of the point, from long and slim, to short and comparatively blunt.

Replacement sandpaper cones may be purchased separately and installed when the original sandpaper wears out. The sharpening action is so gentle, however, that the cone lasts for a very long time.

The lead pointer will not work with a standard, wood-sheathed pencil.

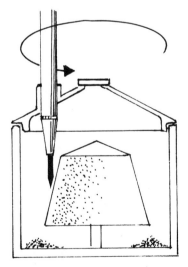

Lead pointer. Central cone is made of replaceable sandpaper which points lead as it is twisted around its surface.

LEADS

Drawing leads are identical to the graphite core found in ordinary wooden pencils, but have no wooden casing. Available in all degrees from 6B to 9H, the leads are held in a lead holder when used for drawing. Using leads and holders eliminates the necessity of sharpening a wooden pencil in a pencil sharpener, and avoids the awkwardness and waste of short pencil stubs.

Layout lettering is a prime example of the value of leads. This lettering technique requires a fine, chisel-shaped lead. This type of lead point wears out quickly and must be reshaped continually to maintain the style and quality of the lettering. Consequently, the lead is used quite rapidly. With an ordinary pencil, the wood must be removed before the point can be reshaped. The sharpener also destroys the basic width and form of the chisel point. Therefore, you must reshape the point from scratch. This is an inaccurate, time consuming, wasteful annoyance that is eliminated with the use of leads and lead holders.

Common Difficulty

Wrong size. There are two diameters of thickness available in both leads and holders. The thick leads will not fit into the thin holders, and the thick holders cannot grip the thin leads. Make sure the leads you buy will fit your holders.

LEADS, COLORED

For those who prefer to use lead holders, colored pencil leads are available. Similar in color range and quality to regular colored pencils, these leads fit most standard lead holders. In addition to the colors, white chalk, sanguine, charcoal, and negro drawing leads may be obtained. Since colored pencils are fragile and difficult to sharpen in a pencil sharpener without shattering the lead, these colored leads—which are interchangeable in the holder—can prove to be more economical to use and much more convenient.

LEROY

The brand name for a system of mechanical lettering tools. One of the earliest brands, the Leroy name is often used generically to describe this method of lettering and the tools involved. (See *Lettering, Mechanical.*)

LEROY LETTERING PENS

The brand name for a type of pen that, used in conjunction with a guide, produces a distinctive form of lettering most commonly associated with drafting. The name is generic and may be commonly found in want ads that call for Leroy letterers. This usually indicates that the job is not creative and requires a strict mechanical skill. (See *Pens.*)

LETRASET

Brand name of a transfer type and the parent organization that produces a complete line of art supplies for commercial artists. Many of these products are provided in the Pantone Matching System (PMS) color range for coordinated presentations. One of the largest and most respected manufacturers in the industry. (See *Transfer Type.*)

LETTERING GUIDES

Solid plastic bars into which alphabets have been impressed. These guides are

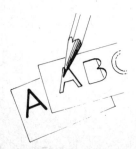

Single-stroke lettering guide.

an integral part of a system of lettering that employs the scriber pen. (See *Lettering, Mechanical.*)

LETTERING, MECHANICAL

An extremely limited form of single-stroke lettering produced by a scriber pen and lettering guides; used mainly in mechanical drafting.

In mechanical lettering, the words are lightly penciled on the finished rendering for position and spacing. A straight-edge (F) is positioned beneath the lettering and a lettering guide (E) is selected and placed against the straight-edge. The tail pin (D) of the scriber is placed in the horizontal slot on the bottom of the guide and the tracing pin (C), located on an adjustable arm, is inserted into the proper letter. The guide, with the scriber held slightly above the paper, is then moved along the straight-edge until the inking point (A) of the scriber coincides with the position of the penciled character. The inking point, filled with ink, is then lowered onto the paper and the tracing point is gently guided around the indentations of the character on the guide by means of the knob (B). This action causes the point to trace the letter form precisely on the paper. Once the letter has been inked, the scriber is raised, moved to the next letter, and the procedure repeated.

With practice, a large amount of lettering can be completed quickly and accurately. Changing the size of the inking point, selecting different guide styles, or adjusting the angle of the arm holding the tracing pin will all vary the kind of lettering produced.

Several organizations produce the scribers and guides used in this system, but you are apt to hear the lettering referred to as Leroy lettering—particularly in the want-ad columns. Since these ads appear in the art section, many beginning artists feel that they should know this type of lettering. However, the jobs being offered are mostly with engineering and architectural firms and the lettering is taught

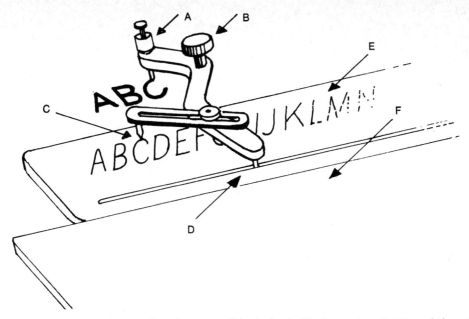

Diagramatic presentation, showing the inking point (A), the knob (B), the tracing pin (C), and the tail pin (D) of the lettering scriber, and the lettering guide (E), and a straight-edge (F).

to drafting students more often than to art students. There is a limited use of this method in the sign field and in charts and similar presentations. But even here the need for a wider range of artistic style has led to the use of transfer type more often than mechanical lettering.

Common Difficulties

The scriber/guide set is a precision instrument that performs well with a simple measure of care and cleaning and offers little difficulty once the knack of coordinating all the necessary movements have been mastered. However, there is one hint that will help you right away. With your free hand, try to hold the straight-edge, the guide, and the base of the scriber all at the same time. This will prevent the pressure of moving the tracing pin from causing slippage anywhere in the items mentioned, and will prevent the scriber from jumping out of the guide.

LETTERING PENS

Pens or pen points that have been designed specifically to produce showcard

or reproduction lettering, usually with a minimum of strokes. (See *Pens.*)

LETTERING STENCILS

Metal, plastic, or heavy paper sheets into which letter forms have been cut. These letter forms are not complete, however, since small connecting strips are necessary to hold the interior shapes of the o, e, etc., as well as weak points such as the angles of the w. These stencils are available at most paint supply and art material stores in single letter and complete alphabet form—though in a very limited selection of styles. The single metal letters have crimped edges that slide together to create stencil words. The alphabet sheets must be utilized one character at a time.

Paint is forced through the stencil with a dabbing stroke whether a brush, cloth, or any other means is used to apply the paint. Aerosol paint cans and spray guns can also be used.

The finished letter will always have the characteristic breaks caused by the connecting strips. This limits the use of

Typical lettering stencil with its characteristic interrupted letter form.

stencils to the crudest kind of lettering, such as carton labels, which has no value to the artist unless this specific effect is needed for illustrative purpose. (See also *Stencils, Lettering Templates,* and *Lettering, Mechanical.*)

Common Difficulties

Bleeding. Paint will bleed under the edges of the stencil openings if too much paint is applied. Always dab the applicator on a test surface first to reduce the amount of paint until it is just sufficient to cover the surface. Continued use of the stencil will also allow the paint to build up on the edges where it can easily smear. Always wipe the stencils clean after each use to prevent this build-up.

Warping. Excess paint on the stencil, particularly the plastic or paper kind, will often cause the stencil to warp so that it will not lie flat on the surface. This warping encourages bleeding, and may also lead to the deterioration of the stencil. Once again, keep the stencil clean and use the least amount of paint possible. Store the stencils in a cool, dry place and keep them flat so that they will not curl before use.

LETTERING TEMPLATES

Plastic sheets into which the shapes of each letter of the alphabet have been die-cut in much the same manner as stencils. However, only the outline—not the interior—of the form, which serves

as a guide for a pencil or pen, is left. Interior shapes, such as in the o and e, are created by keeping the drawing tool pressed firmly against the sides of the template form while drawing. The lettering produced by using these templates, being rather precise and characterless, is not adequate for modern advertising art, and these templates should be used only for simple chart and sign work. While the templates can help a student become familiar with letter forms, their primary value is to the drafter who must do a considerable amount of labeling and titling. This lettering must be neat and accurate, but the engineer is neither trained, nor expected, to be able to execute artistic lettering. A very limited selection of type styles is offered in template form wherever art or drafting supplies are sold.

Lettering templates should not be confused with lettering stencils, since the openings permit paint to fill in all the interior forms. Similarly, stencils cannot be used as templates, for the small connecting pieces that hold these interior forms prevent the drawing tool from making a complete, unbroken outline of the letter form.

Templates also differ from lettering guides, which are solid and which have indented grooves for the tracing pin of a scriber lettering pen. (See *Lettering, Mechanical.*)

To use a lettering template, draw a guide line very lightly on the artwork. Next, sketch the lettering on the guide line, also very lightly and in pencil, to assure layout and spacing. Then take the template and select the proper opening for the first character in the line. Place the opening so that it sits exactly over the indicated letter. Hold the template firmly and place the drawing tool into the opening against an edge, and trace the tool around every edge of the opening. Lift the template carefully to avoid smearing and repeat the procedure until the lettering is completed. If you wish to eliminate the layout lines without danger to the finished lettering, erase them before using the template. This can be done by using a piece of drafting tape to hold one edge of the template once it has been put into position. Now the template can be lifted, the lines erased, the template returned to the same position, and the finished lettering completed.

Although the lettering template can be used with any pencil or pen, the most effective pen is the Rapidograph type, since these pens ink in any direction and can follow the template shapes easily. To prevent blotting while inking, raise the template above the paper by placing tape, triangles, etc., underneath the template. (See *India Ink Pens.*)

Lettering templates are subject to all the conditions of other plastic art tools, such as triangles, and should be treated in the same manner.

LIGHT BOXES

A wooden box with a glass cover containing an arrangement of bulbs or fluorescent lights. The light box is used for transferring art or reference material directly by tracing. The light box is also used for screening conventional color slides and transparencies. Sketches, layouts, reference material, etc., are placed on the glass surface. A clean sheet of paper is placed over this material and the lights are turned on. The light will pass through all these layers, allowing you to trace or modify the material on the clean top surface. This is a particularly handy method for applying transfer type and acetate films, since the guide lines or actual layout are on a separate piece of paper. Thus you can achieve complete accuracy quite easily without marking the finished art. And since there are no guide lines to be removed, you do not risk damaging the fragile film or type during clean up.

Light boxes are available with clear or frosted glass. Frosted glass provides a soft diffusion of the light, a condition that makes working easier because you do not have the glare of the light in your eyes. Some models permit you to move the lights to concentrate the light on the area upon which you are working.

Large light tables are also available. With the exceptions of size and a tablelike support, they are identical to the smaller light boxes. The table permits work with large items and is used primarily in the commercial field to assemble negatives for producing printing plates.

A light box can be improvised with any box, a piece of glass, and a light fixture. When no light box is available, use an ordinary window. Sunlight from outside the window will provide the necessary illumination, and the materials can be held or taped to the glass. (See *Light Tables.*)

LIGHTING

The most important requirement for artists is adequate light. In addition, light should permit colors to appear as natural as possible. (Eyestrain and distorted colors are two things artists should avoid.) Modern commercial artists' wide range of functions have created many different lighting needs, which have been met by a remarkable variety of lighting fixtures. These include standard light bulbs alone and in combination with fluorescent tubes, light and magnifier combinations, and single- or double-tube fluorescent lamps.

The style and kind of lighting artists prefer is not as important as overall lighting quality. All studio areas should be well lit, and the work surface should not produce too much of a contrast with the background. Such contrast is tiring. Combinations of light source, both fluorescent and bulb, tend to allow colors to appear more natural. With fluorescent fixtures, a mixture of two kinds of tubes will be more satisfactory. Experiment with different combinations before making a final decision. (See *Lamp, Fluorescent* and *Lamp, Daylight.*)

LIGHT TABLES

A large, glass-topped table with lighting underneath, used primarily for stripping and assembling photo negatives in printing. (See *Light Boxes.*)

LINEN TESTER

A small magnifying glass mounted on a collapsible, L-shaped stand. Designed for thread counting in textile manufacture, it is used in commercial art by printers and platemakers to check the size, position, and condition of the dots in halftone reproduction. The area magnified is too small for any other practical artistic use.

LINE-UP BOARD

An inexpensive bristol board with a pale blue grid printed on the paper. This board eliminates the need for extensive drafting equipment when preparing simple mechanicals and paste-ups. The light blue lines are sufficiently close together so that any piece of art can be positioned properly by eye, and the pale blue color does not photograph when the art is photographed by the platemaker.

LINOLEUM BLOCKS

Practically anyone who has studied art has experienced the enjoyment of carving designs into a piece of mounted linoleum and reproducing them with ink or paint by simple hand pressure onto paper. Linoleum block printing, the simplest form of letterpress, is too unsophisticated for most commercial art requirements, but it is a delightful hobby and excellent for experimentation. Linoleum blocks and the simple engraving tools used to work them are available at all art supply stores, which will also furnish pamphlets that describe the procedures.

LIQUID WATERCOLORS

A bottled, premixed version of conventional watercolors. (See *Paint* and *Dyes.*)

LITHOGRAPHIC CRAYONS

Soft, greasy, paper-wrapped pencils designed for use with lithographic stones. (See *Crayons, Lithographic.*)

LUCI

Term that describes any large camera-type enlarger-reducer, or the process. For instance, an artist may "luci" artwork when using such a device. *Luci* is an abbreviation of *camera lucida,* a term that was used as the brand name for *Lacey Luci* by the first manufacturer of this equipment. Although no longer produced, the product name is generic. (See *Camera Lucida, Enlarger-Reducers,* and *Viewers.*)

LUCITE

The brand name for a clear, thick plastic that has the visual qualities of glass, but which can be cut or modeled easily with a knife, saw, or drill. This makes Lucite an excellent material for displays and models. Pieces of Lucite may be joined together with Lucite cement.

Apply the cement sparingly, and only to those areas that are to be joined. The cement melts the Lucite slightly and cannot be removed once applied. Press the two pieces together accurately. Once again, improper positioning will cause cement to be spread beyond the area of the joint, marring the surface. Hold the pieces together firmly until they are completely bonded and dry. This will take several hours, so you must prepare a jig—any device or object that will hold the parts immobile—or clamp the pieces together. If the pieces are not too big, a few heavy books may be sufficient to hold the pieces firmly in position. The important thing is to prepare the jig *before* you apply the cement, so that the pieces may be joined and held without risking a slip that will spread the cement.

Acetone, which is a solvent for Lucite, may also be used as an adhesive. Apply sufficient acetone to the areas to be joined so that the Lucite melts slightly. Join the pieces and hold them firmly until the Lucite has rehardened. This adhering procedure will produce an invisible bond if care is taken when applying the acetone. Too much acetone, too carelessly applied, will disfigure the surface of the lucite near the joint, spoiling the appearance.

Using Lucite for displays will mean that art or lettering must be applied to the surface. Make sure that the materials you use are effective on glossy, plastic surfaces. Enamels and lacquers from a commercial paint store are effective, but they are not proper art supplies and you may not be used to working with them. Acetate inks and paints will adhere to the surface, but may be too transparent and streaky when applied with small art brushes and pens. Perhaps the neatest, simplest way is to work with cut, adhesive plastic films and transfer type. Where

renderings and gradations are necessary, the best results will be achieved with friskets and an airbrush. The techniques in these cases are standard, whatever the surface, and are discussed in their respective entries. (See *Plastic Films.*)

LUCITE CEMENT

An adhesive prepared especially for joining Lucite and other similar plastics.

The cement is applied directly from the tube or painted with a small brush onto the specific areas to be joined. Use care in the application—the cement dissolves the lucite, disfiguring the surface. Do not apply too much or the excess will be squeezed beyond the joint ruining the adjoining surface. Wipe off any excess immediately with a clean rag before it can mar the surface. Make sure that you remove it *all*. Any residue will cause a slight haze when it dries.

A solvent may be recommended by the manufacturer—but only while the cement is still wet. Any delay will allow the cement or solvent to melt and distort the clear plastic surface.

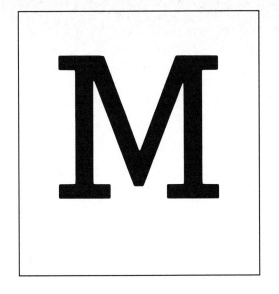

cases. The more deluxe models even include stands that free your hands while working, and some even provide lights for illuminating the working area.

None of these accessories are essential, but they may help you in your work. Inexpensive, unmounted lenses work just as well and may be found in hardware and surplus stores.

Common Difficulty

Eyestrain. Most people tend to squint when using magnifying glasses. Such exertion can cause eye fatigue, or result in double vision, or make focusing the eyes difficult after prolonged use. To avoid this, try leaving both eyes open while you work. Even small lenses will let you work properly in this manner, which is more restful to the eyes.

MAGIC MARKERS

The brand name of one of the first products to be produced in an art material version of this common marking device, the name has come to symbolize any marker of this type. (See *Markers.*)

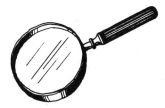

Magnifying glass mounted with a handle.

MAGNIFIER, ILLUMINATED

A circular fluorescent lamp with a magnifying lens in the center. Similar in all other respects to more traditional lighting, the illuminated magnifier is a specialized device suitable only for those who do close work. For most artists, conventional lighting is superior. (See *Lighting.*)

MAHLSTICK

A slender wooden rod with a soft ball at one end. The rod serves as a hand rest when producing art or lettering at unusual angles, while the ball prevents the rod from damaging the surface of the art during its use. (See *Hand Rests.*)

MAGNIFYING GLASSES

These are very helpful when artists must do extremely fine detail work. Even people with excellent eyesight may find magnification handy when doing fine rendering, clean up, retouching, and corrections.

Magnifying glasses come in all forms and sizes, with and without holders or

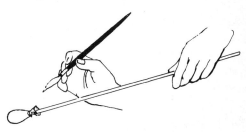

Use a mahlstick to rest and guide the hand while painting.

MANNEQUINS

Either flexible rubberoid figurines, or simplified wooden figures with ball joints.
Usually under 2' tall, mannequins can be
bent into rough approximations of human
postures. Since neither the armature in
the rubber body nor the inflexible wooden
blocks duplicate human structure, these
poses are useful only as a guide and have
no value for accurate detail. The commercial artist who requires accuracy
should use models, skeletons, and anatomical casts. (See *Anatomical Casts.*)

Mannequins do have a certain value
for beginners who are learning to draw
the figure and cannot readily obtain a
model. The mannequin can assume a pose
sufficiently well to serve as a visual aid
in determining the best view of a pose,
foreshortening, and the placement of body
masses.

However, it must be stressed that such
assistance should not be allowed to become a crutch, and that the mannequin
is an approximation at best. Supplement
this help with a scrap file of photographs
or drawings, and with the help of family
or friends who will pose for you.

Only by constant reference to accurate
information can the artist become familiar
with anatomical detail and become edu-
cated enough to realize the limitations
of the mannequin as compared with the
live model.

The paradox of the mannequin is that
once you know enough anatomy to be
able to work with the mannequin—and
compensate for its deficiencies—you will
probably no longer need it to assist you
in visualizing the figure.

MANILA PAPER

A cheap, coarse-textured paper commonly used by schoolchildren. It is useful
to the commercial artist only as an inexpensive sketching paper, and is not
used for finished art, even in the layout
form. (See *Papers and Boards.*)

MAP PINS

Small, straight pins with colored, globular
heads. Traditionally, these pins have been
used to locate salespeople on maps of
the country. However, they can be colorful
elements in certain art and display work.
Some of the larger pins can be used as
alternatives to thumbtacks and pushpins.

MARKERS

Designation for a group of rendering tools
that is indicative of their origin. The first
markers produced black, indelible marks
on laundry and other materials and were
sold in houseware sections. Artists were
quick to use them to produce sharp, crisp
lettering and lines on pastel layouts prevalent at the time. This led to the introduction of colored markers, and soon
marker layouts—with their bright inklike
hues—had completely replaced pastel as
the medium of choice for layouts. Other
companies have joined the original Magic
Marker firm in producing complete color
lines of markers. Modifiers such as "art
markers" and "studio markers" have been
introduced, as have variations in the original, squat metal can. There is a wide
choice of slim, plastic pencil-shapes and
elongated tubes. Nibs have evolved into
a range of fine points, broad chisel shapes,
and even a flexible brush. Solvents are
either permanent, oil-based, or water soluble. Complete sets in various color ranges
and values are sold with desktop stands.
Individual markers can be purchased to
replace empty ones or to create person-
alized sets.

The marker technique completely dominates layouts. Any artist wishing to enter
the commercial art profession must become proficient with these tools. They
are also popular as a fine art medium for
paintings and illustration.

The most common layout method of
applying markers involves drawing a fine,
dark outline and filling the shapes with
flat strokes of color. The secret of a suc-

cessful layout is the preplanned balance of shape, color, and value. This prevents overdrawing and overrendering, which creates a "dirty," scrubbed look that destroys layouts' highly desired, sparkling spontaneity. Despite the hundreds of colors and tints available, a good layout may contain only a dozen or fewer. Producing a crisp layout takes considerable skill and practice. (See *Layouts.*)

Common Difficulties

Drying. Unless the caps on markers fit airtight, the highly volatile dyes evaporate quickly. Be sure to replace the cap the minute you finish with an individual marker; do not wait until your job is done, leaving various markers open during the drawing process. Even with the caps in proper position, the markers are subject to some evaporation, in some colors more than others. Be sure that the art materials store you deal with maintains a fresh stock and test the marker on a scrap of paper before the purchase. The markers do not contain a large amount of dye, so be prepared for a marker to be used up during a large job and be sure to keep a sufficient reserve.

Just before the marker has dried completely, it may be moistened with a dye solvent, extending its life for a brief period. There are no specific preparations on the market designed for this particular use, but a number of liquids in the artist's studio may be effective. Solvents like acetone, lacquer thinner, pen cleaner, and even rubber cement thinner or water may dissolve the dye, depending on the brand of marker you are using.

Bleeding. The colors of the dyes are very intense and tend to bleed through any medium applied over them and through one another as well. Learn to use the colors independently or test the effects of overlapping before using. If you must use paint for lettering or corrections, use a good quality bleed-proof opaque white paint.

Soaking. The dyes in markers are so volatile that they tend to soak through paper very rapidly. The oil-based colors do this invariably, the water-based to a lesser degree. There is no correction for this problem. If the paper you are using allows even the water-based colors to penetrate, back up the paper with another sheet of scrap paper. If art must appear on both sides, render the art on separate papers and adhere them to a third sheet of opaque paper. A special paper, designed for markers—sold at many art supply stores—resists this blotting action. However, the dyes cannot soak into the paper at all and tend to produce a rather thin and streaky coating. Your technique on this paper will have to be considerably different from that which you use on regular layout papers. Practice and experiment.

Erasing. Dyes are impossible to erase by conventional means. Chlorine bleach will work but must be used with care. (See *Erasers.*)

Blending. When a fully rendered comp is desired, certain shading may be required. Skilled layout artists have learned to feather strokes so that smooth gradations of shading are possible. If this proves difficult, try softening the first color with an appropriate solvent before applying the second (or shading) color. With practice, smooth blending can be mastered.

Streaking. Applying flat color to broad areas often leaves visible streaks, particularly if the marker is running dry. Use fresh markers for such tasks, or wet the nib with solvent. Color broad areas with long, straight, parallel strokes that do not overlap. Use a straightedge as a guide. Most important, do not attempt to rectify an error. The effectiveness of the marker technique depends upon a "clean" look. Short, choppy correction strokes and stripes caused by occasional overlaps make the rendering appear labored. It is

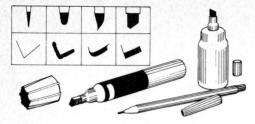

Common marker forms. Representative nib styles and the characteristic strokes they produce are illustrated in the boxes.

better to start over than to have visible corrections.

Lettering. Most layouts require some form of lettering. This is often done with paint. Marker dyes will discolor opaque paints, even those that are "bleedproof." To overcome this problem, render the lettering first with a good opaque white paint. Let the paint dry thoroughly and spray lightly with a workable fixative. Repeat the lettering with the desired color of paint. If the stain still bleeds through, repeat the application of fixative. (Never apply a heavy coat. The solvent will dissolve the rendering and smudge the drawing.)

MARKING PENCILS

Greasy, paper-wrapped pencils in various colors capable of writing on most surfaces. (See *Pencils, Marking.*)

MASKOID

Brand name for a liquid frisket that can be applied with a brush or pen. Once the liquid has dried, it serves as a temporary mask to protect the covered parts of the drawing. When rendering has been completed, the Maskoid can be peeled away without damaging the surface. (See *Friskets* and *Friskets, Liquid.*)

MAT BOARD

A lightweight cardboard covered with a matte or pebbled paper in several muted tones. It is used to mount artwork, or cut out to frame pictures and presentations. A full sheet of mat board is 28″ x 44″, or 30″ x 40″, but smaller sheets may be purchased in art stores. Pre-cut mats in a number of sizes are also sold in many of these stores. Double thick mat board is available for larger jobs. Mat board can be cut with a razor blade, but the preferred tools for preparing a mat are the mat knife or mat cutter. (See *Papers and Boards.*)

MAT CUTTERS

These, with and without straight-edge attachments, facilitate the cutting of beveled edge mats. Though mat cutters vary considerably in design, they consist primarily of a holder that accommodates a blade at an adjustable angle. The blade may be drawn with great pressure over the mat board, producing a clean beveled cut with a single stroke, a difficult task with an ordinary mat knife.

Since the blade can be adjusted, these cutters may be used for scoring as well, a procedure achieved by raising the blade and straightening the angle. This will produce a cut of any depth, regardless of the pressure applied, and will assure an even cut. Scoring is advisable when heavy cardboards and papers must be folded. A light cut, or identation, will allow the material to fold without irregularity or tearing.

Mat cutters do make the job easy, but they require considerable practice before you can use them to their full advantage. Be sure that you allow yourself plenty of practice before attempting to cut a fine piece of board.

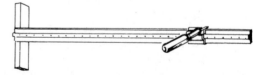

Mat cutter with knife in position to produce a bevelled cut.

MAT FRAMES

Plain, colored, or textured mat boards that have been precut to standard picture frame sizes with a beveled interior opening. These mats are used primarily to frame paintings, etc., prior to their being hung on a wall. However, commercial artists also use them for framing presentation layouts, etc.

To a large extent, commercial art presentations will not be of a standard size, and many formats (booklets, envelopes, folders, etc.) do not lend themselves to a mat presentation. For this reason, most commercial artists prefer to cut their own mats as needed. However, when such artists are preparing a large number of presentations, all in standard sizes, the precut mats are accurate, attractive, and save considerable time.

Many art supply stores and picture framing establishments carry mat frames, and some will cut mats to any desired size. There is an extra charge for such service.

MAT KNIFE

A heavy-duty knife suitable for cutting the heaviest of cardboard with sufficient control and accuracy to produce the clean opening of a mat frame. (See *Knife, Mat.*)

MECHANICAL LETTERING

A system used by engineers and architects for producing lettering on mechanical drawings and renderings. The system employs a lettering guide and a scriber pen. (See *Lettering, Mechanical.*)

MECHANICALS

A mechanical is the final artwork for any job that is to be reproduced. The name derives from the mechanical tools and procedures used to achieve the accuracy needed for such art.

Although the mechanical needs little artistic skill, the requirements of the various reproduction processes make creating the mechanical a very exacting and demanding art. These requirements are too involved for more than a cursory mention in such a work as this; it is necessary to study the books already available on this subject, to enroll in a proper commercial art course, or to obtain professional advice from the technicians involved with producing the reproductions.

Simply stated, the dimensions of the job are inked on a piece of illustration board, and all line art is added (either on the board or pasted on the board) in the proper positions. Next, the halftone material is indicated by using the actual art, a photostatic copy, or by a panel drawn on the board that is the exact size and shape of the material. If the art is not used directly, it is mounted separately and coded to match the indication on the mechanical. All such substitutes should be clearly marked "for position only" so that they are not used by mistake. Finally, special instructions (folds, die cuts, color panels, crop marks, etc.) are drawn on the mechanical in their proper positions, and the finished job is covered with an overlay. This overlay is used for additional instructions (colors, paper stock, number of colors, etc.), and is further protected with a final flap.

Ink is the preferred medium for this work, because of its durability and the fact that ink in mechanical drafting tools can produce very fine, accurate lines.

Three colors are used for the lines drawn on a mechanical:

Black. For all line art, register marks, and crop marks. In short, anything that should be reproduced, even though (as in the case of the crop and and register marks) they will be trimmed away from the final job.

Blue. For instructions that should not reproduce. Guide lines and benday indications are done in blue. Blue does not photograph on platemaking film, so these lines do not need to be removed during the platemaking process.

Red. For all instructions that require special treatment but are not art and will not be reproduced: for example, die cuts. Platemakers know that red means instruction. They copy the shape to reproduce the die, and then remove the red line from the printing plate. Halftone indications are also drawn in red outline, since the platemakers use these lines as a mask for stripping in the halftone negative which will be produced separately. The lines themselves never appear on the final printing plate, but since red photographs the same as black, these lines must be removed by the platemakers. To play safe, these lines can be marked "holding line only," to make sure that they are not inadvertently printed.

The above is only the barest outline of what constitutes a mechanical. There are many ramifications and variations depending upon printing processes and media (television, for example). Therefore, this section should be regarded as nothing more than a *simple* description. Producing mechanicals is one of the time-honored methods of breaking into the art field, and your ability to prepare them accurately will have a strong effect upon your advancement. Make sure that you study this subject with great thoroughness; even though you may graduate from this type of work, you must be completely familiar with it for the rest of your professional career.

Despite the proficiency you may acquire with mechanicals, it should be noted that there are individual variations caused by the working habits of each studio, printer, etc. The wisest course is to always consult with the people who will be producing the job to make sure that you are working in a manner with which they are familiar; the better the cooperation, the better the job.

MINERAL SPIRITS

A traditional name for a group of solvents derived from the distillation of petroleum. These solvents are used to dilute and dissolve many paints, lacquers, varnishes, and shellacs. (See *Solvents.*)

MODELS (LIVE)

A live model is anyone, professional or amateur, who will hold a pose while you paint, draw, or photograph. Professional models are preferable because they are experienced in assuming and holding poses, and their bodies usually have well-defined features which are easy to see and draw. They often have extensive costume collections which will help you to set up specific situations for illustration.

Live models are expensive, however, and may be difficult to locate. If there is an art school near you, it should have a listing of models who work for the school. Many models also leave their names with art supply stores, photography groups, and other organizations of this nature.

The cost of models can be reduced by encouraging others to form a sketch group that works together and shares the expense.

Your own family and friends can often serve as well as any professional for short poses and costume situations. A Polaroid camera is helpful for recording the pose, so that you can finish the details later. Many school and civic groups may also furnish potential models. Theatrical and dance organizations, in particular, will have members who are well-suited for posing; they will have the physical build and costumes to satisfy many requirements. These people will often pose for a small fee—or a donation to their organization. (See also *Anatomical Casts.*)

MOUNTING BOARD

An inexpensive cardboard of several different weights, plain or covered with an equally cheap paper, used to construct displays or mount artwork. The quality of this board is not sufficient to permit its use for any but the crudest artwork. Sold in full sheets, 28" x 44", or cut into smaller sizes by individual art supply stores. (See *Papers and Boards.*)

MULTILINER

A wooden-handled, chisel-shaped tool with regularly spaced ridges on its working face. These ridges act as individual engraving points, which are used to remove the surface coating in scratch board rendering. Multiliners provide a quicker, more accurate way of producing parallel lines on scratch board, than drawing them

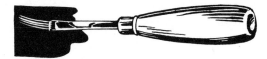

Multiliner, for producing parallel lines on scratch board.

one at a time. Multiliners come in a variety of widths with different numbers of engraving ridges.

Since the use of scratch board as a professional technique has declined in recent years, your art store may not stock multiliners, but will order them.

MYLAR

This is the brand name of a relatively new, clear plastic film that does not stretch, shrink or warp, and is not affected by water. These qualities, referred to as dimensional stability, make Mylar an excellent substitute for other plastic films. The newness of this product and its high cost may make Mylar difficult to obtain, since few stores will maintain a large stock of such an item. Orders, however, can usually be placed at an art supply store. Inform the dealer of your specific need and he/she will be able to help you select the proper product and get it for you. (See *Plastic Films.*)

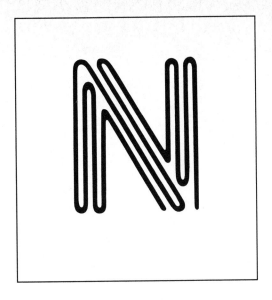

NEWSPRINT

A cheap, buff or gray colored paper used in the art field for drawing or sketching only. Sold in pads in a number of sizes, its low cost makes it acceptable for creative doodling, thumbnail sketches, and other preliminary drawings. (See *Papers and Boards*.)

NON-CRAWL

A brand name for a paint additive that prevents crawling and chipping on glossy surfaces. The descriptive nature of the product has led to its use in a generic sense. (See *Acetate Mediums*.)

NO-SEAM PAPER

This is the paper that is used for creating uniform backgrounds in display and photography. The paper comes in large, wide rolls, so that large expanses may be covered without edges or corners showing. The colors available are generally soft and muted, as backgrounds should be. The paper itself is not unlike construction paper and can be used for booklet covers, etc., although its size makes such use rather expensive. (See *Papers and Boards*.)

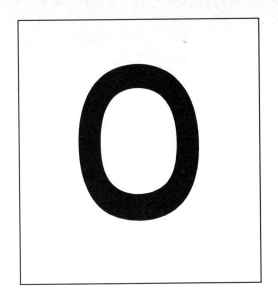

the thinner to evaporate too quickly. In fact, the one drawback of the oil can is the open spout. Thinner is highly volatile and even this small opening allows the thinner to evaporate rather quickly. You can slow this process down by forcing a small wad of kneaded eraser over the tip when not in use.

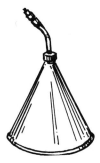

Oil can rubber cement dispenser. Fixture on spout can be closed to prevent evaporation.

OAK TAG

A heavy, durable paper with a slightly glossy surface. This buff colored paper is a standard in most schools for producing covers, cut-outs, constructions, stencils, etc. In the commercial art field, it has a limited value and is usually replaced with other, more specialized papers. (See *Papers and Boards.*)

OIL CAN

A slang term used to describe any rubber cement thinner dispenser. The term derives from the actual oil cans still used by many artists for the purpose, and the similarity of other dispensers now available at art supply stores.

The oil can referred to is the common one with the half-a-hemisphere-shaped can on the bottom and the tall, tapered spout that screws into the top. Inverting the can and pressing on the bottom causes the liquid to be expelled from the small opening in the tip of the spout. The can comes in many sizes with the amount of use determining the size you choose. Remember that too big a can will permit

OIL CHALKS

A fine art pastel with an oil-based binder. (See *Chalks, Oil.*)

OILSTONES

A synonym for whetstone. The name derives from the practice of moistening the stone with oil during the sharpening process. (See *Whetstones.*)

OPAQUE PROJECTOR

A device for enlarging or reducing opaque artwork by brightly lighting the material and projecting the reflection through a lens. The lens itself may be adjusted and the distance from the projector to the screen may be changed. Both factors control the size of the projection. Using the projector permits opaque scrap or reference material to be projected on any surface in many sizes for tracing purposes. Interchangeable lenses produce various enlargements or reductions. Other lenses permit distortions, that is, condensation or expansion. Similar distor-

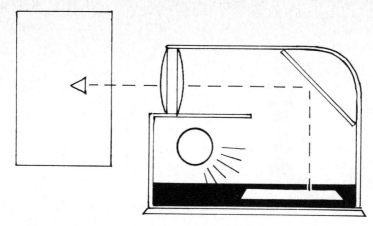

Opaque projector, showing light source illuminating original copy whose image is then reflected by a mirror and projected through a lens onto a screen.

tions can be accomplished by changing the angle of the surface receiving the projection. Tilting this surface in various positions will vary the distortion. Extreme tilting, however, will cause the edges of the projection to go out of focus.

The purpose of the opaque projector is to allow you to trace directly from reference material, regardless of its size. This is accomplished by placing the reference material in the projector and focusing the projected image upon a piece of paper, board, cloth, etc. This material may, or may not be, the final artwork. The projected image may now be outlined or rendered with any medium you desire. As an example, a leading television network produces rendered portraits for its news programs by having an artist draw directly from the projected image of a photograph. This procedure is quick and accurate, a necessary quality for reporting current news. Opaque projectors are also useful for presentation meetings. Since the actual art is used for the projection, film costs (photography, lab, mounting) involved in slides and strip film presentation are eliminated.

There are several brands of projectors on the market. Fully professional models may run to several hundred dollars, but simpler models can be inexpensive and quite satisfactory. (See *Projector, Art.*)

The only difficulties with this manner of projecting and sizing materials are that you need to work in a darkened room—which may be inconvenient—and that your hand will interrupt the light beam as you attempt to trace the image at the screen. However, neither of these difficulties diminishes the effectiveness of the opaque projector.

OPAQUE WHITE

A water-based paint designed to cover other paints, ink, dyes, etc., opaque white can cover other layers in one coat without bleeding; that is, no color applied previously and allowed to dry will be picked up and mixed with the opaque white as it is added on top. In silhouetting photographs, in correcting inked lines, in lettering over painted surfaces, in countless other art procedures, opaque white serves a valuable purpose.

Opaque white may be applied like any water-based paint; that is, with a brush, airbrush, pen, or ruling pen. The manner in which you use it will depend on the specific job. When you are using it to make a correction, repeat the original technique you were using when you made the error. For example, to cover and eliminate a line made with a ruling pen, apply the opaque white with a ruling pen, retracing the original line exactly. This procedure will insure the accuracy of the correction and maintain the finished appearance of the artwork. Although the paint is white, its texture and color will contrast with white paper. The painted surface will attract dirt more easily than the paper, and the resulting smudge can only be cleaned with the application of more paint. The appearance of a job is not helped by irregular blotches of dirty white: they may not reproduce, but they inform the client that you are something less than a professional.

Using opaque white for other tasks requires no special considerations or techniques, just be sure to apply enough. Even opaque white will not be opaque if it is used too sparingly.

Nearly every company that produces paint markets a product that in some way claims to be opaque and bleedproof. The number of these products testifies to the importance of opaque white in art, and also admits to the fact that none of them is everything it claims. Therefore, no recommendation can be made for one product or type of product over any other. Here is a case where experimentation is extremely necessary. It is not just a matter of personal preference; each of these whites performs quite well under certain circumstances and has pronounced faults under others. Some of the whites are gummy and slow drying, some tend to bleed with certain pigments, others cover very well but cannot be worked over, while some really need two coats before they will be truly opaque.

These criticisms are not meant to malign the products. They do the job well within their limitations. The important feature of such a discussion is to convince you that it is necessary to try several brands under many conditions before selecting or rejecting one or all of them.

When you must letter in a light color over a dark background, render the lettering first with opaque white. When applied over the white, the color will have the same brilliance as if it had been lettered on white paper.

OSMIROID

The brand name of a drawing ink pen, similar to both India ink pens and conventional fountain pens. The Osmiroid pen should not be used with India ink (the manufacturer recommends Pelikan fount ink). This pen has a series of interchangeable nibs, including two for left-handed artists, and is used for drawing, lettering, and ruling. (See *Pens.*)

OVERLAYS

A transparent or translucent sheet placed over a piece of artwork for one of three reasons: separation, information, or protection.

Separation. The separation overlay is prepared when two pieces of art of the same color are to be surprinted, or when art of more than one color is being preseparated for the platemaker's camera. In the latter case, an overlay is prepared for each color.

The subject of separation, and the mechanical in general, is a complex one. Before you attempt to prepare mechanicals and separations, make sure that you are thoroughly familiar with them (and printing processes, too) by taking specialized instruction in a good art class or by mastering appropriate text books that are available on the subjects.

The separation overlay must be accurate. Any error on such a mechanical will be repeated or exaggerated in the final printing. To ensure accuracy, use only the best materials. Trade standards require that the overlay be composed of acetate or frosted acetate. The overlay is adhered to the basic artwork by a strip of drafting tape applied across the top. The position of the overlay is permanently indicated by placing three register marks to the sides and below the base art, and in corresponding positions on each overlay. When properly positioned, the register marks (crossed lines within a circle) insure accurate position of the art in all stages of the printing process. These marks are reproduced on the printing plates and thus on the final printed sheet. The printer knows, therefore, when the register marks coincide exactly on the finished printing, that the art is in the precise position it was meant to be. For this reason, you must place the marks with extreme care. If you do not position each mark on the overlay *exactly* over the corresponding mark on the base art, or if you use less than three (three points determine a plane), there is no way for the printer to be sure of the accurate position of the art. Remember that the overlay must be taken away from the base art when the printing plates are being produced. Without proper registration, an overlay can never be returned to its proper position. Artwork is produced on the overlay directly, or on separate papers which are trimmed and mounted on the overlay with rubber cement. The finished overlay is identified with the name and a sample of the color in which the art is to be printed.

Information. Instructions regarding the artwork, directions to the platemaker and the printer, are placed on a separate overlay. Such instructions may include the size of the finished piece, specifications as to the stock and ink, color indications, requirements for scoring, folding, binding, etc., anything that has to do with the final preparation and printing. The purpose of the overlay is to allow these instructions to be presented directly over the areas being discussed without damaging the art. To avoid confusion and misunderstanding, the instructions should be rendered neatly, but with nowhere near the patience and detail required for the art. Since the overlay is

not art, any transparent or translucent stock such as layout or tracing paper may be used. Similarly, the rendering of the instructions may be done in any medium. The most common choices are pencil and dye marker.

No register marks are necessary for this overlay.

Protection. Since the finished art or mechanical must pass through several hands, a final, protective overlay is often included. This overlay not only prevents damage to the art and instructions beneath, but provides a surface for the client to record corrections, modifications, or approval. Once these comments have been acted upon, the overlay may be removed or replaced; the art remains unmarked throughout. Use a transparent stock for this overlay, otherwise the client will have to raise the overlay to view the art. With the overlay raised, the tendency is to write on the art, defeating the purpose of the overlay. (See also *Flap Paper* and *Plastic Films.*)

Common Difficulties

Stretching or warping. Separation overlays may be affected by heat and humidity, causing inaccuracies in fine register. Though thin acetate, vellum, or tracing paper may be sufficient for many jobs, you are advised to stick with the regular acetate or frosted acetate provided for the purpose at all art stores. In cases of extreme distortion conditions, when accuracy is imperative, try Mylar.

Movement. Platemakers and printers must use overlays independently, removing them from the original mechanical. If accuracy of position is important, regardless of the type of overlay, use register marks. Realigning these marks will insure the various pieces of art being returned to their proper position.

Tearing. Since the overlays will be removed and replaced many times in the course of handling, the tape holding them to the artwork must not have too great an adhesion. Scotch and masking tapes are too strong and may tear away the surface when they are lifted. This not only damages the artwork, but destroys the adhesive ability of the tape, making it impossible to replace the overlay. A loose overlay is subject to damage. To prevent this, use drafting or correction tape to fasten down your overlay.

Cutting. Like most plastics, acetate tears easily once the surface has been broken. Trimming artwork that has been mounted on an acetate overlay may score the plastic. Subsequent handling will cause the score to break, the break widens quickly, and the overlay is often destroyed. Trim all artwork *before* mounting.

Bleeding. Dye markers often bleed through thin papers that are used for instruction overlays. This bleeding may discolor the artwork. Use a layout paper that does not bleed. If no such paper is available, sketch the layout lightly in pencil as a guide and remove the overlay before rendering.

Scoring. Writing with a ball point pen on an overlay will cause indentations that damage photographs, airbrush, and pastel renderings. You can't control the habits of others who will handle your art, but, please, don't use a ball point yourself. In fact, avoid the use of any hard-pointed writing tool that exerts too much pressure when you are working with an overlay.

OVERLAYS, TINTED ACETATE

A series of acetate sheets produced by a number of manufacturers that are coated with either transparent or opaque colored inks. These sheets, which may or may not have adhesive backings, are used in the preparation of layouts and product or packaging mock-ups. Since the colors are created from the same inks used in printing, the layouts closely resemble the look of the finished job, eliminating client misunderstanding and disappointment. The range and number of colors available vary from manufacturer to manufacturer, and not all art stores carry more than one brand. However, the convenience of the form and the accuracy of the colors offset any limitations. At least one manufacturer uses colors that match other products in the line, which makes matching combinations of techniques very successful.

These sheets are also useful for creating artwork, collages, and for color separations. They are applied either by cutting shapes from the sheets and applying them to the art, or by applying the sheets to the art and trimming away the excess. Additional art may be added to the sheets using acetate inks or paints. Swatchbooks containing samples of the complete range of colors can be purchased at art stores. These permit accurate planning of a job before the actual sheets need to be purchased.

Common Difficulties

Scratching. The sheets are comparatively fragile and rough handling mars the surface. Store carefully and work with a slip sheet under your hand.

Color. Despite the number of colors offered, inevitably there will be a color that is not available. A specialized sheet may be prepared by airbrushing color on a clear sheet of acetate, using appropriate pigments.

Adhesive. Those sheets that contain an adhesive backing are protected with a wax paper backing. Keep this sheet in constant contact when not in use. Even with the best care, dust and dirt discolor this adhesive. It is better to use a fresh sheet for each job. Long-term storage will render these sheets unusable, with the transparent inks allowing the dirt to show through.

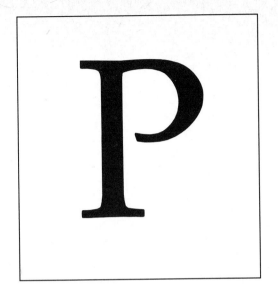

PAINT

Ask a nonartist to describe any kind of artist, and the answer will usually involve some statement about painting a picture. Indeed, art and picture painting have become synonymous, and for a good reason. Anyone who studies art becomes more proficient in picture painting than any nonartist. And even commercial artists who do not paint pictures for a living often paint them as a hobby.

But many aspiring commercial artists misunderstand this emphasis on paint, and the large selection of paints in the art stores is confusing. The result is a tendency for the students to feel inadequate and uncertain, to try to spread themselves too thin educationally, and to expect too much from art education in terms of unraveling the mysteries of the profession merely by learning to handle another medium.

To reduce this confusion, it may help to understand the purposes of the various paints, and to learn which art specialist would be likely to use which, since an artist may spend his/her entire career using only a few kinds of paint. Let us start by dividing all paints into three categories: oil-based, water-soluble, and special purpose.

Oil-Based

The most familiar oil paint is the one used to produce oil paintings, and the many brands available are relatively similar to each other. They consist of a pigment (either natural or synthetic), a ground (to provide body and opacity), an oil medium (usually linseed oil, soluble in turpentine), and a drying agent (which speeds up the time needed for the paint to dry).

These paints differ only in the quality of the ingredients and the proportions in which they are mixed. The commercial brands are usually labeled: "student" or "artist" quality. It is also possible to purchase the materials separately and mix your own paints. Many fine artists do this. However, such procedures are of little value to the commercial artist.

Because of time factors, these oil paints have practically no use for the commercial artist or illustrator. The commercial field is continually limited by deadlines that do not permit the time-consuming procedures required to produce a fine oil painting. Not only do oil paints require lengthy drying times, but toning, underpainting, glazing, and other oil painting techniques consume many hours, both in execution and drying. Another reason for avoiding oil paints in the commercial field is the limitation inherent in all commercial printing reproduction. The subtle values of a fine oil painting are lost in all but the most expensive printing processes. In short, there is no reason for the extra cost in time and effort to produce an oil painting, when another medium will do the job more easily and reproduce better.

If you have read the introduction, you will understand why these oil paints are not discussed in greater detail in this book. This is not to discourage you from using oil for your own enjoyment and edification. There is something about

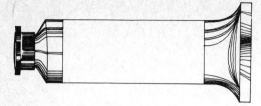

Typical metal paint tube.

working with a fine medium on a fine subject that enhances an artist's ability as no other practice can. By all means, pick up a set of oil paints, some reference texts or instruction, and try out this father of all art techniques.

There are several oil media of value to the commercial artist. But these media are so specialized in their uses that they are better covered in the group of special paints which follows later in this entry.

Water-Soluble

Since we have virtually eliminated oil paints as a practical medium for the average commercial artist, it is obvious that the great majority of paints used in commercial work are water-soluble. Like oils, all of these water paints are composed of pigment, ground, and medium; but all of them dry rapidly, and if anything else is added, it is usually a substance that retards this drying.

There are many water-soluble paints, and it is better to divide them again into four general classifications, each of which has its own section in this book:

Watercolors. Highly refined and transparent, used for layout and illustration. (See also *Dyes.*)

Gouaches. Also called tempera, designer's colors, or poster colors, this group comprises the largest variety of water paints that are most commonly used in the field. Gouache colors may be either opaque or transparent, and are used for layout, illustration, and general design work. (See also *Gouache* and *Tempera.*)

Casein. One of the first alternatives to conventional watercolor and tempera paints, caseins are used almost exclusively for fine art. They are water-soluble, but highly water-resistant when dry. (See *Casein.*)

Acrylics. The most successful of the synthetic paints, acrylics are water-soluble, waterproof when dry, and can be used in any oil paint or watercolor technique, including impasto. Despite this versatility, they have not found great favor with commercial artists and are used largely by fine artists and illustrators. Their major value to commercial artists is its ability to adhere to glossy surfaces without cracking or peeling. (See *Acrylics.*)

Each of these classifications is discussed more fully under its own heading. Since there are many characteristics that overlap, it is suggested that you consult all the listings before choosing a medium.

Special Purpose

There are a number of paints of value to the commercial artist that do not conveniently fall into either of the above categories. However, without exception, these paints are for very specialized areas in the commercial field. Some of these are carried by general art stores and, when available, you may wish to experiment with them. Many of these, however, have so little use for the average artist that they are stocked only by professional suppliers dealing directly with the firms that use them. This is as it should be. The nature of the work is so specialized and difficult, that you should not attempt to do it professionally without extensive training and supervision. Since few schools have classes in these subjects, most of the training comes on the job. Should you acquire such employment, you will receive ample instruction in the materials and how to use them. Let us discuss some of these specialized products on the facing page.

Textile paints. these may be either oil-based or water-based; and they may be applied directly to fabrics with a brush, or silkscreened, printed, or blocked. Outside of the professional clothing manufacturers, this is largely a hobby field. Therefore, the materials and instructional literature are available at art supply stores and hobby outlets. There may be occasions in presentation and display where such paints will help the commercial artist, but they are not a staple item.

Sign writer's paints. For producing indoor signs and showcards, sign writers will use many of the standard designer and poster colors. For outdoor signs there are a number of oil-based paints that are produced primarily for the sign painter. Since the sign market is large and varied, a number of these will be carried by the average art supply store. The most common are Japan colors and silkscreen paints. Both of these adhere well to metal and other outdoor sign materials, and withstand weathering. Most paints of this nature are soluble in turpentine, although some silkscreen paints require mineral spirits. Additional paints and enamels are found less frequently and may have to be purchased from sign writing supply firms. Sign writing is an excellent example of apprentice training. This is not a subject that is taught at art schools, and yet there are a number of simple tasks in a sign shop that a beginning artist can perform to earn a small salary while learning the sign writing art.

Silkscreen paints. As mentioned above, silkscreen colors are useful in sign work, whether hand-painted or screened. But in general, silkscreen is a specialized printing process, a fine art technique (serigraphy), or a hobby. These areas are not consistently encountered in commercial art, and silkscreen is not a necessary talent for the commercial artist. But the materials and instructional literature are easily purchased at all art and hobby outlets. Silkscreen paints are pro-duced with three different bases, soluble in water, turpentine, or mineral spirits.

Enamels. Outside of the conventional enamels sold in paint and wallpaper outlets, there are some enamels sold in art supply stores for limited hobby and commercial art situations. Typical of these is Flo-Paque, an enamel sold in small bottles, that is quick-drying, waterproof, flexible, light-fast, and opaque. These enamels will adhere to most any surface including glass, ceramics, fabrics, metal, wood, plaster, plastics, and leather. Flo-Paque additionally offers a thinner (called Dio Sol), a glossy waterproof glaze, and a high gloss, alcohol-proof coating called A1 Pro-Cote.

Animation paints. Paints of this category, often referred to as cartoon colors, are designed primarily for use with animation cels in producing animated films. Their characteristics are identifical to acetate and acrylic paints, which they usually are, and they adhere well to most glossy surfaces. These paints are all water-soluble, and some, like the acrylics, are waterproof when dry. For these reasons they are used in many other areas of commercial art besides animated films. Preparing overlays and presentations on plastic films is easily accomplished with animation paints.

Acetate paints. Like animation paints, acetate paints are designed for work on glossy, nonabsorbent surfaces. But while animation paints are universally opaque, some acetate paints may be transparent, permitting a wider range of rendering techniques. (See *Acetate Ink, Acetate Mediums,* and *Paint, Acetate.*)

Opaque white. Covering errors on mechanicals, silhouetting photographs, etc., are procedures that occur constantly in commercial art. This frequency of use has led to the development of special water-soluble white paints for use in all cases where an opaque covering is necessary. (See *Opaque White.*)

PAINT CUPS

Paint cups—containers for paint—may be either permanent or disposable. Both are recommended whenever large amounts of a color must be premixed or the consistency of the paint is such that it will run on a normal palette. Permanent cups are larger and more stable than disposable cups; however, they must be cleaned. Disposable cups must be placed in a holder of some type, but are inexpensive and can be thrown away after using. The box in which the disposable cups are sold makes a fine holder. Simply cut away the part of the box above the base. Disposable cups also fit into egg crates or into multiple-opening trays that are sold to hold them.

Common Difficulties

Deterioration. Be careful with media other than watercolor. Some synthetic paints, lacquers, acetone, etc., dissolve plastic paint cups. Use metal, glass, or ceramic containers for these liquids.

Evaporation. Paint will dry out rapidly in the small paint cups. Since there is no way to seal them, mix only enough paint in the cups to accommodate your current work. If it is necessary to leave the paint after it has been mixed, try placing a wet cloth over the cups. This will slow down the evaporation.

PALETTE

The conventional palette is a square or oval board with a thumb hole. This type of palette has been developed for an artist who stands at an easel; as he paints, he holds the palette and extra brushes in his free hand. Since few artists in the commercial field stand while they work, the palette is not essential for the commercial artist; and even if they prefer to stand, they generally work with a taboret. Therefore, anything that comes to hand—like an old dinner plate—is usually satisfactory for use as a palette. However,

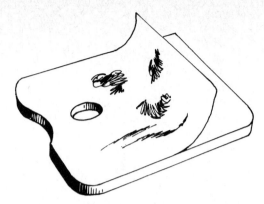

Pad of disposable paper palettes. The dirty sheet is torn off.

if you do paint with any frequency, you may prefer the traditional palette to hold and mix your paints.

Palettes fall into two categories; permanent and disposable. Permanent palettes are made of wood, metal, glass, or plastic, and must be cleaned frequently. The tight deadlines and pressures of the commercial field make this chore annoying, time consuming, and unprofitable, and have led to the marketing of disposable palettes. These disposable palettes usually consist of a pad of coated papers shaped like the conventional palette. The papers, which may be torn off and thrown away after using, do not absorb oil, but will absorb some water. The amount of water absorbed may cause water-soluble paints to dry faster on the palette, but will not affect the cleanliness of the sheets beneath.

Perhaps the most successful alternative to the palette is the common butcher's tray, found in the houseware section of any department store. Since nearly all the commercial pigments are water-soluble, and the tray is enamel or porcelain-covered metal, you can clean the tray easily by soaking it in water. Naturally, the tray is inconvenient to hold while painting, and is usually placed on a work table or taboret. There the weight of the tray becomes an advantage; it tends to remain immobile when used, freeing both hands for work. The edges of the tray are an additional benefit, preventing the paint from running onto the working surface. Lighter, flatter palettes may be difficult to hold steady, and may allow the paint to run over the edges.

There are many occasions when the tray and the conventional palette are not adequate. Thin fluids and large amounts of any pigment are not easy to handle on such flat surfaces. In these cases, use paint cups, egg crates, etc.

PALETTE KNIFE

A small, flexible, spatula blade attached to a wooden or plastic handle, the palette knife was originally designed to mix paint on a palette. The palette knife could also be used to scrape dried paint off the palette when it was being cleaned. However, any thick paint (such as oil, casein, or acrylic) will produce a variety of interesting textural surfaces when applied to a painting with a palette knife. This has led to the development of a large number of variations of this knife with larger or smaller blades in several shapes and degrees of flexibility. Palette knifes are used as alternatives to paintbrushes, and an entire painting can be produced with palette knives without ever using a brush.

The conventional palette knife is still valuable for its original purpose, however, and many commercial artists find them useful, even if they are not illustrators or fine artists.

PANTOGRAPH

A mechanical device used for direct rescaling of artwork by means of tracing. It is composed of two adjustable units made of wood or metal. One unit has a base (A) which is held stationary, and a stylus (C) which is moved over the original artwork by hand. The second unit, which is attached to the first with bolts or screws at points (B), contains a draw-

ing tool (D). As the stylus is moved over the original, the drawing tool duplicates the action, but in a different proportion. Placing a sheet of paper under the drawing tool allows you to record this newly proportioned drawing. Altering the connections of the two units changes the proportional relationship and produces a drawing in a different scale. These alternate positions are marked next to the holes on the two units, and the resulting proportions are described in the instructions which accompany the pantograph. The pantograph may be used to enlarge or reduce artwork, and some models have interchangeable pens and pencils at the drawing point.

Common Difficulties

Awkwardness. With moderately large artwork, the copy paper may have to rest on part of the original. This will make it necessary to work on only a part of the drawing at a time. Trying to move the pantograph to a new position during a job can cause inaccuracies and is inconvenient.

Limitations. The positions of the pantograph are limited by the holes to a number of predetermined settings, and rescaling cannot be accomplished in in-between proportions.

For these reasons, plus the fact that the pantograph must be reassembled and taken apart for each job, most professionals prefer one of the other methods of rescaling artwork. (See *Projectors, Opaque; Photostats; Lacey Luci;* and *Camera Lucida.*)

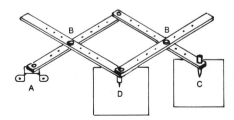

Pantograph, showing the base (A), the screws (B), the stylus (C), and the drawing tool (D).

PANTONE MATCHING SYSTEM

The most accurate color matching and specification system ever produced, PMS is used for coordinating colors of layout presentations to correspond exactly with the inks used in most printing processes. There are 505 Pantone colors, each identified with a PMS number. Printers can create these colors by following exact recipes for blending ink colors. Artists can specify these colors by numbers obtained from Pantone reference books, or by detaching small perforated samples from a book containing all the colors printed on both coated and uncoated stocks. Pantone reference books on other aspects of four-color process printing are also available. Presentation papers and tinted acetate overlays in Pantone colors are sold at many art stores. In addition, many Letraset products, including markers, are produced in Pantone colors.

PAPER CLIPS

Paper clips are a familiar item and I assume that you know what they are and how to use them. They are included in this volume for one very important reason: *never* use a paper clip on a photograph. Paper clips create indentations in the emulsion of the photograph. These are permanent marks that cast shadows in the strong side-lighting used by engravers and platemakers. Therefore, these shadows show up when the photo is used for reproduction. While this may seem obvious and elementary, a remarkable number of photographs, intended for use as finished art, are provided to the artist with a sheet of copy neatly paper-clipped to the print.

If it is necessary to identify a photo or provide written copy or instruction on the photo, front or back, use a marking crayon. The soft wax of such a crayon can be wiped off easily, while any other marking may destroy the photograph.

PAPER CUTTER

A metal-edged board with a hinged knife blade. Drawing the blade down will cut material with a scissors action. An exception is the Nikor, which has a rotary blade instead of the knife arm. Paper cutters come in all sizes, styles, and prices. The higher the price, the larger the cutter and the size of paper that can be cut. Better quality cutters will also be more expensive. Personal preferences will dictate which model you choose.

You should, however, pick a cutter with a good cutting knife and a strong, easily adjusted spring, the first two features to deteriorate with use. Also look for a bed ruled into ½" squares which contains an adjustable guide. These features facilitate positioning the paper for accurate cutting.

An additional feature on some models is a protective shield on the cutting arm. As the knife is drawn down, the shield is rotated away from the cutting edge.

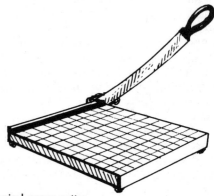

Typical paper cutter.

Common Difficulties

Binding. The paper will be grabbed, instead of cut, if the blade is dull, or if the knife is improperly adjusted. Make sure that the spring is tightened properly so that the knife makes clean contact all along the cutting edge. Remove and sharpen the blade whenever necessary.

Folding. As the spring loses tension, the knife will not cut cleanly, and will fold or tear the paper even though the knife may be quite sharp. Forcing the knife blade against the edge of the board during the cutting stroke will offer temporary relief. But the best solution is to adjust the spring, restoring full tension and holding the blade in proper position throughout the cut.

PAPERS AND BOARDS

Paper is the commercial artist's medium just as canvas is the painter's medium. Although there are exceptions in illustration, film, and television, commercial artists use paper and not much else. From the first doodled sketch up to the final printed piece, paper is the only substance involved. The paper may be white or colored, smooth or textured, coated or uncoated, mounted on cardboard or plain. Even what we refer to as board is either heavy paper or paper that has been stiffened with a cardboard backing.

Naturally, this means that there are literally hundreds of kinds of paper. You *must* have a working knowledge of this all-important material; and fortunately, the *basic* kinds of paper are limited. So some simple generalizations are possible to help you gain an understanding of this complex subject.

Paper is produced by pouring a mixture of water and fibers of natural or synthetic origin onto a fine wire screen. The water drains off and the fibers interlock in random patterns that give the paper its strength. The sheet is then allowed to dry naturally, or is finished by a process called calendering—forcing the paper through rollers that can be smooth or textured, hot or cold. Where the fibers extend over the edge of the screen, they create a ragged edge called a deckle. Handmade papers have a deckle on all four edges. Commercial papers are produced in a continuous sheet so the deckle occurs only on the sides, and this is usually trimmed off with knives as the paper is gathered in rolls. Handmade papers may have, in addition to the natural texture of the fiber, an impression of the screen. This shows up as delicate parallel lines, called laid lines, and the paper is referred to as a laid paper. Where the screen is even, and no pattern occurs, the paper is called a wove paper. Commercial papers duplicate the richness of these details by incorporating them in the calendering rolls. Commercial papers have one other distinctive characteristic—the grain. Since the paper is formed continuously, the fibers tend to lay more frequently in the direction of the moving machinery. This is the grain. Folding the paper against this grain causes the fibers to break, creating a ragged seam, and disrupting any printing that may cover that area. As the paper is made, additional characteristics can be imparted by coating it with clay, varnish, or plastics. And, of course, the paper may be bleached or colored while still in the liquid stage.

Within the limits of this over-simplified description of the papermaking process, paper companies produce about a half dozen *general* categories of paper:

1. Bristols and vellums. Superior quality papers, more often white than not, quite heavy and opaque.

2. Covers and texts. Lighter, less expensive papers with a wide range of colors, textures, deckles, etc., that are used for booklets, folders and the like. The cover stocks are about twice as heavy as the texts, and usually come in the same colors and treatments.

3. Bonds and writing. The most common papers in everday use. Stationery, typewriter paper, and the bulk of inexpensive printed pieces are made of bond. It is comparatively light and tends to be translucent.

4. Thin papers. Onionskin and second sheets are prime examples of this category. These are the lightest papers and the cheapest. They are usually quite transparent.

5. Card stocks. Ledger and index are the most common names in this area, and they are used to make file cards, etc. They are essentially cheap bristols.

6. Specialty papers. A rather haphazard category in which to lump all the remaining papers that do not fit neatly into the above descriptions. It would include the newer plastic papers and any other unusual specifications that prevent the papers from being common standards.

All of the above papers may be altered in the manufacture to include any or all of the variations of texture, color, coating, etc., to produce countless hybrids that defy convenient classification. However, the basic papers are those listed above and no others.

Once finished, the papers are cut into sheets and boxed. These sheets are about 2' x 3' in size, and the packages contain reams or parts of reams. A ream is 500 sheets, the basic unit of measure in the paper industry. A quire is twenty-five sheets, generally the smallest unit considered. Regardless of the size or number of sheets, the paper will be identified by a basis. This basis will include the size of the full sheet and the weight of a certain number of sheets, usually a ream or a multiple thereof. The heavier papers will usually have a smaller number of sheets involved in the figuring of the basis weight. For instance, "cover stock," which is heavier than text, will have a lower basis number. Sixty-five pound cover is about twice as heavy as eighty pound text, since fewer sheets are used to determine the basis for cover stock. This may seem confusing, but you will soon get used to it. Another item covered n the basis is the grain. "Grain long" means that the fibers tend to lay in the same direction the long way on the sheet. Therefore, a text paper, basis eighty, 25" x 33", grain long, tells you that the paper is much heavier and more dense than bond, that the largest sheet you can buy is 25" x 33", and that if you plan to

produce a folded piece, the printer should lay out the job so that the fold runs parallel to the long side of the sheet to prevent cracking.

There are two reasons for you to know these papers. First, you must work with them when your art is printed. The printers will produce your art on one of them. The different prices and characteristics of these papers will often determine what you do and how you do it. There is no book, no course of study, no special way at all that you can learn about paper. It comes with experience. But you can hasten that knowledge by becoming a friend of your printer and your paper distributor. They want a good job, too, and they will do all they can to help you pick the proper paper for each job. Listen to them, get samples from them, collect the booklets that the paper companies distribute through the paper merchants. In this way you will accumulate a vast storehouse of valuable knowledge about a very important area of your work.

Second, you must understand these categories because the same paper companies produce most of the papers that are sold in art supply stores. In older days, artists' papers were produced by specialists who produced only art materials. Economics has made this impossible; the costs are too high, and the demand is too limited to support separate companies. Therefore, the bulk of *all* papers are now produced by the leading paper companies and the art papers are usually their standard papers, or minor variations of them. These papers are sold to art supply houses who pad or package them under their own names. This leads to confusion, for each company attempts to make its product appear unique. Once you understand that there are only a few basic papers and learn the characteristics of these papers, you will be able to assess them and make better choices.

Perhaps the best way to discuss the papers you will use as an artist is to take the various functions of an artist and examine which papers are used in these areas. We can then do the same with the boards; for although the boards are composed of identical papers with cardboard backings, their functions may be changed in the process.

Let us set up four arbitrary categories of paper use: layout, artwork, presentation, and construction. Naturally, there will be overlapping functions within these categories but, for the most part, papers will be used pretty much in one category or another.

Layout Paper

In preparing preliminary sketches, the main considerations are economy and speed. You will use a lot of paper trying out ideas, and there is no sense wasting money on superior papers. Also, you will save time if you can slip a previous drawing under a clean sheet and make corrections, variations, and refinements in the old drawing by tracing directly. For these reasons, you will use a light, transparent, and inexpensive paper. These papers are the bonds and onionskins, or though they are quite expensive, the transparent vellums. But in the art stores you will find them referred to by different names:

Tracing paper. This is composed of highly transparent onionskin entirely.

Tracing vellum. This is never called tracing paper; it's expensive and they want you to know why.

Visualizer paper. This is a catch-all category that may include several different weights of either the onionskin or bond papers. It will be more translucent than transparent.

Drawing paper. Usually a more opaque bond.

Layout paper. About the same as drawing paper.

Bond paper. This will be any of the various weights of bond that are available

as writing paper in stationery stores. It will usually be opaque and will often be quite heavy.

All of the above papers are satisfactory for producing layouts. There are no special preferences, although you will find that most artists and art studios will stick to a few particular items through choice or habit. Often it will be the ones on which they can get the best deals from the art supply houses. Don't be confused by the various brand names. Nine times out of ten they will have been manufactured by the same company. If you buy them in sheets you can save a considerable amount of money. You pay a lot for the pad, and for the store name—neither of which is particularly important. The pads are convenient and come in all sizes from 4″ x 6″ up to 19″ x 24″. The art stores will rarely stock single sheets or even reams, but it may be possible to place an order through them. If not, take a sample to a paper wholesaler, if you can. He will probably be able to match it quite closely, and you can buy a full ream for a fraction of the cost in pad form.

All of these papers are meant for use with dry media, that is, pencil, charcoal, pastel, etc.; and hedging a little bit, dye markers, which dry so quickly that they are really not a wet medium. In all cases the surface texture is smooth and matte with a gentle tooth that takes these media very well. The exception is the dye marker. Most of these will bleed through the paper, or at least spread and blot more than you can control. A special visualizer paper is offered that resists this bleeding action.

Since the papers tend to be transparent, layouts rendered on them must be backed for presentation. Any opaque white paper will do very well. For stiffness, mount them both on a piece of board, or frame them with a mat. (Mats are covered later in the book, in the section on boards.)

Artwork Paper

It would seem that this group would include the largest number of choices, but oddly enough, the basic choice is very limited. Commercial artists, as opposed to illustrators, have little call for extensive rendering past the layout stage. Whatever pictures are called for are usually supplied by the illustrators and photographers. Therefore, the commercial artist usually has little need for anything other than:

Bristol. This is the same bristol that has been previously described in this entry. However, the quality is extremely important. There are a wide range of bristols and the artist should use only the best for most finished art uses. The standard for the industry is Strathmore bristol, available in sheets of 1-, 2-, and 3-ply in kid finish (matte and slightly rough) and plate finish (smooth and glossy). Bristol of this quality is excellent for use with any medium, wet or dry. It is this universality that makes bristol so widely used. What you lose in cost, you more than make up in the fact that you need waste nothing on alternatives. Although a high quality bristol is recommended, there are many jobs and situations where the quality is not that important and the budget will not stand the expense. There is nothing wrong with using a cheaper bristol if it works for the job. Bristol is available in both single sheets and pads of all sizes, and in many grades, from student to Strathmore. You will have to try several before you can make a proper choice. But remember that a good bristol will take considerable abuse without damage. Abrasive ink erasers will not damage a fine bristol, and ink can even be scraped away with a razor blade on the best ones.

Newsprint and manila. There are many papers sold in the art stores that find their uses in commercial art, but to a very limited degree. These range from the very coarse newsprint and manila papers, which are good only for rough sketching and are not even used for layout in the field. Newsprint is, of course, the same paper which newspapers are printed on. It is quite cheap and you should use it only for your own practice and development. Newsprint comes in pads of many sizes. Manila paper is a student item and is not used by commercial artists. Most grade schools use this paper and that's about its level. Even for practice, you will do better by becoming familiar with the better quality stocks.

Bond and ledger. These may be used for cheap budgets. The heavier opaque bonds are not too different from light bristol, but they wrinkle when used with wet media, like inks and paints, and do not stand up when erased. Even a gentle eraser will break and fray the fibers, producing a ragged, messy appearance which should be alien to commercial artists. Ledger papers, which are like cheap bristols, also fall into this category since they are of too poor a quality to withstand much abuse. They do have sufficient strength to withstand being wet, however, and low budget jobs that require painting with paints, inks, dyes, and watercolors can be done on some ledger stocks. These papers will be sold in sheets as well as pads in a wide choice off sizes.

Remember that if the price is low, you will be getting an inferior bristol, a ledger, or a bond. Good bristol is expensive, and there is no way around it.

Your art store may also carry some special stocks, like clay coat paper. These specialties are designed for use with particular media and may find a limited use, if you are doing extensive drawing. But for the most part there is no need for you to stray very far away from a good bristol; it will handle any job that you are called upon to do.

Watercolor paper. If bristol is the commercial artist's standby, watercolor paper is the illustrator's. Of course, many other surfaces are used, but watercolor paper is the primary medium. Here again, the best quality will produce the best results. Watercolor paints are preferred for commercial illustration since they dry quickly (for tight deadlines) and reproduce with a greater degree of fidelity than oil paints; but they will not be successful on cheap, low quality papers. One of the finest papers available is the imported French paper, D'Arches. Like all watercolor papers, this excellent, handmade stock is available in three weights: 72 pounds, 140 pounds, and 300 pounds (remember the basis weights?), and in three surface finishes: rough, fine (cold pressed), and smooth (hot pressed). This refers to the calendering rolls; remember that a hot iron presses more smoothly than a cold one. The paper comes in sheets 22″ x 30″, but you can cut this into smaller sizes if you wish. The papers are also available in pads of several smaller sizes and in watercolor blocks. A block is a pad that is bound on all four sides. This binding holds the paper firmly, as it would be if it were stretched. All watercolor paper should be stretched before using. Do this by soaking the paper in clean water and laying it flat on a sturdy wooden board. Fasten the edges to the board with gummed paper-tape. Let the paper dry slowly and naturally. As the paper dries it will shrink, stretching tightly against the tape. This will provide a drum-taut surface for painting, and will not buckle and create valleys into which the paint can run. If you have trouble getting the tape to hold against the considerable force of the drying paper, reinforce the glue with a little vegetable paste. Do not take the paper off the board to work with it. Leave it stretched until the painting is finished and then cut it loose.

The descriptions and procedures have been described for D'Arches paper, but there are many fine grades of watercolor paper that are less expensive and as good as need be for most commercial work. Your art store dealer will be able to recommend the various brands and qual-ities that he carries, and you can experiment with them.

Fine art papers. This is a subdivision of artwork papers that is of concern to the illustrator only. Other than for practice and experimentation, these papers are too limited and expensive to be used in any volume by the commercial field. However, they are important to the artist, if only so that he can make recommendations to illustrators working with him. These fine art papers include Oriental rice papers, parchments, tissues, pastel and charcoal papers, and etching papers. These are often quite exotic and limited in their use, even to the fine artist. They are all distinguished by the fact that they are produced to work with different fine art media, and the beautiful and subtle effects they permit are not capable of being reproduced by commercial printing methods. Therefore, I suggest that you avoid them, except for your own private practice, development, and enjoyment. Visit art stores, find out what papers they carry, and experiment with them at your leisure. Nothing that this book could provide will be able to suggest their richness, nor the thrill that comes with employing the finest materials to create the most artistic results. Commercial art does have many limitations, but that does not mean you should neglect your own artistic growth—the development and maturation of your own taste and discrimination.

Presentation Paper

Finished artwork usually goes to the printer to be reproduced, but the commercial artist must also prepare presentations, either layout or finished, that require the art to have a completed, printed appearance. Comprehensive layouts and one-of-a-kind displays are examples of this type of work. For these purposes there are several art papers that enable the artist to work with his standard tools and media to create artwork that has a finished feeling. Perhaps the most common in the field are:

Color-Aid and Colorama. These are papers prepared by silkscreening oil-based paint on a plain white stock. The result is a fairly heavy paper with a soft, matte surface that is available in over 200 tints, shades, and colors. Although full sheets, 24″ x 36″, are sold, the most popular sizes in stock are 18″ x 24″. One characteristic of the full sheets is a thin, white border left uncolored during the-manufacture. This border has been trimmed away in the smaller sheets. Each sheet has an identification number printed on the back. The only practical way to select the paper is to consult a swatch book—small sample-sheets of the paper bound with a single metal rod through the corners so that individual sheets may be fanned away from the group for comparison. Even this method has its drawbacks. The colors change with age and exposure to light; and the papers are rarely produced with exactly the identical colors. This can make it difficult when you are attempting to match a color precisely. The best procedure is to take a sample of the desired color to the art store, so that you can choose a paper that matches it as closely as possible. Also, if you need a large number of sheets for one job, it is wise to check beforehand. Many stores, in refilling their stocks, have accumulated sheets from several different production runs. These sheets may differ in color sufficiently to affect the presentation. In such a case it is better to order the sheets far enough in advance so that they can be delivered in one order—all from the same batch. These are small criticisms when balanced against the advantages of the product. The wide range of colors and the basically good working surface make these papers invaluable. You can work with virtually any medium on these papers, but you must be careful. Fingerprints, guide lines, errors, etc., show up very clearly and are almost impossible to remove. Make sure that your hands and tools are clean, draw your guide lines gently with chalk or pastel that can be wiped off easily with a clean coth or cotton, and use a sheet of paper under your hand when you work to protect the surface from fingerprints and dropped paint. If an error must be removed, use a kneaded eraser with a blotting motion (rubbing will produce a shine that is very unsightly), wipe away paint with clean water and cotton (change the cotton frequently so that no residue is left), and scrape off India ink with the flat of a razor blade (the thick paint coating will allow a small amount to be removed without revealing the paper backing, if you are careful). Once you are finished, any minor shines, scrapes, fingerprints, etc., can be minimized by spraying the surface with a fixative. This will dull the color of the paper somewhat, but it will also tend to blend and hide any discoloration. These papers are very brittle, and will break and crack if bent. When you buy, carry, or store them, make sure that they are flat; a limited amount of rolling is also possible. If you are preparing a folder cover, etc., that must be bent, score the back of the paper first. Using the back of a scissors blade, or the back of a single-edge razor blade, draw a line where the fold is to occur—but on the white side of the paper. If the fold must be bent many times in use, protect the paper by applying invisible Scotch mending tape over the fold. The tape *will* show a little, but it will be less objectionable than the cracked paper. Once the paper has cracked, it becomes quite weak, as well, and will tear easily. As with any art medium, practice first with a scrap piece of the paper. As you become more familiar with it, you will find that its limitations are easily overcome and the final effect is worth the bother.

Flint paper. Flint papers are similar in many respects to Color-aid and Colorama papers in use and handling. However, flint paper is produced in less than a dozen colors and these are very glossy. Therefore, these papers are used in the more limited areas where a glossy, varnished, printing job is being imitated. The paper is much thinner and will fold fairly easily without breaking or cracking. Paints and other media do not take too well on a glossy surface and you may have to add Non-Crawl or a similar acetate medium to get complete coverage. The best materials with which to work on this surface are the pressure sensitive transfer types and shading sheets. These hold very well to the smooth surface and produce a highly finished effect. This may limit the type of artwork you can do with the paper, but there are not too many times when you will want to do rendering, etc., on this kind of surface. There is no medium that matches the glossiness, and a dull, matte rendering looks wrong on the shiny paper. On the other hand, a color photograph mounted on a dummy package covered with flint paper is practically indistinguishable from the finished item. The glossy photo blends in with the flint paper perfectly. Flint papers are only sold in one size—20″ x 26″.

Flocked paper. Flock is composed of a velvety pile of very short fibers, usually rayon. There are a small number of papers prepared with an even coating of flock which are used for display purposes as a background. No medium takes on this surface, and any artwork must consist of other papers that are cut out and pasted to the flocked surface with nearly any adhesive *except* rubber cement. (You have to coat both surfaces with rubber cement, and you can't remove the excess from the flock paper.) Since the uses are limited, there is not much call for the paper, and you will have to check and see if your art supply store carries it or can get it for you.

Naturally, just about any material can be used for presentation, even surfaces that you have prepared yourself. The adaptation of other papers and coatings

is limited only by your imagination and experience. However, outside of obtaining samples of commercial printing papers from wholesale paper houses, the few examples discussed here are more than sufficient for most of the presentation work done in the field. Also, the use of art media with these papers is not really different from the manner in which you would normally use them, so you can follow the same instructions that occur in the sections that discuss them.

Construction Paper

Since paper has little strength for building models or displays, the word construction is used in the sense of preparing something.

Oak tag, stencil, and frisket paper. The most common construction in commercial art is the preparation of a stencil or frisket. This method of creating an opening in a mask that protects the art surface not being worked on is important enough to have been covered in separate sections. You should familiarize yourself with them. In any event, the papers used with the process are common and easily obtained at any art store. Oak tag and stencil paper are very similar. They are stiff, durable papers that cut easily and resist deterioration when used with liquid media. Some stencil papers have been treated with wax or oil to improve this ability to withstand wetness. While they perform their jobs very well, you can substitute any heavy paper for them when preparing most stencils. Frisket papers are much more specialized. These papers, usually transparent, allow you to see what you are doing and permit you to cut them over the artwork, itself, for greater accuracy. Frisket paper can be purchased with or without an adhesive backing, in sheets and in rolls.

Pressure stick. A number of plain papers are sold with an adhesive backing. These papers, both transparent and opaque, are designed to be used for labels and art that can be adhered to another surface. In the preparation of displays and presentations, you can create the art on such a paper, working on a smaller, easily handled piece that has the characteristics of conventional drawing paper and add the finish to another surface by cutting it out, removing the backing sheet, and pressing it down on the final presentation. These papers are usually sold in small sheets, although some of them may be available in rolls.

No-Seam. This is a matte paper offered in several subdued colors that comes in large, wide rolls. The size of the paper, and the muted tones, make it an ideal background for photographers and window dressers. As the name implies, you can create a large background surface without any interruptions. In photography this produces what is called a limbo background—the object seems to float in space. For catalogs this is the preferred method of showing merchandise, free from ground lines and other distractions. In display the paper allows for easy, inexpensive change of background without any of the time and labor necessary to build and paint a complex display. For example, a square-shaped display window can be altered into a curved space by merely stapling a free standing piece of no-seam to the front edges of the window. The paper is strong enough to stand by itself and light enough to be held by a few staples. By varying the size of the paper, you can create a deep curve, an S-curve, or many other variations.

Kraft paper. Kraft paper is wrapping paper, and this is its most common use in the field of commercial art. Its strength and low cost make it adaptable to some other uses such as stencils, flapping finished art, and printing novelty pieces; but for the most part it is used to wrap artwork and other packages.

Construction paper. Construction paper, despite its title, does not serve any useful purpose in commercial art—even

for construction. This cheap paper has a very limited range of colors, mostly dull and unsuitable for sophisticated artwork. Only the black paper is used to any extent. Since black is black, the low cost of this paper makes it convenient to use the black sheets when a matte black surface is needed, for layout or presentation. The paper is also highly opaque, so that it can be used in photography where light must be blocked out. The sheets of construction paper can be purchased singly or in packs of several sizes and assorted colors. The most common colors, like black, can also be purchased in packs.

Once again, there are few limitations on the choice of paper used in construction work. Very few artists or studios maintain a large selection of any of these papers, but with a little imagination and ingenuity, you can make do with whatever is on hand. The items discussed here are offered only to familiarize you with what is available, and in no way is meant to suggest that these are the only papers used.

As mentioned earlier, most boards are composed of papers that have been backed with cardboard for greater durability. But it will be wise to discuss them again in sections as we have done with the papers, since the added cost of the boards means that there are fewer and more specific uses for each. For instance, there are no layout boards. Layouts are quick and cheap, and there is no need to make them durable for display. If it is necessary to take a particular layout and show it, it can be mounted on any clean white board and matted or framed with any other board that is available, so long as the finished result is neat, clean, and attractive.

Artwork Board

Boards used for finished art are, like artwork papers, quite few in number, consisting primarily of the same bristols mounted on cardboard.

Illustration board. This is the work horse of the commercial field. It is used for everything from mounting layouts and creating artwork to assembling mechanicals. The largest sheet of illustration board is 40″ x 60″, but the most common size is 20″ x 30″ and most stores will sell it in several smaller sizes. There is also a double-thick illustration board in which the cardboard is twice as heavy for display work, and a two-faced illustration board with bristol on both sides and cardboard between. As with unmounted bristol, illustration board is ideal for use with all media. The only area of difficulty with illustration board concerns the quality. There are usually three qualities available: student grade, commercial grade, and high grade. The finest grade, Whatman board, is no longer available, which narrows the choice considerably. Student grades are very cheap, which means that a low-grade bristol was employed. Except for mechanicals and paste-ups, this can be a false economy. The poorer paper deteriorates quickly while being worked on and erasures cannot be made with any vigor. A good bristol will allow you to scrape away errors with a razor blade with little damage to the surface; a poor bristol frays, creating a rough surface that not only looks bad but will cause any subsequent work to be ragged and blurred. For the most part this leaves the commercial grades, which are all about the same. Each store, however, will tend to carry its own brand. Don't be confused, there won't be that much difference between them. The only other consideration will be the surface, itself. Hot press means a smooth or plate finish. Cold press means a kid or rough finish. There isn't much to choose from between the two. Theoretically the smooth should be better with pen and ink work, and rough should be better with paint and brush. However, they both work rather well on either surface, and you should base your choice upon your own personal preference.

Textured boards. Coquille board and Ross board are the primary examples of these boards, which consist of a large variety of textured drawing papers which may or may not be mounted on cardboard. Essentially, these are bristol boards with pebbled, ridged, or grained textures impressed on them.

The effect of these textures is to prevent pencil or crayon from penetrating to the bottom of the valleys between the raised portions of the texture. Pencil or crayon marks appear only on the raised portions of the paper; the result is an overall black and white design which is determined by the textural pattern of the paper chosen. Some of these patterns are bold and open; others are subtle and fine.

These textured boards facilitate the gradation of shading in fine rendering, since the texture causes an effect similar to pen and ink cross-hatching or stippling. Almost any medium may be used, but the boards work particularly well with black lithographic crayons. These greasy, wax crayons come in varying degrees of hardness and thus permit great control by the artist. Litho crayons are intense black; variation of pressure only produces a larger or smaller mark, not a lighter or darker one.

Since the finished rendering is composed entirely of solid black marks on pure white paper, the finished drawing may be reproduced directly as line art, which does not need to be broken up into dots by the halftone screen. Thus, textured drawing boards allow complete control by the artist, and permit cheaper printing costs.

Presentation Board
Presentation boards are quite few in number. There is nothing comparable to Color-Aid or Colorama in board form. To create these effects, you must mount the paper yourself. However, there are a few choices.

Poster or showcard board. These are inexpensive boards with thin papers mounted on them. The range of colors is small and not very good. Although there are a number of metallic colors and the surface can be glossy or matte, the boards are really for sign work only and lack a degree of sophistication normally expected in commercial art. A full sheet of this board is 28″ x 44″ and some stores carry smaller sizes or will cut them for you. They take most liquid media, but oil colors tend to soak into the board showing a dark ring around the work. The boards are too thin to stand alone and must be mounted. A double thick showcard is offered in a few colors, but even this will not be too strong. For the most part, you will be better off preparing your own presentation board by selecting an appropriate paper and backing it with a cheap cardboard.

Mat board. Mat board comes in the same sizes and thicknesses as illustration board, but has a small selection of muted colors. This board is used to mount or frame artwork, but the colors are pleasant and provide neutral backgrounds for a number of other presentation requirements. In many cases, mat board will produce better looking signs than poster board, and most media will work on their soft, matte surface. When using them for such artwork, treat them in the same manner as you would a less expensive illustration board.

TV board. This is a specialized board that was prepared for use in television artwork before color TV became prevalent. The board is essentially a poster or mat board with a selection of grays that are the working range of values suitable for television reproduction. They are still useful for preparing title cards, etc., for television where basic gray values are necessary for visual separation.

Construction Board

This is the largest section of boards, as you might expect, since the strength of board makes construction possible. You will find these boards under a large range of names, but they are essentially grouped into a few categories. If you will describe your job to your art store dealer, he/she will be able to help you select the one that does the job best for you. Some of the best are covered below:

Foamcore. This is a sheet of Styrofoam plastic that has been faced on both sides with an inexpensive paper. The plastic gives the board great strength and is quite light. The paper facing is also much lighter than on comparable boards, so that the overall sheet weighs very little. However, the strength and durability of the combined sandwich is much greater than any construction board. This permits large signs and displays to be created without the necessity of any heavy framework. Also, a number of these cards, 40″ x 60″, can be carried easily, without any strain. Foamcore's surface will take any medium, but is difficult to erase or correct. The surface is very shiny and comes only in white, but the light weight allows you to mount other papers on the board without creating too bulky a package. Another advantage of this board is the ease with which it is cut. The plastic foam slices easily with a razor blade, unlike heavy illustration or sign board that must be cut with a heavy knife and great pressure.

Corrugated board or papers. This is the conventional packing material that is used to protect fragile items in shipping boxes. Like foamcore, it is useful because of its great strength as compared to its light weight. Used primarily in display, corrugated board or paper has a distinctive brown color and texture, caused by the ridges of paper that constitute the inner core and provide the strength. This means that corrugated products must be covered with some other material when used for display. Corrugated board comes in sheets, and the paper in rolls, and is available at wholesale paper houses and stationers, if not at your art store.

Mounting board. This covers a wide range of products whose function is to serve as a base for other papers and boards in displays and presentations. The cheapest are the chipboards or newsboards, which are untreated cardboard conglomerates. Their surfaces are too rough and unattractive for any use except as a backing, but they are sturdy and inexpensive. A piece of such board makes an excellent surface on which to do your own cutting to protect table surfaces. The boards then range all the way up to high-grade cardboards that may have paper facings on one or both sides. In many cases these may serve as cheap sign boards, although they only come in white. They are much stronger than showcard, though, and will stand without buckling. A sheet of this faced mounting board is a fine covering for your drawing table. It will protect the surface and can be changed often when dirty, since it costs so little. None of these mounting boards is suited for art media, and must be cut with a heavy mat knife or the equivalent. Sizes will range from 8″ x 10″ to 40″ x 60″ and there are a number of weights and thicknesses.

Line-up board. This is a lightweight board with a prepared surface like cross section paper. It is used to prepare mechanicals and paste-ups, since its light blue lines act as a guide in placing art assemblages but will not reproduce when the printing plates are made. The value of the board over the paper lies in the strength of the board. Paper may stretch or shrink under different conditions of humidity and may tear easily if subjected to extensive handling. The board reduces the possibility of such misfortunes.

PARALLEL RULING STRAIGHT-EDGE

Often abbreviated to "parallel rule," this is a mechanical drafting alternative to the T-square. As can be seen in the diagram, the parallel rule is a straight-edge containing four pulleys that travel on a wire framework, which is arranged like an open-bottomed figure-eight.

The parallel rule is mounted on a drawing surface by placing the closed, upper loop of wire over hooks (C) and (D). The ends of the wire are secured to the edge of the surface at A and B. The straight-edge is adjusted to an accurate horizontal position and a clamp (E) is tightened over the wire. As long as this clamp is tight, the straight-edge can slide up and down the wires without losing its horizontal position; that is, any line drawn with the straight-edge in one position will be parallel to any other line drawn in another position. Adjustments can be made at any time simply by loosening the clamp.

Most people using the parallel rule for the first time are upset that the wires do not prevent the straight-edge from being lifted off the surface, but this action does not distort the accuracy of the parallel rule. In fact, leaving a little slack in the line allows you to lift the straight-edge over pencils, triangles, etc., which may be lying on the working surface. A further advantage of leaving slack is that, while retaining its parallel position, the leading edge of the rule can be tilted up to act as a guide for ruling lines with a paintbrush.

Less expensive than the drafting machine, more accurate than the T-square, the parallel rule is available at all drafting supply stores in a number of sizes which are adaptable to all kinds of drawing boards and tables.

Common Difficulties

Inaccuracy. Although the wires may be slack without hurting the accuracy of the parallel rule, there must be no slippage. Most people have difficulty understanding this. It seems that if the wire is slack, there ought to be slippage; but this is not so. As long as the clamp on top is holding the wire firmly, the parallel rule cannot get out of true line. This is not just a post that the wires goes around, it must grip the wire tightly to be effective.

Jamming. Sometimes a sudden jolt will cause the wires to jump off the pulleys, preventing the rule from moving. This

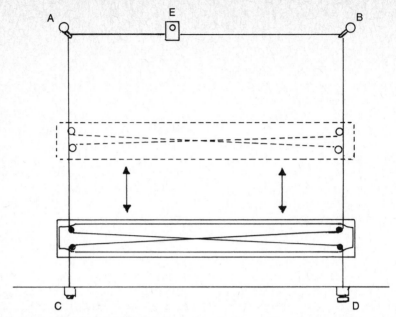

Parallel ruling straight-edge. The wires, which pass through the straight-edge on pulleys, are secured at A, B, C, and D. Make sure that the resulting rectangle is just as wide as the wire outlets on the straight-edge or undue wear will break the wires. The lock at E is left open until the straight-edge is forced into proper alignment. Once the lock is tightened, the straight-edge can be moved to any position (even lifted slightly) and the edge will always produce parallel lines.

can be corrected easily by removing the screws on the bottom of the straight-edge. With these screws out, the cover may be lifted off exposing the pulleys. It is a simple job to replace the wires, remembering the figure-eight diagram. (You will probably have to unfasten the wires from the table first, so that there will be enough slack to turn the straight-edge over to get at the screws.)

Worn or broken wires. The wires used with the parallel rule are comparatively brittle and will break easily if flexed too often. To prevent this, the wires are wrapped in braided threads. However, these threads are subject to wear and fray, causing the threads to clog the pulleys and stop the movement. Several conditions will contribute to excessive wear that can damage either the fabric or the wire.

In the first place, the installation diagram must be followed exactly. Points A, B, C, and D must form a perfect rectangle which is precisely as wide as the rule. Any variation from this pattern will cause the wires to pass the pulleys at too sharp an angle producing undue flexing, which will break the wire.

Too much slack in the wire will permit the wires to rub against the cover, which will fray the fabric covering.

Sharp projections on the table, fastening the wires to a table by bending them at right angles around the edge of the table, or slamming the rule sharply against the bottom limit of its travel, will all subject the wire to excessive strain. In time, these conditions will break the wire.

Should a wire become worn or damaged, it should be replaced. The wire can be purchased at the same store that sold you the rule, and the new wire can be installed by removing the cover on the rule as described above and replacing the entire set-up as shown in the diagram.

Inconvenience. The one drawback of the parallel rule is that it is blocked by anything left on the drawing surface. If you intend to use this handy tool, you must have a working surface that will allow you to store supplies out of the way of the rule.

PARCHMENT

The name given to a wide range of natural or simulated sheepskin papers commonly associated with diplomas and testimonials. Outside of an occasional presentation or printing job, this is the only use for these distinctive papers. (See *Papers and Boards*.)

PASTE

The term used to cover a wide range of adhesive substances, largely water-soluble, used to adhere paper, cardboard, etc. (See *Adhesives*.)

PASTEL

A rendering medium composed mainly of chalk, pigment, and a binder. Pastels are available in round sticks, square sticks, and pencils. The round sticks are called artists' pastels, and are extremely soft and crumbly. Used principally for fine art, they are much too messy for average commercial use, being totally unsuited for lettering. The square sticks and pencils are commercial art variations, which contain higher percentages of binder, allowing them to maintain sharper edges and produce cleaner strokes.

Both the sticks and the pencils are available singly or in sets of from six to ninety-six colors, as well as in a range of grays. Some manufacturers have sets of pencils that have exactly match the sticks; on a job that requires the larger sticks, the pencils may be used for the fine detail.

Chalk will not adhere to glossy surfaces. Thus, pastels are used only on papers having pronounced texture or "tooth." Charcoal and pastel papers are sold for this specific purpose and may

be asked for by these names. Tracing and visualizer papers are also satisfactory. Some papers, like Color-Aid and Colorama will take pastel to a small degree and can be used for limited effects. A small amount of experimentation will help you discover which surfaces give the results that appeal to you most, and at the least cost.

Pastel is extremely dusty and smudges easily. Finished renderings must be protected. The ideal method—primarily for fine art—is to cover the rendering with glass. This is not usually possible with commercial work; the alternative is to spray the rendering with a coating of fixative. Although the fixatives are clear liquids, they will affect pastel by darkening the color values.

Pastel's use is declining in the commercial art field. Once the technique of choice for layouts, pastel also enjoyed a certain popularity in illustration. The advent of markers has virtually eliminated pastel layouts, and student illustrators rarely are trained in the medium. Acrylics, too, have developed and the growing possibilities of computer art have probably ended the likelihood of a significant revival. Pastel remains a very popular medium for fine artists and amateurs. The one exception would be comp artists who use pastels in conjunction with other mediums to create special effects on their marker comps.

Pastel is primarily used as a layout medium. Its ability to cover large areas quickly, cheaply, and with even intensity, make it ideal for fast sketches. Although it may be used for illustration, pastel has a number of limitations. Pastel colors do not mix readily, producing a dirty smudged appearance. The necessity of fixing or protecting the final rendering, and thereby darkening it, robs pastel of its greatest value—brilliance. And the difficulty of working with a dusty medium makes pastel suitable for only the most expert and experienced illustrator.

Pastel requires no complex preparations for use; its technical simplicity is one of its great advantages. However, a degree of planning will produce superior results. Since the number of colors is limited, and these colors may not be mixed, you should determine beforehand which colors will give you the best effect. These colors may not be identical with your subject, but with practice you will be able to choose a palette that gives the proper over-all impression. Once you have made a stroke on the paper, do not go over it again. Repeated handling will only produce a smudged, amateurish result. Even if you have made a minor drawing error, the total appearance will be more effective if the spontaneous nature of the drawing is not disturbed.

Where is is necessary to produce a perfect edge, you may use a frisket. If you use an adhering frisket, be sure to spray fixative on the other areas of the drawing that have been rendered. A workable fixative will allow you to work over these areas in the future. A dry frisket, or merely the edge of a piece of paper, may be used if you work carefully. Always stroke the pastel over the frisket into the working area so that chalk does not get under the edges of the frisket. If chalk does get outside the proper places, correct this by using a reverse frisket that covers the rendered area. This will have to be a dry frisket. Hold it carefully, so as not to smudge the drawing, and blot the excess chalk by pressing gently (not rubbing) with a kneaded eraser. When no more chalk is removed by this method, rub the eraser gently away from the frisket until the paper is clean.

Where a tint area is desired for backgrounds and the like, use a frisket and a stomp. In large areas, even your fingers will do. Do not use the pastel stick directly, but work with powdered color. This powder may be produced by drawing the pastel stick over a clean sandpaper pad. Strokes from the stick, drawn directly on the paper, may dig deeply into the paper and may not be smoothed out, producing a streaked effect.

To correct errors, use a kneaded eraser, blotting with the eraser first to remove the excess chalk. Rubbing directly with any type of eraser will only dig the grains of color deeply into the paper so that they will not come out.

When the drawing or any part of it is finished, and you are preparing to use fixative, blow dry air (by mouth) over the places where no chalk is wanted. This will clear away invisible grains of dust that will have settled on these spots. If this dust is not removed, the fixative will spread the pigment and produce a visible stain that cannot be removed.

When using pastel to indicate lettering, a chisel edge works best. To ensure a fine edge throughout the entire job, shape the edges of the pastel frequently on a sandpaper pad. If pastel pencils crumble when they are sharpened in a mechanical sharpener, use a razor blade and finish the point with a sandpaper pad.

Although pastel sticks and pencils are very fragile, no special care is needed to preserve them. There is nothing to dry out and the colors do not fade. Even if the pieces become broken, they are still effective. Most artists *prefer* to use smaller pieces and break the whole sticks before using them. However, the colored dust that accumulates with use can discolor the sticks and create smudgy drawings. All pastel sets come with partitions and a covering pad. Try to get into the habit of returning the sticks to their proper slot and keep the pad in place.

Pastels are an exciting and enjoyable alternative for quick sketches and figure drawing exercises, which any commercial artist constantly needs to be practicing. Pastel sketches on inexpensive newsprint paper are an excellent and economical way to do it. Similarly, pastel roughs and thumbnails offer a cheaper way of exploring a design idea, while sacrificing none of the sparkle and spontaneity of markers. When you have acquired some skill with them, you may find that you can combine pastels with markers, just as skilled comp makers do. (See also *Oil Pastels.*)

Common Difficulties

Streaked color. If the color remains streaked, even after being smoothed by hand or with a stomp, try applying the pastel with a softer touch. The binder that hardens and holds the chalk together may cause one edge of the stick to bite too deeply into the paper. Once dug in, this pigment cannot be smoothed out to the same degree as chalk that lies more loosely on the surface.

Dull or muddy color. Excessive rubbing or blending too many colors together will produce a dull, muddy result. Pastel, like watercolor, depends for much of its brilliance upon the reflection of light from the paper through the pigment. Avoid rubbing whenever possible. Never mix colors. If that is unavoidable, mix as few colors as possible within the entire composition; mix only two colors together in any one spot.

Darkened color. Fixative, although necessary to prevent smudging, has a pronounced darkening effect. Try to plan your rendering with this in mind. When spraying fixative, use several very light coats, rather than one heavy coat. This will prevent the fixative from dissolving the pigment and forcing it deeply into the paper. Instead, the pigment will receive an adequate amount of fixative, become firmly adhered to the surface, but remain on top of the surface, and thereby retain the brilliance of the light reflected from the paper.

Additional strokes will not take on fixed drawing. You have used the wrong fixative or too much fixative. Several fixatives on the market can fix pastel colors without destroying the roughened surface necessary for pastel work. Make sure you are using one of them. The label states that they are "workable" or "reworkable." Even these fixatives, if used to excess, will create a clear, glossy surface that will not take further pastel. When fixative must be used many times during a job, try to mask off those areas that do not need fixing, so that they do not receive too much. If they are too heavily coated, roughen the surface lightly with fine sandpaper. When applying sandpaper, avoid heavy pressure or long positive strokes; they will create grooves which the pastel will settle into, causing heavy streaks.

Paint will not take and forms beads. One of the common procedures when preparing a pastel layout involves adding paint over a pastel drawing, particularly when a lighter color is needed. A white headline over a dark illustration is an example. If the paint will not lie flat and cover the desired area, you have used too much or too little fixative. If too little, add several quick and light coats of fixative until the surface is not too chalky to receive paint. If the paint will not take because the surface is too glossy from too much fixative, add one of the commercial products made for making paint adhere to acetate. In an emergency, add a little soap; the glycerine in the soap has the same effect. Do not use too much or you will get suds. Do not use a detergent.

Bleeding color. The dust from the normal application of pastel is not necessarily visible while you are working. These granules of colored dust will dissolve in the fixative spray, however, and spread considerably, becoming very pronounced. Try to work with some sort of frisket to prevent the dust from settling on clean surfaces. Before fixing an area, use a clean kneaded eraser and wipe or blot the dust away. If you use the eraser too heavily or smear the dust around, you may force the pigment into the paper, where it will become imbedded. Fixative will then cause the colored granules to show.

Corrections. A limited amount of correction can be made on pastel that has been fixed. The primary difficulty is removing the fixative without disturbing the pastel too much. Lacquer thinner, acetone, or nail polish remover will dissolve the fixative, but great care should be taken. Moisten a small piece of cotton or cotton swab with the solvent. Dab the cotton on the area to be corrected. Repeat the process several times with clean cotton and solvent. Do not rub. Let the area dry thoroughly, and then erase with an ink eraser. Follow up with a kneaded eraser. If the procedure has been performed carefully, most of the color will be removed, new pastel may be applied, and the entire area recovered with fixative.

PASTEL HOLDERS

Pastel, even the hard varieties, is a soft crumbly medium. The sticks break easily and are worn down quickly. Although pastel is cheap and most artists prefer to buy new, clean sticks—rather than work with small and often dirty fragments—a metal holder is sold that will enable you to get the most from your pastel. Made of aluminum, this holder takes the piece of pastel and holds it in a chuck device at one end. The effect is like working with a mechanical pencil, allowing you to do extensive drawing with a piece of pastel of any size.

PASTEL PAPER

This usually refers to the same paper that is more commonly called charcoal paper. However, the term also applies to a flocked, dark-colored paper whose velvetlike texture creates a rather glowing effect. Except as a drawing or sketching medium, neither of these papers enjoys any use in the commercial art field, since the soft, delicate effects do not lend themselves to reproduction. (See *Papers and Boards*.)

PASTE-UP

A common term in commercial art used to describe the procedure of any artist producing a mechanical—assembled art ready for the platemaker and the printer. The procedure involves coating art, type, photostats, etc., with rubber cement and adhering them in the proper positions on the mechanical board, which has also been coated with rubber cement.

This is a simple process, but it has implications in the commercial field that require a considerable amount of expertise. Since the finished paste-up, or mechanical, will be used as finished art by the printer, a previously drawn layout must be followed as a guide, and the work must be clean and accurate. Various elements may need subtle alterations in size and position since the layout was drawn before the elements were created. Some art elements may actually be lacking. These conditions, and others too numerous to even begin to list, make it necessary for the paste-up artist to be familiar with photostats, type, fixatives, rubber cement pick-ups, etc. He must also be capable of creating simple art—rules, borders, spot illustrations; and have good artistic taste so that he can assemble the units without supervision and make the constant judgments in spacing and size that are continually required.

PEN CLEANER

A soapy liquid that effectively dissolves dried and caked India ink that has clogged and impaired the usefulness of a pen or other drawing instrument. To be completely effective, the item to be cleaned should be left in the liquid for a considerable period of time. As the cleaner becomes darkened with dissolved ink, it may be difficult to locate and remove small items like pen points from the bottom of the small-mouthed jar. For this reason, some jars of cleaner contain a plastic tray, permitting you to lift the soaking pieces from the bottom of the bottle without fuss. While this feature does eliminate some annoyance, it is hardly essential. If you do not have such a tray, or cannot find a suitable substitute that will fit into the jar, pour the cleaner into a shallow bowl. Then the items being cleaned will be easy to handle and the cleaner can be poured back into the jar after you have finished. The cleaner rinses off easily with water. The cleaned parts should be dried immediately and coated with a light oil. To prevent oil stains on the artwork, wipe the tool with a clean, dry rag. If there is any ink still remaining on the tool, repeat the process.

In an emergency, if you do not have pen cleaner, use ammonia or even warm soap and water as a substitute. These will soften the ink to some extent and vigorous wiping with a cloth or chamois should remove enough of the ink to permit normal use of the tool.

PEN FILLING INKSTAND

A metal desk stand that holds a small bottle of India ink, the cap of which is placed in one end of a lever that is attached to the stand. Placing the heel of your hand upon the free end of the lever raises the bottle cap, so that an inking tool, held in the fingers of the same hand, can be held under the filling device of the cap. The entire procedure allows you to refill an inking tool with one hand, while the other hand holds the inking guide steady. (See *India Ink Dispensers.*)

PEN HOLDERS

Tapered wooden cylinders that have an opening at the large end into which pen points are inserted. Holders are inexpensive and come in all the varieties necessary to accommodate any pen point. Some, in fact, come with a pen point already in place. This type of holder

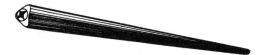

Triangular pen holder.

provides a certain stability that is lacking in the loose pen point and holder combinations, but the entire assembly must be replaced when the point is damaged.

Common Difficulties

Improper fit. It may be impossible to insert the pen point properly if the holder is clogged with ink. A poor fit will cause the pen point to wobble or drop out while drawing. Such a holder should be cleaned with water, ammonia, or pen cleaner. To prevent these conditions, do not dip the pen too deeply into the ink. A clean ink bottle will help, since you will be able to see when the point has been filled with ink—before the holder is covered. The same conditions can be caused by rust or corrosion. High humidity and frequent washing without drying will rust the holder deep inside where it is impossible to clean. Such a holder should be replaced.

Dipping troubles. Incrustations of ink on the side of the holder and the ink bottle opening may make it difficult to dip the pen into the narrow neck of the ink bottle. If the pen goes into the bottle at all, it may pick up ink on the side, which transfers to the fingers and then to the drawing. Keep bottles and holders clean. It is wise to keep spare holders and ink bottles on hand so that a faulty one can be replaced immediately without interrupting your work.

PEN POINTS

Pen points fall into two general categories: drawing and lettering. The pens in each of these categories come in two types: reservoir and plain. Within these four groupings there are literally hundreds of variations.

The simplest and most common pen point is the curved piece of metal that has been shaped to a point and slitted. The metal used, the shape of the point, and the size of the slit determine the nature of the line produced. There are no rules for determining which of these points to use. Although the manufacturer will often attribute certain specific characteristics to each shape, the artist can often create many variations with a single nib. Practice with all nibs until you are able to choose a favorite or favorites. Almost all of these simple forms are what are referred to as drawing pens.

The simplest addition to the ordinary pen point is a reservoir designed to hold more ink. This reservoir is a hinged or flexible flap that covers the top of the nib. The flap stores ink between itself and the top of the nib, and the ink flows from this storage area through the slit. The hinge makes cleaning easier. Reservoirs of this nature are available on nearly all the simple pen point styles. However, they cannot be added to an existing point; they must be purchased as a reservoir nib.

The lettering pen points are distinguished by the shape of the point. In most cases, this point will be bent at an angle to the nib and will be larger than any of the drawing pen points. The larger size permits you to letter with a single stroke, and the size and shape of the bent nib determines the characteristic of the lettering style. All lettering pens come in boxes or on cards that show the type of line or lettering that can be created. The most famous of these pen point sets is the Speedball series. Speedball pens and those like them come in four basic shapes: chisel, square, oval, and round. Each series contains about six nib sizes. All pens of this nature have reservoir attachments, either hinged or stationary, but flexible.

Another variety of lettering pens is typified by the Coit series: the nib is formed by a flat loop of metal which is slitted. The greater the width of the loop, the more slits provided, to insure an even flow of ink. The virtue of the Coit pen is that the slitted loop works quite well with paint, unlike the Speedball variety that works only with ink. However, the Coit pens must be bought complete; the nib is permanently attached and is not interchangeable. Moreover, the loop is limited in its ability to produce lines of differing characteristics for different styles of lettering.

Under different brand names, there are countless variations of the points described above. Some have angled points, some are created particularly for left-handed people, and some provide reservoirs of unique design. But most of them will fit into the standard pen holder and the differences between them are minute. Get as many nibs as you can and try them. What can artist can do with a pen may be entirely different from what another can do. (See also *Pens*.)

Common Difficulties

No line. Most new nibs, and some that have been used before, may fail to create a line, even though they have been freshly dipped in ink. On a new nib, failure to produce a line is generally caused by a very fine film of preservative which was added during manufacture to prevent rusting or discoloration. This coating causes the ink to bead, like water on a freshly waxed surface, drawing the ink away from the tip. The harder you press, the wider the nibs are forced apart and the more the beading pulls the ink away. To remove the film, moisten the nib in your mouth *before* dipping it in ink. If you prefer not to put the nib in your mouth, dip it in ammonia. Water will not remove the coating, nor will wiping it with a cloth. If the nib has been used before, but will still not produce a line, it may have dried ink on the nib, preventing the flow of fresh ink. This can also occur while the pen is being used. In this case, clean the pen point. Water will dissolve freshly dried ink, but ammonia will be necessary if the ink has been on the pen for any length of time. It is a good practice to dip the point regularly in ammonia while you are drawing. The ammonia dissolves the clotting

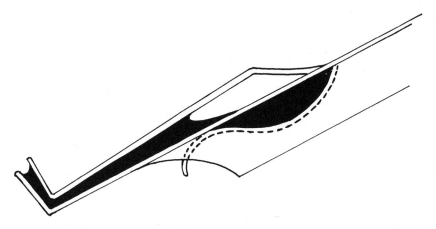

Two ink reservoirs on a typical lettering pen point. Such reservoirs must be kept clean if the ink is to flow.

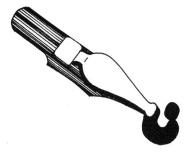

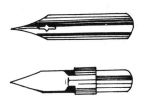

Flicker pen point with ink reservoir.

Speedball lettering pen point.

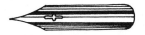

Drawing pen point.

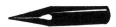

Crow quill pen point.

ink and slows its drying so that you may draw without any slowing of the flow.

Spattering. Most of the fine quality drawing points are made of hard metal, which provides spring and snap in the nib and preserves the original shape of the point. If the metal were softer, the nibs would not spring back when pressed apart and would not create the necessary fine line. However, this hardness makes the fine metal points of the nib very sharp, which means that when any pressure is applied to the nib, these points dig into the paper. As the pen is moved, these points are suddenly released and, springing back, spatter ink. This can be avoided if you apply only slight pressure on the point, just enough to prevent digging in. If spattering still occurs, the paper is probably causing it. Be sure that you use the finest quality bristols for drawing with these fine pen points and stay specifically with the plate finishes, which have the smoothest possible surface. Other finishes and other types of paper have tiny fibers exposed on the surface, which catch the points of the nib as it is drawn over the surface.

Clogging. Clogging, which causes an uneven line, is the result of reduced flow from dried ink. Keep your pen points clean. Clean them frequently while in use and clean them thoroughly after use. If the pen points are cleaned often, water will suffice. If the ink dries too long, use ammonia. If the ink has hardened too much, or too thickly, it may be necessary to use pen cleaner.

Raggedness. If everything else is right, the presence of a spotty, ragged, or spattered line will be caused by the nibs themselves. Even with the best of care, it is possible to bend the fine points of the nib in normal use. When this occurs, the points will not return to their proper position and the slit will be enlarged or distorted so that the ink cannot flow properly. In some cases, it may be possible to bend the points back together.

But this is a stop-gap measure at best. Throw away a bent nib and use another point. Like paintbrushes, pen points will not last forever and must be replaced.

PENCIL POINTER, METAL

The metal pencil pointer is essentially a broad, flat nail file. Performing the same function as sandpaper, this tool is excellent for pointing and shaping pencils, pastels, charcoal, and crayons. The big advantage of the metal file over sandpaper is that it does not wear out and need not be replaced. (See *Sandpaper Pad.*)

Although it is durable, the metal pencil pointer will become dirty quickly, which makes it difficult to use when many colors are required or when soft or chalky materials fill the cutting surface of the pointer. Being metal, the pointer is easily cleaned with a stiff-bristled brush, but this is a nuisance many artists try to avoid.

The metal file is not satisfactory for smoothing cut edges you have made on a board, nor is it suitable for cleaning mechanical tools.

Choosing a metal pointer or sandpaper is entirely a matter of personal preference.

PENCIL SHARPENERS

Pencil sharperners comprise a large group of devices that are designed to produce a fine point on an ordinary lead pencil. The simplest of these devices is the small plastic cube containing a knife blade fastened at an angle inside a hole. When a pencil is inserted into the hole and twisted, the angled blade cuts into the pencil and produces a point. These familiar sharpeners are available at any dime store, and are handy to carry about with you.

However, most artists find these simple sharpeners too clumsy to use and too crude for producing a fine point. The most common sharpener for general use is the wall- or desk-mounted sharpener with a series of blades which are rotated by a hand crank, a container for collecting shavings, and an adjustable guide for accommodating various thicknesses of pencil. This sharpener is also very familiar.

The more popular is the electric sharpener. The basic construction and action of the electric sharpener is little different from the hand sharpeners, but the electric motor produces a much quicker, smoother action and permits finer control and less likelihood of pencil point breakage.

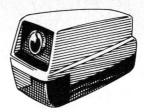

Popular style electric pencil sharpener.

Common Difficulties

Uneven point. Occasionally, you will find that your pencil sharpener is producing a point that is off-center; the point is half-wood and half-graphite. This uneven point is caused by the blades in the sharpener becoming loose or out of position. On the cheaper hand models this condition cannot be corrected. The only remedy is to purchase a more expensive model in which the craftsmanship will insure a longer life, and in which some adjustments are possible.

Frequent breakage. If the sharpener tends to break the point during the sharpening, the blades are out of position or too dull. Once again, get a more durable model or one in which the blades can be replaced.

Clogging. Any sharpener will become clogged occasionally with the broken point of a pencil, particularly with the softer leads of graphite or colored pencils. To clear the obstruction, insert the point of an already sharp pencil into the sharpener, and proceed as though it required sharpening. This will take a little more force than you would normally use to sharpen a pencil. However, the pressure will cause the blades to disintegrate the blockage. Be sure that you use a hard pencil for this operation, preferably a 4H. If you use another soft pencil, the added pressure will simply break its point.

Shattering. At times, the wooden casing of a pencil will shatter in a sharpener,

clogging the blades, and ruining the pencil. This shattering may occur in any type of sharpener, and is caused by dull blades that grab the casing instead of cutting it. The rotary action of the blades will then tear the wood, which comes away from the lead in long, jagged pieces. The only cure for this problem is to replace the blades with a new set. Many higher quality sharpeners have replaceable blades, which are available at art or stationery stores. Replacing blades requires dismantling the sharpener and removing the old blades. Instructions are provided with both the sharpener and with the replacement blades. The process is not difficult and is accomplished with the simple tools found in any home or office. If immediate replacement is impossible, the sharpener can still be used, but with caution. Reduce the pressure you apply to the pencil while sharpening, and make sure that you start the rotary action of the blades *before* any pressure is applied. In this way, the dull blades will have a greater length of time in which to accomplish their function.

Slow action. Any sharpener will lose efficiency when the collection area is filled with shavings. These shavings slow the rotation of the blades and tend to push back against the newly formed shavings. Simply empty the shavings and its efficiency will improve. If the cutting action is still slow, check the blades.

PENCILS, CHARCOAL

Charcoal pencils are similar to lead pencils in appearance, but contain charcoal in a hardened form. Such pencils are often used in layout. (See *Charcoal.*)

PENCILS, COLORED

Thin sticks of colored pigment in wooden pencil casings. A waxy binder holds the pigment together, producing a relatively firm lead which may be handled in much the same manner as the more familiar graphite pencil. (See *Leads, Colored.*)

Although colored pencils should be familiar to anyone who has studied art, they are not commonly used by commercial artists for finished renderings. However, many artists still use them for layouts, specifically for lettering and fine line detail, usually in combination with other mediums.

Red and blue pencils are used extensively for preparing mechanicals. Since blue does not photograph, light lines drawn with a blue pencil make an excellent guide for positioning the elements of a mechanical, and do not need to be erased. Similarly, the red pencil lines— which photograph like black—can be used for holding lines and for other instructions to platemakers, which must be retained during the platemaking process.

Colored pencils are also available with broad, flat leads similar to sketching pencils. Although limited in the range of colors, these broader colored pencils are superior to pastel for rendering colored lettering on layouts.

Common Difficulties

Fragility. Colored pencils are fragile, and if they are dropped, the leads will shatter. This fragility makes these pencils difficult to sharpen in a mechanical sharpener. Even normal sharpening can cause the lead to break and jam the sharpener. In both cases use a knife or razor blade, making a fine point with a sandpaper pad.

Smudging. Some colored pencils are water-soluble, which may be handy for wash effects, but be careful when you are using them. If your hands are moist, they will smudge the color. Avoid handling the artwork as much as possible and use a slip sheet under your hand while drawing.

Streaks. Most colored pencils are difficult to apply evenly to large areas. Try to keep all the strokes parallel when rendering, and avoid excessive pressure. This procedure will produce an even but light tone. To darken the tone, repeat the process as often as necessary. One method that works quite well is to sharpen the point so that it is flat. Use a straight-edge as a guide and overlap each stroke onto the previous one. A little practice will enable you to produce a steady tone without streaks.

Shine. Repeated stroking with excessive pressure may build up areas of the waxy pigment. This build-up produces a disturbing glossiness or shine, which may be avoided by using the methods described above.

Muddiness. The colored pencil pigments do not mix readily with one another. If the colors overlap, their brilliance is dulled and the result may look unprofessionally muddy. This problem is avoided by using a set of pencils that includes a larger choice of colors or by altering the color scheme of your drawing to accommodate the colors you have. In rendering, the effect is always more satisfying if the colors are pure, even though they may not be entirely accurate.

PENCILS, LEAD

One of the artist's primary tools, the lead pencil is composed mainly of graphite and clay, the mixture of which determines the degree of hardness or softness. For comparison, the common lead pencil is usually 2B if soft, or 2H if hard. Artists' lead pencils come in a range of 6B soft to 9H hard. In the middle of the range are two classifications called HB and F. There is no rule for selecting any classification.

Remember that the softer pencils tend to erase with less difficulty, make a darker mark, smudge easily, and do not dent the paper surface. The harder pencils leave a more permanent line, may actually score the surface, produce a lighter mark, but do not smudge as much. The hardest pencils hold a fine point best and are excellent for tracing, while the softer pencils deposit more graphite when you make your own tracing paper.

Lead pencils can be sharpened by any pencil sharpener, and the point can be refined with a sandpaper pad. It is also helpful to have a razor blde available for sharpening a point of unusual length or shape.

Common Difficulties

There is little that can go wrong with a pencil, and once you have tried all the varying degrees of hardness and softness, you will be able to select one that suits your purpose under any circumstance. However, there are two conditions that may merit discussion:

Breakage. A pencil—particularly a soft one—that has been dropped repeatedly may break frequently when sharpened in a mechanical sharpener, because the lead has shattered inside the wooden case. Such a pencil may still afford satisfactory use if the pencil is sharpened carefully with a knife or razor blade. Expose only the amount of lead you need to work with, without removing so much wood that the next break in the lead is exposed. In this manner, you may avoid the breaks and the pencil can be used in the normal way.

Repeated sharpening. It may become tedious to sharpen a point continually when a great deal of fine work must be done. For this reason, you may prefer to use a lead holder with a lead pointer.

PENCILS, MARKING

Marking pencils, also called China markers, consist of a waxy core wrapped in a durable paper cover. The paper is scored so that one section may be removed at a time to expose more of the wax point. Available in black, white, red, yellow, and blue, the pencils will write on any surface. Despite this advantage, the pencils are not often used for finished renderings. Crayons and oil chalks produce a similar texture with a much wider selection of colors. The artist uses a marking pencil to write instructions to printers, etc., on fragile surfaces like photographs and overlays. The soft, waxy mark takes well to a glossy surface, will not crack or dent a photo emulsion, and can be wiped off easily with a clean cloth—leaving no stain. For these reasons, you should always have a marking pencil on hand.

PENCILS, SKETCHING

These resemble carpenter's pencils from which they are derived. Thinner than a graphite stick, thicker than a regular pencil, the sketching pencil is a broad, flat graphite lead in a wooden casing. They are available in three degrees, all soft: 2B, 4B, and 6B. Since the shape will not fit any pencil sharpener, sketching pencils must be sharpened with a knife or with a razor blade. Final adjustments in the size and shape of the lead should be made with a sandpaper pad or metal pencil pointer.

The sketching pencil has two principal functions: layout and illustration. As a layout tool, the point is kept chisel-shaped and sharp. This shape produces a pencil technique that is similar to those of pastels and dye markers, which are the primary layout tools. That is to say, working on the edge of the point produces a fine line, while the full point creates a broad line; the one drawing tool produces any line or variation used in layout indication.

Since both effects can be produced in one stroke, the sketch pencil is the recommended tool for rendering single stroke lettering, regardless of style.

In illustration, the broad lead is valued for the ease with which it allows you to create rich, character-filled lines and broad areas of tone. In both layout and illustration, the wooden casing keeps your fingers clean while working, a distinct advantage over a graphite stick. (See *Chisel-Point Pencils.*)

Common Difficulty

Dullness. The soft lead dulls quickly, requiring continual pointing and sharpening to maintain ideal layout technique. There is no way to avoid this. Keep a blade and sandpaper always at hand and learn to use them frequently.

PENS

A pen is a pointed drawing tool that uses a liquid medium fed to the point from a reservoir. Within that basic definition there are a number of variations. Commercial artists use India ink, drawing inks, dyes, and paints that cannot flow through conventional writing and fountain pens, so a large number of specialized pens have been created for their use. The most common, frequently used pens are the ruling pen and the pen point inserted in a pen holder. These have been covered in their own sections, and you should become thoroughly familiar with them.

There are also several categories of pens that have specialized value to the artist. These may be grouped rather broadly and arbitrarily as India ink or drawing ink pens, lettering scribers, dye marker pens, felt-nib fountain pens. Each pen has been created for specific uses and has its own characteristics. Let us study them separately.

India ink or drawing ink pens. This is the largest group, and contains some names that have become virtual standards in the field, such as—Rapidograph, Graphos, Osmiroid, and Wrico. These pens have special mechanisms incorporated into their construction to facilitate the storage and flow of India and drawing inks, which dry quickly and clog conventional pens. There are three variations: hollow-point, ball point, and modified fountain pen.

Ball point pens. Professional quality ball point pens work like any conventional ball point pen, but use a form of black, indelible ink that closely resembles India ink, or a limited range of colors that can be used to produce mechanicals. Some of these pens have an ink cartridge that can be replaced when empty, the others are thrown away when they are dried out. Since they are so similar to conventional writing pens, there is little that needs to be said about them. Your art supply store will probably carry any number of them, and you may try them and select the one that suits your needs.

Hollow-point pens. Nibs consist of fine tubes with finer wires inside them. Ink flows from a reservoir into the nib, and the wire can be moved inside the tube point to start the flow and break up any clogging. The hollow-point pen's nib is, of course, inflexible and produces only one weight of line. However, different size nibs can be purchased and screwed into the pen once the original nib has been unscrewed. Hollow-point pens are the finest drawing tools made for ruling and inking with templates, curves, and straight-edges.

Fountain pens. Come with a single nib and resemble an ordinary fountain pen in almost all respects, or they can have interchangeable nibs in a wide variety of sizes and shapes. These pens are used for drawing, lettering, and drafting.

There are no criteria for selecting pens within this group. Personal preference and the kind or job you are doing will dictate your choice. You are advised to investigate all of them; your art supply dealer will be glad to demonstrate them for you. Remember that any tool of this nature will require practice and familiarity before it can provide you with the best results.

Lettering scribers. These are specialized pens used almost entirely to produce mechanical lettering and they are discussed in that section. They are included here because the brand names are often the same as those of the drawing ink pens, and you should not confuse them. When you buy a pen, or any piece of art equipment, you should discuss the purpose with your dealer. Not only will this prevent misunderstanding, but the dealer will be able to introduce you to any new products that have come into the market that may perform better. (See *Lettering Pens* and *Lettering, Mechanical.*)

Marker pens. Markers have come into wide use over the last several years, and a section has been devoted to them. This popularity has led to a number of variations of the marker in pen form, such as the Pentel. These pens differ from the conventional marker in the slender shape of both the nib and the holder. But unlike most pens, they cannot be refilled; they are thrown away when used up. These pens are used primarily for fine detail drawing and layout, but their felt or nylon nibs are not fine enough for ruling. There is a growing range of colors now available at art stores to match the markers as they increase in popularity. It is this choice of color that gives these pens their chief distinction and superiority over other pens.

Felt-nib fountain pens. These pens combine the characteristics of both the fountain pen and the marker pen. Like the fountain pen, you can add its own special ink to a reservoir; and like the marker, this ink is dispensed by capillary action through a felt nib. These nibs, which are interchangeable with a variety of shapes and sizes, are held by simple friction and fed by a valve in the pen. Pressure on the nib opens this valve and allows ink to soak through the felt. There are only a few colors of ink that are sold for use with this pen. A solvent is also sold that cleans the pens and softens the felt tips if they dry out. In action, this pen acts much like a dye marker, and is excellent for use with them in doing layout work. The different nibs provide a wide range of treatment. However, it is messy to change the nibs in use, and you may prefer to buy a separate pen for each nib that you use with any frequency. (See also *Pen Points.*)

Common Difficulties

India ink or drawing pens. The only problem with these pens, excluding actual breakage, is clogging. Virtually none of these pens is truly what it is claimed to be. Regardless of the ink used, the pens will clog—both in use and while being stored—and you must become accustomed to this frailty. It in no way detracts from the value of the pen or from its function. It is merely a condition that you must accept. The only way to reduce this shortcoming is to keep the pen *clean.* This means disassembling the pen and washing it thoroughly and often. Use water with a little ammonia in it to dissolve the old ink. Several brands will also sell a pen cleaner for this purpose, but if the pen is cleaned frequently, clean water will do. Wipe the parts carefully and completely to remove any vestiges of old ink. Use a cotton swab to reach the insides. But get it clean. When you reload the pen, use fresh ink and shake it up well. Choose your ink with care. Regardless of what the pens are called, the popular brands of India ink do not work well in these pens, and even the manufacturer's recommended inks may not perform as well as others. Ask advice from your art supply dealer and experiment yourself. Remember that a drop or two of ammonia will dilute the ink so that it will flow better and help to reduce clogging. When the pen clogs while in use, the common tendency is to shake the pen vigorously. Indeed, the mechanism within the hollow-point pens is designed to respond to this treatment. However, this may cause the pen to leak. Shake the pen gently. If this does not immediately start the ink flow, try dipping the point in water or ammonia to dissolve the drying ink. Repeat this dipping and tap the point on a pad of paper or into a rag (so as not to damage the point). Usually the point will clear after a few seconds of this treatment. If not, take it apart and clean it.

Marker pens. Dyes are highly volatile and dry quickly if left exposed to the air. Always keep the cover on when not actually in use, even while drawing. Once a pen has dried, you may be able to extend its life for a brief time by soaking it in a solvent for a few seconds. Acetone, lacquer thinner, pen cleaner, even rubber cement thinner will often work, depending in the brand of pen used.

Felt-nib fountain pens. There are few troubles with this pen if you use it continuously. Some of the difficulties you may encounter are listed below:

1. Clogging. Long inactivity will cause the ink to dry and clog the valve action and harden the nibs. While the solvent/cleaner will remedy these problems, its action is diminished the longer the ink has dried. Unless you use the pen steadily, you should dismantle the parts and clean them thoroughly before storing.

2. No ink. The felt nibs are comparatively long and the ink takes quite a while to soak through, particularly after the pen has been used and allowed to dry. Allow time for this soaking before attempting to draw. If the nib has hardened too much, soak it in the cleanser provided by the manufacturer. Be sure that the ink is fresh. If allowed to sit too long in the pen, the ink will thicken and the flow will be slowed.

3. Fuzzy line. Repeated use will cause the felt to fray at the point of the nib. A razor blade or knife may be used to trim the nib, particularly when the felt is dry and hard. If this does not work, replace the nib.

PENS, BAMBOO

The oriental bamboo pen is simply a piece of bamboo that has been sharpened to a point and slitted. The fibrous texture of this point is capable of producing a range of line treatments that vary in character between those of a pen point and those of a brush. Since the pen is simple to use and clean, and works well with any number of liquid mediums, it has become popular with illustrators. With practice you can learn to produce an interesting assortment of line techniques with this pen, all in one drawing.

Bamboo pens tend to break or lose their points rather quickly, but they are inexpensive and can be resharpened with a knife or a razor blade by shaving the sides of the tip in much the same manner that you would sharpen a wood pencil with these tools. Remember to lengthen the slit in the nib, if it has been shortened during the sharpening, so that ink will flow smoothly and the tip will produce the proper variations in the line.

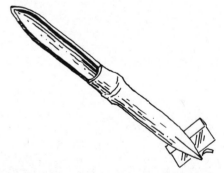

Typical bamboo pen showing how a blunt or damaged point is renewed with a razor blade. Do not forget that the slit in the point must be kept open for best results.

PENTEL

The brand name of a dye marker pen, and is representative of many other similar pens that have begun to be sold in art stores. These pens are convenient, economical, and work well as both an art tool and conventional writing instrument. (See *Pens.*)

PERFORATING WHEELS

Perforating wheels may have a number of names: trace wheels, pounce wheels, and even roulettes. They are all the same, made of a handle and a freely turning disc with sharp projections, much like a fancy horse spur. Drawing the wheel over a surface will produce a series of evenly spaced perforations. These perforations are used primarily for patterns. A paper pattern that has been so punctured may be dusted with pounce powder which then sifts through the small openings and leaves a delicate and easily removed du-

plicate of the original design. Pouncing is an excellent method of transferring lettering layouts to window glass.

Another, less frequently employed, use of the perforating wheel is to produce the effects of scoring or perforating on comp layouts. By using this wheel, coupons and return mail cards may be indicated on such layouts.

Perforating wheels come in several sizes with different sizes and numbers of perforating prongs on the wheels.

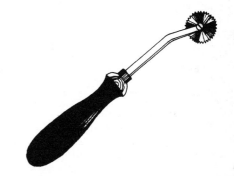

Perforating, or pounce wheel with sharply pointed rotating wheel.

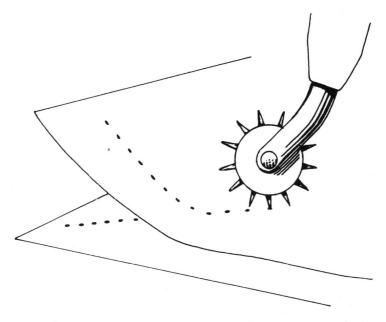

The dot pattern created by dusting powder through the holes made by a typical perforating wheel.

PERSPECTIVE LINEADS

Used to construct lines in perspective when the vanishing point lies off the drawing surface, perspective lineads resemble T-squares, except that the heads are Y-shaped.

To use the linead, place two pins on the board above and below the horizon line. As long as the blades of the linead are kept in contact with these pins, any lines drawn will, if continued, cross the same vanishing point. By using two sets of pins at either end of the drawing, it is possible to construct a complete perspective drawing.

One word of caution. Although the perspective lineads are easy to use and require no more care than you would give a T-square, the creation of a perspective drawing is not a simple matter and should not be attempted without a complete understanding of the subject. If you have not studied perspective, or do not understand the principles thoroughly, do not attempt to use the linead or any other device or procedure until you have had an opportunity to read a good book on the subject or to take a class of instruction.

PHOTO DULLING SPRAY

A matte finish varnish that is used to coat photoprints and similar glossy material that must be subjected to bright lights, when glare can be disruptive. TV is a prime example. The numerous lights used in a TV studio make it impossible to position a photo so that no glare is produced in the camera. The dulling spray prevents the glossy surface from reflecting such a glare. Photo dulling spray is sold in a conventional aerosol spray can in most photo and art supply stores.

PHOTOLETTERING

Used almost exclusively with display type, such as headlines, photolettering employs cold type principles—with two notable exceptions. The basic film negative is much larger, and the operations are performed by hand, instead of with computer-aided equipment. The matrix negative for photolettering needs to be large, because display type is large. The lens systems of cold type machines can enlarge characters, but you should be aware that enlarging tends to magnify errors. (Sometimes enlarging actually creates errors where none existed in the original negative.) Since it is one of the most important design elements, display type must be perfect. It is better to start large and reduce to size.

Photolettering's hand operation permits extremely careful spacing and positioning of letters. The automatic kerning features of cold type systems are not subtle enough for the delicate spacing such important elements require. Finally, no previous type system has been able to produce an effective script alphabet that can be set mechanically. The very nature of script is a certain handwritten irregularity. Except for formal Spencerian scripts, hot metal types have been unsuccessful with scripts. The necessity of having each connecting stroke occur at exactly the same spot to coincide with the matching stoke of the next character destroys the flowing nature of most freehand scripts. Photolettering relies on hand positioning, and can be modified with original art. Thus, highly individual characteristics can be accommodated. Ink and white paint can be used to overcome difficult juxtapositions. The final design can then be rephotographed and a clean proof submitted to the client. In a similar manner, objectionable features of an existing alphabet can be modified.

The photolettering process is comparatively simple and inexpensive, mainly requiring a good knowledge of type and the ability to draw well with a fine brush or pen. A number of photolettering machines can be purchased by the individual artist, which is very effective if there is sufficient volume of such lettering to be produced. These machines are not sold through art stores, although art store personnel may be able to help you contact the appropriate manufacturer or distributor. Trade magazines also carry advertising for vendors. Many typographic suppliers maintain such equipment and will offer photolettering with their services. In larger metropolitan areas, independent photolettering firms may be found. For unusual and specific designs, a layout should be submitted, as normal type specifications cannot describe their characteristics. (See also *Cold Type* and *Type*.)

PHOTO PRINTS

Normal photographic copies of art or photography. They are too expensive and slow for use in sizing and positioning artwork, but may be necessary for retouching and for color work.

The best processes for making photo prints of color are the dye transfer and the carbro. The cost makes both of these prohibitive for most commercial artwork, and they have been replaced by the less accurate C-print. C-prints can be made by most photographic studios, but specialists produce the best quality. Considerable investigation will be necessary to find such an organization in your community. Even in the larger cities, the quality of C-print work varies considerably. However, the inexpensive cost and reasonable quality make C-prints the standard of the industry. For more information about these complex processes, check with your photographic service, either lab or studio.

PHOTOGRAPH CLEANERS

Photographs being displayed, retouched, and reproduced must be absolutely clean. Retouch paints, for example, are water-soluble and will not adhere properly to a dirty photograph. In addition, the strong lights used with reproduction cameras will pick up and exaggerate any surface stain on a photograph that is being copied.

The most common discolorations on photographs result from fingerprints, grease pencil markings, or merely from the chemicals used in processing the photograph itself. Any solvent that will dissolve these materials can be used to clean the surface of a photograph. Since there are many existing solvents (including water, ammonia, and rubber cement thinner) that will remove these discolorations, there has never been a need to manufacture one specifically for the purpose. However, many retouching specialists have devised mixtures of their own, including such exotic substances as ether, and have had it prepared privately. If you intend to handle photographs extensively, you may wish to prepare a similar solution yourself. You might also check with your art or photo supply store dealer. Many of these stores will carry solutions that serve as photograph cleaners. (The Marlene solution from the Marshall Oil Photograph Coloring sets is an example.) Their experience may help you select a satisfactory cleaner. Actually, any liquid that can be used to remove dirt, grease, or chemicals from the surface of a photographic print is properly a photograph cleaner; experience and personal preference will dictate what solutions you use.

When cleaning a photograph, it is preferable to have the photograph mounted on piece of illustration board or mounting board. This may be accomplished with a dry-mount press or with rubber cement. Mounting insures a smooth surface and prevents curling or buckling which can damage the emulsion. Apply the cleaning liquid with a piece of cotton, and rub it quickly and gently over the entire surface. Do not scrub or exert undue pressure. Such actions may damage the delicate surface of the emulsion. Repeat the cleaning with fresh liquid and clean cotton until all evidence of dirt has been removed. Wipe off the excess fluid with clean cotton and let the photograph dry by itself.

When nothing else is available, a piece of cotton moistened with saliva is an excellent substitute. But most important; never use anything but cotton or an extremely soft rag. Anything else will scratch the surface.

Common Difficulties

Scratching. Even following the procedures described above may not prevent the photograph from being scratched. The emulsion of a photograph is extremely delicate, particularly when it has been softened with water. If the cleaning fluid you are using does soften the emulsion, you must use extra care. Work as fast as you can and allow the emulsion to dry and harden between steps. In this way you will not be touching the surface when it is soft and vulnerable.

Streaking. Many times, after cleaning the photograph, whitish streaks or blotches may remain. These are caused by the residues of the cleaner itself drying on the photo, or by dissolved dirt and grease left by imperfect cleaning. In either case, take a *clean* piece of cotton and repeat the cleaning process. It may be necessary to do this several times before the streaks disappear. If they do not, you are probably using too much cleaner. Make sure that the cotton is only damp and do not allow puddles of cleaner to sit and dry on the surface. Maintain a gentle wiping motion until the cotton and the photo are both quite dry. If the stains still do not disappear, flush the photo with clean water and wipe it gently with clean cotton. Allow the photo to dry thoroughly before doing any further work. The emulsion will be quite soft.

Beading. If retouch paints bead or do not lie smoothly on the print, repeat the cleaning process. There is probably still too much grease on the surface. If further cleaning is insufficient to eliminate the beading, try a different solvent. If no cleaner seems to be effective, try saliva. Often the residue of the cleaner itself may be the cause of beading. Saliva will remove this residue and does not interfere with any paint. If there is still a tendency to bead, add a drop of acetate medium to your paint, since the paint may have difficulty taking on any glossy surface.

PHOTOGRAPHIC TAPE

A matte black drafting tape designed for use in photography and all other situations where it is necessary to prevent the passage or reflection of light.

PHOTOSTATS

Photostats (stats) are black-and-white, high-contrast copies produced by an inexpensive, opaque-paper photographic process. They are used to enlarge or reduce existing line art or lettering, to obtain paper negatives in which the values are reversed, and to create reasonable copies of continuous tone art or photography for paste-up and positioning on mechanicals. At one time, the photostat process was unique in commercial art. Progress in chemistry and photography, however, has introduced alternatives, such as the direct positive (DP), which are single-step processes that eliminate the negative (saving time and money) and gradually are supplanting the photostat. In addition, DPs can produce copy on transparent film and create a single-step paper negative. If you are in doubt about which process to use, or which might be available, ask your copy service for advice. (See *Direct Positive.*)

The photostat camera is a large, bellows type mounted horizontally on a stand that includes a movable, horizontal platform on which the original is placed. This original is held fast by a sheet of glass, and the platform and the camera are adjusted to obtain the proper focus. Strong light is flooded on the original, and the image is relayed to the camera by a prism lens. The camera records the image of a continuous roll of sensitized paper, the width of which is determined by the size of the camera. The paper is exposed for a specified period controlled by a timer, and a crank is turned to advance the paper out of the exposure area. A knife in the machine is activated to trim the exposed paper, which is now cranked out of the camera, where it falls into a tray of developer situated on the back of the machine. After developing, the print is washed and treated with a weak solution of bleach to heighten contrast and remove minor discolorations that usually appear during the process. The print is then washed in clean water, fixed in hypo, washed again, and dried on a drum type print dryer. If a positive is required, the process is merely repeated with the negative in place of the original on the copy board.

Several papers are available for use with stat cameras, but two are conventionally used for the vast majority of stat work. These are the matte and glossy papers. Matte paper produces a soft, dull copy and is the cheapest. Glossy paper has a bright, shiny surface and produces the strongest contrast. Special papers and finishes are available at extra cost, not only for the paper, but for the time spent unloading a camera, inserting the paper, and returning the original paper to the camera after the shot. The finishes are usually controlled by chemicals and the drying procedure. These finishes are rarely optional, depending instead on the procedures at any particular stat facility.

The stat camera has a limit of 400% enlargement or reduction. Further changes in size can be obtained by repeating the entire negative/positive process another time. Or the original may be placed on a vertical surface farther away from the camera, and the prism replaced with a conventional lens. This procedure is referred to as an easel shot and entails an additional charge. Similarly,

copy may be reversed or flopped by means of another form of lens. Here again, there will be an additional charge for the service.

The stat camera cannot photograph blue, and red will photograh as an intense black. All other colors will be more or less accurate in value. This is important to remember when copying colored originals. If red or blue must be copied, ask for the cooperation of the stat personnel. With varied exposures, they can overcome these limitations to a degree. But remember that all the other material in the original will be affected by these variations. It may be necessary to get several stats and cut them apart.

Photostats are used for many copying purposes in all industries, but they have specific functions in commercial art. Line material can be reproduced on a glossy stat with great accuracy, so type, line drawings, etc., are often enlarged or reduced in this manner when used in preparing a mechanical. Photos and other continuous tone material which must be sized and positioned on a mechanical are usually copied with a matte stat which can be pasted directly on the mechanical. Since these stats are used for size and position only, the matte stat, which is cheaper, is used although the quality may be slightly inferior. Glossy stats are used when material must be reversed in value, as when light lettering appears in a dark panel. And, finally, reference material is often statted to the exact size of the artwork, so that it may be traced directly.

Material that is being submitted for photostating should be flat and clean. If the original is too small, it is wise to mount it on a larger sheet that it is not lost during the processing. The larger paper also provides room to place the necessary instructions. These should include your name, organization or address for identification purposes and delivery instructions, the kind of stat (matte, glossy, etc.), negative or positive print, the number of prints of each kind, and the size each of the prints should be. There are two ways to indicate size. Either you furnish the focus percentage (150%, 50%, etc.), which you have determined with a proportional guide; or you mark an area with two lines and a connecting arrow (←— —→). The size you wish this space to be in the final print is written near this marking (that is, 2″ BM, for between marks). The stat operators will translate this into the percentage, themselves. Either way is acceptable, but the BM method allows the stat house to check the accuracy of the print. You may make a mistake figuring out the percentage, and they will have no way of knowing that an error has been made; but the stat people will be able to measure the distance of the marks on the final print and correct any error they have made.

The prices of stats are determined by the various processes just described. However, the basic cost is based on the size of the paper used to produce the stat (not the size of the original) and on the particular stock selected. An 8½″ x 11″ sheet is the smallest size available. The largest size will be determined by the size of the camera and the kinds of paper stocked by the copy service. Remember, the photostat is a two-step process, and while one step may be less expensive than a direct positive, two steps will cost more. Actual prices vary with location, and the extent of the services available. Check with a photo studio or blueprint firm if a photostat house or copy service is not available.

Common Difficulties

Instructions. Since the negative stat differs from the original only in value, some confusion can result when ordering copies of reversed art. "Negative" tends to mean white on black. If you wish copy art that is white on black, the stat house may mistake your art for a negative and produce only a "positive" (black on white) from it. It is usually safer to refer to the number of steps desired; for example,

first print for negative, and second print for positive. This is more descriptive of the steps involved and causes less confusion.

Fading. Most stats are produced quickly to meet commercial deadlines. Therefore, they are not left in the hypo/fix for more than a few minutes. Consequently, the paper will turn brown with age. Depending on the length of the fix, this may occur in a few weeks, months, or even a year. If you wish to use a stat for extended periods, include this information with your instructions, so that they can fix the stat permanently.

Distortion. Speed, again, may cause the print to be mishandled in the drying process. This abuse may cause a large stat to stretch or shrink in places. If accuracy is essential, stress this in your order, as well. Extreme enlargement or reduction may cause similar distortion, due to limitations of the lens. You can avoid these extremes by having intermediate-sized copies made.

PICA RULER

A ruler, the divisions of which are marked in the point and pica scale used by printers and typographers. (See *Rulers.*)

PINK PEARL

A brand name for a pencil eraser, similar to the eraser found on common pencils. The name is generic for most erasers of this kind, regardless of color. (See *Erasers.*)

PLASTIC FILMS

Plastics are being used in ever-increasing numbers of products in the world today, and the art field is no exception. But their greatest use is in plastic sheets. These sheets may be made of a wide range of plastic materials, but the two most common and successful are acetate and Mylar. Both of these products have great dimensional stability, which means that they do not tend to stretch or shrink in extremes of heat and humidity. This is important in the art field, where art must be reproduced by the printer and where changes in the size of the art can cause errors of register. I am sure that you have seen pictures that seem fuzzy or out of focus, and colors that run over their borders. One cause of these imperfections is art that has stretched or shrunk. Mylar, the brand name for the newest of these products, is the best in this respect, but it is still the most expensive.

Plastic films are used as the basis for several products commonly used by the artist. These include Bourges sheets, transfer type, and frisket paper. But the primary use of plastic sheets is for overlays, an essential part in the production of layouts, finished art, and mechanicals.

There are not many differences between the materials that are sold for these purposes in art stores. Whether you buy a single sheet, a pad, or a roll, the products now available work very well; the only way to find your favorite is through practice and experience.

Plastic films are sold with and without adhesive backings, and some films have a surface that has been frosted to accept conventional mediums. Shiny plastics will require acetate or acrylic paint and ink, or they will not hold the pigment. Acetate mediums can be added to conventional paints and inks to help them adhere, but they tend to distort the covering qualities. A great deal of practice is necessary to learn to use these additives correctly.

Plastic films can also be purchased that are colored or have a coating of color applied to them. (See *Overlays, Tinted Acetate.*)

POINT RULER

A ruler, the divisions of which are marked in the point and pica scale used by printers and typographers. (See *Pica Ruler* and *Rulers.*)

POLAROID

The Polaroid camera, which takes photographs that can be developed in the camera in seconds, has become a familiar and popular item. Because the Polaroid camera delivers a photograph on the spot, it has become the artist's standby in the field of reference. Used directly to copy details for later study, the camera is also useful for testing set-ups for more conventional photographic procedures. The more expensive models produce a print with sufficient quality to be used directly for reproduction on many occasions. These more costly models also permit the use of a wide range of attachments for close-ups and other specialized photographic procedures. Obviously, the more versatile the camera, the more value it can offer you as an artist.

The operation of this camera is quick, relatively inexpensive, and requires no particular training. The main value of the camera is speed—always important to commercial artists. For instance, you can assume a pose and take your own picture with the help of a cable-release attachment on the camera shutter button, and have the picture for drawing reference in just a few minutes. This is cheaper, quicker, and just as accurate as hiring a model, and easier than working with a mirror. In addition, you can obtain a photostat copy of the print enlarged to the size of your drawing, which will permit you to trace the details directly. Such prints are available for about one dollar at any photostat or blueprint shop. These shops are located in most cities—check your local Yellow Pages or ask advice from your local printers and photographers. These people use such services and will know where they are available and often can provide them themselves.

POLYETHYLENE

A plastic used extensively in the form of thin sheets for modern packaging. This plastic is not readily available and cannot be purchased at art stores. It is necessary to get the material from the manufacturer or from a packaging firm. However, since so much packaging is done with plastics of this type, you should have some knowledge of its properties when designing with them. Special inks and printing processes have been invented to work with polyethylene and the only way to become familiar with them is to actually work with an organization that uses them. If you are confronted with a design problem involving plastics, be sure that you contact a manufacturer who can provide the necessary samples and technical information.

PORTFOLIOS

The term portfolio covers a wide range of folders used for carrying artwork, for delivery or presentation. The simpler portfolios are merely two large cardboards joined by a cloth hinge and tie strings. These are available with flaps large enough to cover the tops of any art pieces in the folder and to protect them from the weather. The fancier portfolios are leather cases with sturdy handles and a zipper which seals all openings. These portfolios usually contain a loose-leaf binder and come with presentation sheets and acetate covers which have been punched to fit the binder rings. Additional sheets may be purchased separately.

Somewhere between these two types of portfolio are presentation books. These books have some method of securing presentation sheets with their covers, but do not have carrying handles, nor do they close with zippers or tying strings.

All three of these forms come in many different sizes, based upon the paper sizes used most frequently. Which one you choose is therefore dictated by the material you intend to carry. Illustrators more often need the larger portfolios to accommodate their full-sized renderings, while the smaller sizes are usually sufficient to satisfy the needs of a layout designer.

The artist has continuing need for a neat and orderly method of carrying and presenting artwork to clients and employers, and the portfolio is literally a must. Which form you choose will be dictated by the amount you wish to spend and by your own personal design preferences. Any art store will have a large selection. (See *Attaché Cases.*)

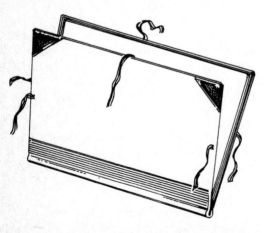

Common, reinforced cardboard portfolio with string ties.

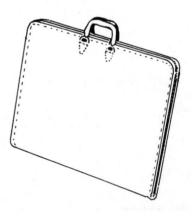

Portfolio of good-quality leather with zipper closure and carrying handles.

POSTER BOARD

An inexpensive cardboard covered with colored paper with either a matte or glossy surface. Used for display and sign work, a full sheet of poster board is 28″ x 44″, but can be purchased in half and quarter sheets as well. Available in two weights, 14 and 28 gauge, for light or heavy duty. Also known as showcard. (See *Papers and Boards.*)

POSTER PAINT

The name given to inexpensive tempera paints commonly used in schools and in the commercial art field when quality is not as important as cost. (See *Paint.*)

POUNCE POWDER

A pulverized, dry medium that can be dusted through a pattern which has been prepared with a perforating wheel. The powder is purchased in a small bag, and is applied by dabbing (or pouncing) the bag over the openings of the perforated stencil. This action dislodges a fine dust through the mesh of the bag, which sifts through the pattern holes onto the working surface. Guide lines produced by this technique are easily removed once the artwork is completed.

Chalk, charcoal, and pastel, in their powdered forms, may all be used as pounce powders.

Common Difficulty

Obliteration. Working over a design that has been transferred by the pounce method is not easy. The fine dust is wiped away by a touch. It is usually essential to use some form of hand rest.

POUNCE WHEELS

A small wheel with sharp points used to punch holes in paper through which powder may be forced. The process, called pouncing, is used to transfer designs from a paper layout to any material. (See *Perforating Wheels.*)

PRESS, MOUNTING

A pressure and heat device for permanently bonding paper surfaces using a separate adhesive sheet. (See *Dry Mount.*)

PRESSURE GRAPHICS

Term that refers to the entire category of typographic fonts, symbols, tints, colors, and other graphic devices produced on sheets with self-contained adhesive backing. They are applied by rubbing. (See *Transfer Type, Overlays, Tinted Acetate.*)

PRESTYPE

A brand name for a transfer type of the rub-off variety. Since it was one of the original products of this nature, the name is often used in the generic sense. (See *Transfer Type.*)

PRINTING INKS

Inks that are produced for, and distributed to, commercial printing firms for use on their presses. (See *Inks, Printing.*)

PROGRESSIVE PROOFS

In the printing industry there is a great necessity to proof, or test, the quality as the job progresses, particularly before the actual press run begins. Corrections or revisions after this point are excessively expensive. Simple two-color jobs can be easily checked by blueprints, but four-color process printing is another matter. There is only one adequate way to be certain of the quality, and that is to make the plates and try them out. First, each plate is inked and proofed by itself. Then the plates are proofed in sequence, in the order of the actual press run, adding a plate for each step. For instance, the yellow and magenta (red) plates are printed together; then the yellow, magenta, and cyan (blue) plates are printed together; and finally, all four plates—yellow, magenta, blue, and black—are printed. In this manner the printer can see what the final job will look like, and if there are errors or revisions necessary, can find out at which step and on which plate the alterations must be made. These proof sheets—seven in all, the four individual colors plus the yellow/magenta, yellow/magenta/cyan, and the yellow/magenta/cyan/black—are referred to as progressive proofs or progs.

It takes a highly skilled craftsperson to read these progressives, but there are things that you can discern very quickly. As a commercial artist, you will be called upon to evaluate them. Looking only at the last sheet, you can check to see what the final impression looks like. Skin tones and product colors should be reasonably accurate, remembering that commercial printing can rarely come within 25% of actually matching the original. And the image should not be fuzzy. Often errors in these areas can be corrected easily with minor adjustments in the actual press run, particularly if you call them to the attention of the printer. But others may cause considerable trouble. Remembering the limitations of the medium, you cannot have your cake and eat it too. If the faces are too red, you can lighten the red, but this may make the product color look wrong, etc. It's much like trying to tune a color television set. There are limits to what can be done. If you insist on too many finicky adjustments, you may force the printer into extensive revisions or even new plates. This costs money and someone must pay.

Even the progressives are expensive to make, and many printers are trying to avoid this step on less important jobs. One of the more successful ways they have at their disposal is the 3M color-key-proof. The 3M Company, manufacturers of Scotch brand products, has invented a system of producing proofs on transparent plastic sheets in the actual colors of the plates. The method is similar to the blueprint in that the plate *negatives* are used with sensitized sheet of plastic. When the sheet is developed the plastic remains clear, and the image appears in one of the four process colors. By exposing all four process negatives with their corresponding 3M color key film, a set of proofs is produced that replaces the first step of the progressive proofs. But these proofs are transparent, and stacking them in sequence allows you to see all four colors at once, just as you would with progressive printing.

There are limitations to this process, however. The thickness of the plastic sheet distorts the color to some extent, there can be slight differences in size caused by the developing that prevent perfect register and impart a soft fuzziness to the final image, and the colors themselves are not quite the same as inks printed on paper. These are all very small aberrations, though, and the process has found a great deal of acceptance on lower budget jobs.

PROJECTOR, ART

A term that applies to any of a number of devices used to enlarge or reduce an image and project it upon a glass surface within the device (to rescale research material), or upon an independent screen (to present graphic material to an audience as well). (See *Opaque Projector, Camera Lucida,* and *Lacey Luci.*)

PROJECTORS, OVERHEAD

Devices that project light through transparent graphics, against an angled mirror, and onto a screen or other surface. Used for business meetings and lectures, overhead projectors permit the use of rapidly prepared art work in a large and convenient format, which does not need extensive photographic reproduction. The machines and materials necessary for overhead projection are specialized, since their use is limited. Art supply stores usually do not stock projectors, since business organizations tend to deal directly with the manufacturers. However, the associated graphic processes and procedures are very simple and can be mastered quickly on the job.

PROPORTIONAL DIVIDER

An X-shaped device, the legs of which are marked with a scale and joined by a movable set screw. The opening between one pair of legs will be proportional to the opening in the other legs. For instance, an opening of one inch between one pair of legs, with the scale set at two, will produce an opening in the other legs of two inches.

For another example, let us assume that you have drawn a layout sketch of a figure, but it is too small for the finished art—the sketch is 3⅜″ high and the final must be 9¼″ high. Adjust the legs of the proportional divider until one pair is 3⅜″ apart and the other pair is 9¼″ apart. As long as the point where the legs join is kept constant, any movement of the legs will always remain in the same proportion and you may transfer any dimension from the sketch directly to the finished rendering.

However, this procedure is slow at best. Most commercial artists use photostats or enlargers which allow you to see the full sketch in its new dimensions all at once. (See *Lacey Luci.*)

PROPORTIONAL SCALE

A device for obtaining accurate dimensional ratios. These devices come in the form of slide rules or movable disks (called "scaling wheels"). In either form, setting the scale to a known ratio will permit you to read off the correct figures for any unknown dimension. For instance, if you have a piece of artwork that is 5″ x 7″, and you wish to enlarge it one and one-half times, set the scale to 150% and the readings opposite the five will be seven and one-half, and opposite the seven will be ten and one-half. In fact, at any point on the scale, the figure opposite a number will be one and one-half times the original figure. In a like manner, any other ratio may be established.

Conversely, these scales may also be used to determine percentages. When both figures are known, but not the percentage, reverse the procedure. Setting the numbers nine and twelve opposite each other will cause the percentage scale to register either 75% or 133⅓% depending on which number is set first. This illustrates the most common confusion with these devices. Always establish a regular habit—set the original figure first, the new figure second, and you

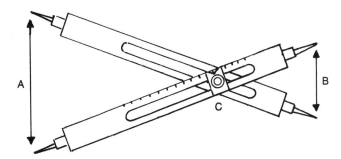

Proportional divider. Once the ratio has been set at C, no matter how the legs are spread, A and B will always be in proportion to each other in that same ratio.

will avoid this confusion. Thus, if twelve is the original .number, nine is 75% of twelve. If nine is the original number, twelve is 133⅓% of nine.

These scales need not be expensive and they are available at all art stores.

PROTECTIVE COVERINGS

Artwork, models, and package dummies frequently require protection from handling. The most common methods are to spray them with fixatives or cover them with plastic films. (See *Fixatives* and *Plastic Films.*)

PROTRACTORS

Templates that divide a half circle into 180°. While simple and easy to use, the protractor is more effective when incorporated in a protractor angle or with a drafting machine.

Protractors are used when lines at definite angles must be drawn, as in the construction of geometric shapes—an accurate five-pointed star, for instance. Draw a circle and divide its circumference into five equal parts. In other words, divide 360° by five. The answer is 72°. With a protractor it is easy to mark five points on the circle, each 72° from the next, and connect the points to form a star.

PUSHPIN

The commercial artist's thumbtack. The difference is the pushpin's head, which

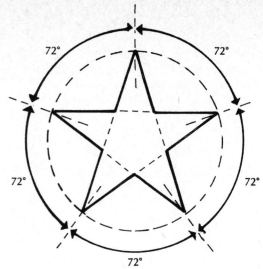

A five-pointed star created by using a protractor.

A pushpin.

is a long, cylindrical shank, rather than the thumbtack's flat head. Although the height of this shank makes it impossible to slide a T-square or triangle over a pushpin, as you can over a thumbtack, the shank is easily gripped and thus makes it simpler to remove without damaging the item being held.

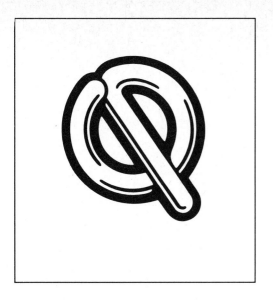

QUADRILLE PAPER

A light bond paper upon which has been printed a grid of light blue lines. The size of the grid may vary from ⅛″ to ½″, and differs from cross section and graph papers in that none of the grid lines are accented. Used to prepare graphs, charts, etc., and to assemble paste-ups where the light blue lines act as a guide for proper alignment, but will not be picked up by the reproduction camera. (See *Papers and Boards*.)

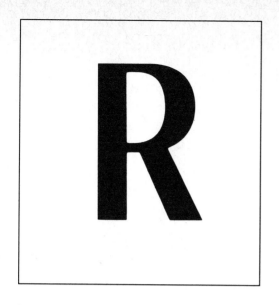

RAPIDOGRAPH

A brand name for a series of drawing pens of both hollow-point and ball-point design. Available at all art stores, the pens may be purchased individually and in sets. The hollow-point pens are made to resemble fountain pens and come in single holder/interchangeable nib style. These pens are excellent for ruling, particularly with templates and curves. Some are designed for use specifically with India ink. (See *Pens.*)

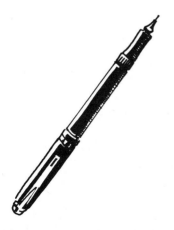

The fountain pen style of the Rapidograph pen.

RAZOR BLADES

The most commonly used commercial artist's cutting tool. Unlike razor blades used for shaving, these industrial blades have only one cutting edge, and the opposite side of the blade is protected with a heavier flange of metal that makes them safe and easy to handle. These blades are inexpensive and may be replaced as often as the cutting edge dulls. Contrary to expectations, paper and cardboard dull a blade very quickly. Knives must be constantly resharpened or the blades replaced and they are much more expensive than razor blades, factors which make razor blades more popular.

Many artists use the razor blade instead of tweezers for moving paste-up material. The point of the blade's edge is inserted lightly into the paper, providing a grip that is sufficient to make the small moves necessary for such a technique. The fine edge is also excellent for slipping under paper while lifting. The thumb is pressed against the side of the blade to grip the paper. An old coffee can is usually provided in an art studio for discarded razor blades. Remember, people must handle the trash, and such a blade can be dangerous if thrown into an ordinary waste basket.

Common Difficulties

Nicking. The razor blade is relatively flexible and may bend into the edge of a straight-edge while the cut is being made. This will cut or nick the edge of the blade and of the straight-edge, destroying the accuracy of both. Try not to

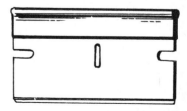

Common, commercial razor blade with single cutting edge.

use good drawing equipment as an edge for cutting. Also, while making the cut, keep the edge of the blade low, as nearly parallel to the paper as possible. This reduces the drag of cutting and tends to prevent the bending that produces nicks.

Breakage. The edges of razor blades are fragile and any lateral pressure while cutting may snap the tip of the blade. Keeping the blade low will help to reduce this error. Once the blade is broken, throw the blade away. New blades are too cheap to make it worthwhile saving a damaged one.

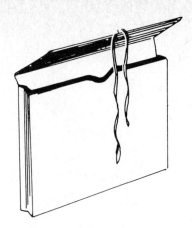

Red rope envelope with string ties.

RED ROPE ENVELOPES

An inexpensive catch-all container for artists. Composed of a simple, expandable envelope of durable construction, the red rope envelope gets its name from the distinguishing red string, stapled to the flap, with which the envelope is secured. This envelope is extremely handy for storing materials and artwork in the studio and for carrying artwork on deliveries, and is available in sizes from 9″ × 12″ to 20″ × 26″.

REDUCING GLASSES

These are more essential than magnifying glasses, regardless of your eyesight. Commercial artists often must work larger than the size of the finished printing. For this reason, you may wish to check as you proceed to make sure that the detail will "hold up" in the final reduction. Since the reducing glass is only used for a moment at a time, there is no need for any fancy mount or case.

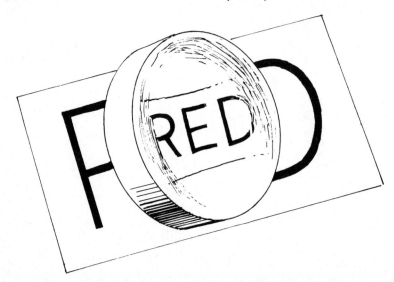

An unmounted reducing glass. These lenses also come with frames for easier holding.

REGISTER MARK

A circled cross used by printers and plate-makers to ensure the proper registration (position) of art throughout the reproduction process. It is necessary for artists preparing mechanicals to provide these registration marks whenever a separation overlay is used. Although these marks may be drawn by artists, the frequency of their use and the high degree of accuracy needed make the already prepared register marks invaluable.

Printed at frequent intervals on a roll of transparent plastic tape, the prepared register mark permits easy and accurate placement on the artwork. These prepared rolls usually come in a metal tin which keeps the tape clean and undamaged when not in use.

An alternative is Double Cross, a transfer typelike mark consisting of two complementary shapes printed on opposite sides of a single plastic sheet with adhesive backing. The sheet is adhered to the base plate and rubbing pressure is applied to the top of the overlay over the mark. The portion of the mark on the top of the sheet is transferred to the back of the overlay in perfect register.

The procedure is easier than trying to affix two separate marks to separate (and movable) layers. However, the part of the compound mark on the underside of the overlay is as fragile as transfer type and can be damaged.

Common Difficulty

Tearing. Like most plastic tapes, the free end of the register mark roll has a tendency to adhere firmly and invisibly to the roll. Trying to discover and undo this end often leads to tearing the tape, an annoying process at best. Since you may lose several marks before the tape is free, it is recommended that you turn under the unmarked portion of this end, adhering it to itself, after completing a job. This practice will assure the easy opening of the roll and prevent time loss and waste.

RETOUCHING COLORS

Retouching photographs and transparencies requires special paints and dyes that are compatible with photographic papers and films. They are not to be

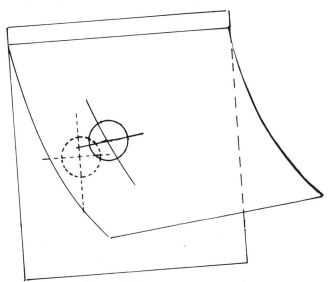

Register marks, here mounted on both base copy and overlay to assure proper positioning.

confused with photographic coloring kits, which are used to tint black-and-white prints. Photo retouching requires the correction or modification of the original subject and must not be distinguishable from the rest of the photo. Black-and-white prints are retouched with opaque paints that are sold in sets of graduated grays, which may be applied with brush or airbrush. Color retouching is more complex and usually requires transparent dyes which resemble those of photographic emulsions. Color retouching often requires bleaching the errors before adding new color. Whether on color prints or transparent film, this procedure requires expert knowledge and practice, particularly with the airbrush. The colors, bleaches, and other chemicals needed to prepare or fix the surface are sold at most art stores with instructions.

RICE PAPER

Product of the Orient, where it is the standard for all kinds of art and printing. There are many distinctive patterns in these fine, hand-made papers, and most art stores will carry at least a few of them. They cannot be described, but must be seen—with their subtle textures and handsome deckled edges. These papers are meant to be used with watercolor paints and will take many dry media as well. Although they have a limited use in commercial art for booklets, presentations, and displays, rice papers are highly prized by artists and illustrators as a beautiful ground. (See *Papers and Boards.*)

ROSS BOARD

A heavy bristol board with a pebbled surface that produces a line technique when worked on with a dry medium such as crayon or pencil. This allows the artist to produce a halftone drawing with full shading effects which can be reproduced directly and inexpensively as line art.

Available in several sizes and textural patterns. (See *Papers and Boards.*)

ROTO TRAY

The artist's version of the Lazy Susan. Made of plastic and mounted on a swivel base, the roto tray permits you to store a considerable number of pencils, brushes, pens, etc., in upright holes. There are also a number of trays in the base, in which you can store any manner of art supplies.

The roto tray provides a convenient method of keeping your tools clean and undamaged, close to your work and instantly available. About ten inches in diameter, it provides a large amount of storage area without taking up too much of your working space.

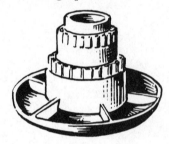

Roto tray with opening for tools and trays in the base.

ROULETTES

A small wheel with sharp points used to punch holes in paper through which powder may be forced. The process, called pouncing, is used to transfer designs from a paper layout to any material. (See *Perforating Wheels.*)

RUBBER CEMENT

A liquefied rubber adhesive, equally effective for temporary or permanent bonds. Since rubber cement does not stain and may be removed easily without damaging the surface of the paper, it has become the primary adhesive for all commercial artwork.

Rubber cement may be used with any art material that must be adhered to any other surface. Rubber cement thinner is used to dilute rubber cement to a proper working consistency and to separate items that have been rubber cemented together. Since both the cement and the thinner are extremely volatile and evaporate rapidly, they work best when applied from small, closed containers. An adequate reserve for refilling these containers may be maintained in proper condition in large cans, since these cans will not be opened so often. (See *Rubber Cement Dispenser* and *Rubber Cement Thinner Dispenser.*)

Excess rubber cement is removed by wiping it away with a rubber cement pickup, once the cement has been allowed to dry.

The main purpose of any adhesive is to stick two items together. In commercial art, most adhesive problems are handled best with rubber cement. In particular, rubber cement's ability to effect a temporary bond makes it ideal for preparing friskets. And the fact that it can be removed from a surface enables rubber cement to be used directly as a frisket, itself.

Apply the cement thickly with the dispenser brush where you wish the surface to remain clear. After the pigment has been applied, let it dry thoroughly, and remove the cement. Do this by rubbing your finger lightly over an edge of the cement towards the center. This will roll up a small accumulation of cement which may now be picked up with your fingers. If you lift slowly and carefully, all the cement will come away in one piece, carrying the unwanted pigment with it. If you move too quickly, the dried pigment will flake away or the cement will tear. In either case, you will then have to try to remove the pigment carefully so that it does not mark the clear area.

When adhering two surfaces, first make sure that both are clean; then coat each surface with rubber cement and allow to dry. The rubber cement should flow freely without being too thin. If it has become too thick, add rubber cement thinner. If it is too thin, add more rubber cement or let the container remain open until the cement thickens by evaporation.

Apply the rubber cement with a brush. The best type of brush is the one that comes with the rubber cement dispenser. Spread the cement evenly and do not let any dirt settle on it while it is drying.

When the rubber cement on both surfaces is thoroughly dry, carefully position the item to be adhered. Do not press. A small amount of movement is possible until the two items are pressed firmly together. This movement allows for minor corrections of position. Make these corrections by moving the surface to be adhered with the point of a razor blade or with a pair of tweezers.

If the pieces being cemented are very large or difficult to handle, place a slip sheet between the pieces after they are thoroughly dry. Any light piece of paper will serve as a slip sheet, and the dry rubber cement will not stick to it. Place this sheet on one of the cemented surfaces so that about ⅛″ of cemented area is exposed. Now the piece to be adhered may be placed over the slip sheet and adjusted without adhering to more than the exposed ⅛″. This small bond is readily shifted without destroying the adhesiveness of the two pieces.

When the accurate position has been attained, press the cemented ⅛″ surfaces firmly together. This will prevent the two pieces from shifting when the slip sheet is drawn out. Remove the slip sheet *gradually;* as you withdraw the slip sheet, stop often to smooth out the adhering surfaces and press them together, a few inches at a time.

When the slip sheet is fully removed, place it on top of the two cemented pieces. Take a triangle; with one edge flat on the paper, draw the triangle firmly from the center to the edges until the entire area has been smoothly pressed down. The bond is now complete.

If an error of placement has been made, you can separate the two pieces by wetting them thoroughly with rubber cement thinner. Using your finger, a tweezer, a razor blade, or knife point, gently lift one corner. Squirt thinner from an oil can or a dispenser on the cement between the pieces. Keep applying the thinner between the two pieces as you peel them apart. Let all surfaces dry completely and repeat the adhering process.

Any excess rubber cement, on either piece, may now be removed with a rubber cement pick-up.

Rubber cement can also be an effective resist frisket. Merely apply the cement to the surface, let dry, and proceed with your painting. Let the paint dry and then remove the cement with a pick-up, revealing the surface beneath. You can achieve a great many different effects by the manner in which you apply the cement. Try dribbling it directly from the dispenser brush or by dry brushing.

Rubber cement dries rapidly and should be stored in a container that can be tightly sealed. If this is impossible, or if constant usage keeps the cover off, the cement will thicken. Check the consistency before using, and add enough rubber cement thinner to allow the cement to flow freely. Practice will tell you what the best mixture is.

Common Difficulties

Weak bond. If rubber cement is too thin, it will not hold properly. Try applying a second coat of cement. However, if cement has been thinned too often, it will lose much of its adhering ability. Either throw out this batch and start fresh, or, if your container is big enough, add an equal amount of fresh cement. This mixture may now be diluted without losing effectiveness. If a piece has been lifted

with the thinner several times, the same weakening will occur. Clean off the old cement with a pick-up and apply a new coat of cement.

Discoloration. Although rubber cement will not stain, it will *itself* turn yellow with age. If it has been applied properly and the bond has been made firmly, rubber cement will last for years. But some papers and other materials are so porous that air can still get at the cement, and then discoloration will occur. Remove the old cement with a pick-up or with thinner and apply new cement. The discoloration is only in the cement itself; the paper will be untouched. Some discoloration will be noticed if the pieces are bonded while the cement is still wet. This is not really a change of color, but merely the wetness of the paper. If left long enough, the cement will eventually dry and the discoloration will disappear. If it does not, lift the pieces apart, using thinner to separate the dry parts. Let everything dry thoroughly and press together again.

Bubbling. Under certain temperature conditions, air bubbles will form on a layer of cement while it is drying. These bubbles can prevent a smooth bond or cause lumps. If the bubbles do not disappear by themselves, place a little thinner on them and smooth them out.

Lumps. It is often impossible to avoid working on a surface after it has been coated with cement, in preparation for a future operation. This additional work can cause bits of dirt, or even beads of dried cement to collect on the surface. These will cause lumps in the final bond. Try to protect the surface while you are working by covering cement coated parts with a sheet of paper. Inspect the surface carefully before adhering any new item. If you discover potential lumps, remove them with a pick-up, moisten the surface with thinner, and smooth out.

Stains. Although rubber cement will not stain, it can cause a slight darkening of certain prepared surfaces, like Color-Aid or Colorama papers. This darkening cannot be removed; for all practical purposes, it may be considered a stain. Since there is no correction, the best procedure is to cover the entire surface with rubber cement and then remove the cement with a pick-up. This at least equalizes the effect by making the discoloration uniform. If some mottling still remains, spray the entire surface with fixative. Once again, this darkens the color and tends to hide any defects.

Impermanence. Other than imperfectly applied cement, two things will cause rubber-cemented bonds to fail. The first is age. Time and the presence of certain chemicals in paper, photostats, and photographs will cause the cement to harden and become brittle. But even under these conditions, rubber cement should last for at least a year or two. The other condition is heat. Not only does heat make the cement dry and brittle, but it causes the pasted pieces to wrinkle and curl. The pressure of this curling helps to force the bonded pieces apart. Whenever a paste-up job must be subjected to heat, use another adhesive. (See *Adhesives.*) And remember that the sun is one of the greatest sources of heat. Window displays are particularly vulnerable. In the sun, rubber cement is lucky to hold for a week before the edges start to curl and peel away.

RUBBER CEMENT DISPENSER

When rubber cement is purchased in small quantities, it generally comes in a can with a brush attached inside the cover. This brush is usually small and very inadequate for commercial work. Therefore, all commercial artists buy rubber cement in large gallon cans and use a rubber cement dispenser.

There are several kinds of dispensers; the type of work you are doing will determine which dispenser is best suited for you. Art studios and bullpens use an open can with a cone-shaped cover that sits loosely on top. This arrangement does not seal the can completely and does permit evaporation. However, the dispenser is in constant use in these shops, and the cement does not get a chance to dry out and harden. Even so, it is common practice for most studio personnel to start their day by adding thinner to the cement to return it to its best consistency.

A separate brush is used with the open dispenser: a large, flat brush, very soft and capable of covering large surfaces quickly and easily. It is by far the best tool for applying rubber cement. The brush does not sit in the rubber cement can, but rests on the edges; some of the cans have a wire across the top for this purpose. Again, constant use prevents the brush from drying and becoming unusable.

The most common dispenser is a glass or plastic jar with a screw cover and a brush whose handle goes through the cover. The brush may be adjusted so that it reaches down into the liquid cement to any desired level and does not become overloaded with cement. This brush is usually of average quality and is only an inch or so thick. However, it is adequate for most purposes, except when large surfaces must be covered. Since the cover can be tightly closed, there is little evaporation or hardening. For this reason, the screw cover jar is the most practical dispenser for most artists.

A plastic jar, with the same screw cover and adjustable brush, is available. This plastic jar has the added virtue of being unbreakable. Once you have tried to clean up a broken rubber cement jar, you will realize the value of having one that will not break.

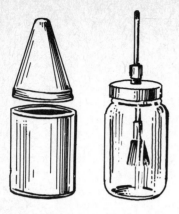

(Left) Rubber cement dispenser with a cone-shaped cover, which fits over brush and helps prevent evaporation. (Right) Rubber cement dispenser with applicator brush attached to the cover.

Common Difficulties

Hardened cement. Even in covered jars, some evaporation will take place, particularly if the level of the cement is kept low. A small residue of thickened cement will accumulate in the bottom of the jar. This residue does not thin out well and is useless. Dirt, brush hairs, and scraps of paper (that drop off the brush) will get mixed into this sediment and will eventually become a nuisance. Dried cement will also build up on the sides and lips of the jar top, making it difficult to move the brush in and out of the jar. When these conditions become too annoying, remove the usable cement by pouring it back into the can. Allow the open jar to sit upside down for a few hours until all the remaining cement has drained out or hardened. While this drying out is going on, keep the brush submerged in rubber cement thinner to clean it and keep it from hardening. When the cement in the jar is dry, it can be stripped out of the jar in much the same manner as you would remove cement from paper. The bottom of the jar may be hard to reach; use the end of a paintbrush or any convenient stick. Once the cement has begun to adhere to the stick, it will work

the same as a pick-up and will remove all of the dried cement.

Dropped brush. On the adjustable brushes, the head of the brush is screwed onto the handle. Normal use of the brush may cause this handle to become unscrewed and the brush will fall off, usually into the cement itself. It is not difficult, but extremely messy and annoying to fish out the brush, screw it back on, and return to work. Nothing will make this operation any easier. Therefore, while you are working, get into the habit of checking the brush frequently to make sure that it is screwed on tightly. Lay the brush on a piece of paper and twist the handle clockwise as hard as you can. If you will do this occasionally, the brush will never come loose.

RUBBER CEMENT THINNER DISPENSER

The thinner dispenser, or "oil can" to the trade, is just that, any long spouted oil can with a removable top that can be filled with thinner and used for applying the solvent in small amounts, exactly where needed. No other method has been found which does the job as well as squirting through a spout. Thinner is extremely volatile and has a capillary action that makes it difficult to pour or brush with any control. An oil can, however, cannot be sealed and the thinner will evaporate quite rapidly from the can. In busy studios, where the thinner is in constant use, this is not a problem. But if your use for thinner is limited, a specially designed thinner dispenser is available at art stores; this has a screw closing on the tip of the spout to close the can and prevent evaporation.

Common Difficulty

Spilling. The opening in an oil can is always small and it is next to impossible to pour thinner into it without spilling. No matter how neat and careful you are, the capillary action of thinner makes the simple act of pouring quite wasteful. Get yourself a small funnel; most hardware stores have a range of sizes, and you should be able to find one that will fit into the oil can opening. If not, get a plastic one that comes reasonably close and soak it in the thinner for a few minutes. This will usually soften the plastic enough so that you may force the tip of the funnel into the opening with a screwing motion. In this way, you will probably "cut threads" on the funnel so that it will attach perfectly in the future. To fill the can, pour a small amount of thinner into the funnel and let it settle completely. Shake the oil can to complete the settling. Continue to pour in small, quick spurts, and there will be no spill or leakage. If a funnel is not available, take a sheet of bond paper and roll it into a cone. Make sure that the paper is large enough so that the sides of the cone are several layers thick. Hold the cone in shape with tape or paper clips, and cut off the tip so that a small hole is made. This will serve as a temporary funnel. Again, pour carefully in quick, small amounts. Some thinner will leak from this makeshift arrangement but with practice you will find that you will not lose too much.

RUBDOWN TYPE

Descriptive term referring to a method of applying the majority of transfer types. Despite the accuracy of this term, and its easy-to-remember brevity, most transfer types are called by their brand names, particularly the popular ones. (See *Transfer Type.*)

RUB-OFF TYPE

A term used to describe a form of transfer type in which the individual characters, composed of solid ink adhered lightly to a plastic sheet, are transferred by means of a rubbing pressure which causes an adhesive on the back of the ink characters to bond to the surface of the art—freeing the character from the plastic sheet. (See *Transfer Type.*)

RUBYLITH

A darkly translucent, deep-red plastic film bonded to a sheet of acetate that is used to prepare overlays for color separation mechanicals.

To use, a full-sized sheet is taped to the mechanical board and registered with registration marks. The desired shapes are accurately (but lightly) scored with a sharp blade and the unwanted material is peeled away, leaving clear acetate. Since both the red and amber photograph as black in the copy film, the shapes act as masks for photographic copy and tint or color panels.

The virtue of these films is the extreme accuracy they provide. The cutting blade is narrower than any pen line, and cannot blot or smudge. Corners are clean and trim without any pen line overextension. Only the unwanted material is touched, and that is simply removed without leaving any residue to attract dirt or require additional clean up.

Common Difficulties

Confusion. The bonding is so firm and the film is so shiny that it is hard to discern which side is the film and is the proper side on which to work. Try scraping each side at the extreme edge of a sheet before beginning the mechanical.

Control. It is difficult to cut the film without scoring or slicing the base sheet. Such marks can destroy the sheet, as they expand quickly with any handling. This damage cannot be repaired easily, although small cuts can be stopped with a piece of Scotch tape on the reverse side. This kind of patching is extremely visible, however, and looks unprofessional. It is better to begin with a new sheet. Use a sharp blade and a very gentle stroke. Never repeat a stroke in the same area. Practice on a scrap before final work is attempted.

Fragility. Once the film has been lifted from the acetate base, it cannot be reattached. Great care and practice is necessary to trim this film without damaging corners and fragile shapes. Obviously, this makes mistakes very costly, since an error requires the use of a fresh sheet. Minor errors, such as a loose corner of a large shape, can be repaired. Apply a little very clean, thin rubber cement. Let both surfaces dry completely and press the corner down firmly with a slip sheet. Clean the excess rubber cement with a pick up, being careful to use gentle strokes that move away from the shape. Don't overdo it. Excessive rubbing will tear the fragile film. (See also *Amberlith.*)

RULERS

A ruler is a straight-edge with a measuring scale on one or more of the edges. There is a wide range of rulers in terms of sizes, materials, and scales available. The most common is the wooden ruler with a metal ferrule; this ruler is usually divided into sixteenths of an inch. This type of ruler is not particularly satisfactory for commercial artists. Wood is not a durable material; it swells or shrinks considerably. The metal ferrule is easily dislodged and does not retain its accuracy as a straight-edge for any length of time. The width of this metal ferrule makes it difficult to make a measurement precisely at the mark, which is on the wood, not on the metal. Therefore, most artists use a metal or plastic ruler.

This still leaves a considerable choice, largely because of the number of different scales (systems of measurement). The artist must work with many other professions that have their own systems of measurement, and these systems will determine the ruler used. Many rulers combine several of these systems, having a number of scales marked on all edges of all sides.

Inch ruler. Most rulers will have normal inch divisions, regardless of what other measurements they have. Whether you use a six, twelve, or thirty-six inch ruler will depend on the size of the job you are doing. The thirty-six inch ruler, of course, is the common yardstick, although you *should* use a metal one. These rulers can come with divisions as small as $\frac{1}{64}''$. Such accuracy is not particularly useful for artists. The normal $\frac{1}{16}''$ division is usually sufficient.

Pica ruler. Printers and typographers measure in picas. There are approximately six picas to the inch, and it is possible to estimate pica measurements quite closely, using a regular inch scale. However, it is wise to use a pica scale directly, if you do much business with type or printing. The pica scale is broken down into half picas, which are about $\frac{1}{12}''$.

Point ruler. The point is the smallest division of the pica. There are twelve points to a pica, or about seventy-two points to an inch. This $\frac{1}{72}''$ is too small to be marked clearly on any scale. For this reason, there is no true point ruler. Instead, common point sizes of type are grouped into individual scales. For instance, machine-set type is available in just a few sizes, usually six to twelve point. Since twelve points are a pica, and six points are half a pica, these sizes can be measured directly with a pica ruler. Only the eight and ten point scales need to be added to this kind of ruler. Typographers have a more complete ruler that also includes the odd sizes: seven, nine, and eleven point.

It should be noted that the point size of type measures not the height of the *type,* but the height of the *metal* on which the individual letter sits. Therefore, these point scales measure the distance from the bottom of one line of type to the bottom of the next line of type.

Agate ruler. Newspapers measure the depth of an ad in terms of agate lines; hence the term, advertising linage. There are fourteen agate lines to an inch. This measurement cannot be approximated by any method other than the agate scale. However, agate lines are included on many point and pica rulers.

Architect's scale. The architect's scale is prism-shaped; that is, it has three sides excluding the ends. By using both edges along each of the three sides, there is space for a number of different scale markings. One edge is used for the normal handling of a twelve-inch ruler. The remaining five edges each have two separate scales. This means that there are eleven separate scales provided on the architects' scale. These extra scales are all divided into specific units of standard measure ($\frac{1}{16}''$, $\frac{1}{8}''$, $\frac{1}{4}''$, $\frac{1}{2}''$, etc.), and each scale provides a different proportion. Therefore, one scale may be composed of divisions actually measuring $\frac{1}{4}''$, but this $\frac{1}{4}''$ is marked with the same divisions of a normal one foot ruler. Any drawing done with this scale will produce a final rendering which is in the ratio of $\frac{1}{4}''$ equalling one foot. Again, using the three-inch scale will produce a drawing that is a quarter size, since three inches equals $\frac{1}{4}'$. These scales can be very valuable in doing renderings of large objects, such as cars, planes, buildings, etc.

Engineer's scale. The engineer's scale is prism-shaped, like the architect's scale, with the same six surfaces and eleven proportional scales. However, each of these scales has been divided into tenths of an inch. Since our system of mathe-

matics produces decimal answers to division, the engineer's scale can be extremely useful to the artist. Say you have a space seven inches wide and you would like to divide it into five equal parts. The answer to this division is 1.4″. There is no way to translate this decimal number accurately and simply into sixteenths or thirty-seconds of an inch. But with the engineers' scale, the answer may be read directly: $\frac{4}{10}''$ is four units on the engineer's scale.

One added virtue of the prismatic architect's and engineer's scales is that the markings do not begin at the end of the ruler, but slightly in from the end. All rulers—plastic, wood, or metal—are easily damaged, particularly the ends. Starting the measurements in from the end prevents minor damage from destroying the accuracy and usefulness of a ruler. With rulers that lack this feature, many people allow for this inaccuracy by starting to measure from the one-inch mark. This is effective, but there is always the danger that you will forget to subtract that one inch from your final reading. Even if you do not use prism-shaped rulers, try to find a ruler that has the added safety margin at the ends.

Good rulers are expensive. Choose only the best and take care of them. There is always the tendency to use the ruler for all manner of drawing and cutting jobs. Used with care, rulers will serve these purposes well. But they do become damaged, and an inaccurate ruler is worse than none at all.

Before spending a lot of money to acquire a series of rulers in all sizes and scales, check with your local suppliers:

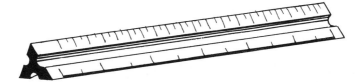

Pyramidal ruler with scales on all six edges.

printers, typographers, newspapers, and anyone else who might be interested in gaining your business. Many of these organizations have rulers of excellent quality, which they distribute free for advertising purposes.

RULING PEN

A device for producing lines of controlled width. The pen is constructed with two steel nibs; color flows between the nibs and the distance between the nibs can be adjusted to vary the line. The ruling pen will work equally well with any medium—ink, fluid paint, etc.—that flows with comparative ease. The ruling pen is not flexible; it is a mechanical tool that must be set in advance, but which will draw constant lines that range from very fine to very broad.

Designed primarily as a drafting tool, the ruling pen is used mainly with India ink. However, the commercial artist will find that paints, dyes, and watercolors will work just as well. The paper used may also vary considerably. Only a few substances—like newsprint paper, which blots easily, or acetate, which has a totally nonabsorbent surface—are difficult materials on which to work.

Commercial artists use ruling pens for finished art or comprehensive layouts where the quality of line must be perfectly exact. This tool is indispensable for the production of mechanicals in which accuracy and fine detail are imperative. The pen has also become an interesting tool in the hands of experimental artists and letterers; used on its side, instead of in the normal manner, it creates a line of delicacy and charm, both in line drawing and in script lettering. There is no way to describe the manner of doing this. Individuals must try for themselves and discover the many effects that are possible.

Always be sure that the ruling pen is clean, that the nibs are sharp, and that they are of equal length and shape. Pre-

pare a sufficient amount of the drawing medium you are using, testing first to make sure that it is the right consistency. When using ink that has become old, add a drop or two of common household ammonia to make it flow smoothly; this also prevents drying and clogging in the pen.

Prepare your working surface so that it is free from dirt or grease that will interrupt the lines. Make sure that your pen is guided by good straight-edges or curves that have no nicks or obstructions that will hinder the free movement of the pen. Prepare your preliminary drawing lightly but adequately in pencil, so that you will not be in doubt about where you are working once you start a line.

Fill the ruling pen so that the fluid stands no higher than about ¼″ between the nibs. Do not dip the pen into the liquid color; fill the nibs with a brush, eye dropper, or the dropper device that is built into many ink bottle caps. Too much fluid will often cause the pen to blot once it has started to flow. Note that mediums like India ink tend to dry rapidly when exposed to the air; they will clog the pen if they are not used quickly.

Hold the pen lightly but firmly, keeping the pen upright, but leaning slightly in the direction in which you are drawing; thus, you will *pull* the pen, not push it. Be sure that the angle you assume with the pen can be maintained. Dropping the angle of the pen, leaning it into or away from the ruling edge, will disrupt the constant flow of ink and create an uneven line. Place the pen lightly on the paper and begin to rule as quickly as possible. Heavy pressure, or holding the pen in one spot too long, may cause it to blot. Rule with constant speed and pressure to insure an even line. Know where you intend to stop the line so that you may do so quickly and smoothly, again to prevent blotting. Since the nibs are sharp metal, do not press them too hard or they will cut the paper.

Clean the pen frequently while you

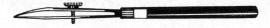

Ruling pen. The blades are positioned by turning the screw.

work with a pen wiper, chamois or cloth. Keep your mediums well mixed and at a proper consistency.

Always keep the points of the nibs clear of the ruling edge. If this edge does not have a ferrule or a bevel on the bottom, place something under the edge to lift it off the paper. Many artists tape coins on the bottom of T-squares and angles that they use frequently for inking. This prevents the ink at the point of the nibs from coming into contact with the straight-edge. Since the ruling pen is fed by gravity, once the ink starts to flow in contact with the straight-edge it will run under the edge and cause a blot.

Always ink curved lines first. It is much easier to connect a straight line to a previously drawn curved one than the other way around. Make sure that you allow time for the ink to dry before working again in the same area. Be careful when you lift your ruling edge from the paper; the straight-edge may slide into a wet ink line and smudge it.

When you must draw with different color inks that touch or cross each other, work with the dark colors first. Inks tend to run and bleed very easily. As a new line is drawn, the ink will run into the existing line and discolor it. If the dark lines are inked first, later discoloration will not show. However, this tendency to run may cause the ink to get under the straight-edge again and smudge. Take *extra* care that the nib is far from the ruling edge, so that the ink does not get near the edge.

Paint, fortunately, does not present any of these difficulties. However, paint must be cleaned out of the pen more often as paint clogs more easily. Dyes react much the same as inks.

Like all mechanical tools, the ruling pen must be kept clean to function well. If the pen is of reasonable quality, the tool will require little care. So that it will not rust, wipe it after each use. A very light film of any oil or vaseline will protect metal surfaces and help the ink or paint to flow freely. Simply wipe the metal with a rag moistened with oil. To prevent smearing oil on your work every time you handle the pen, wipe it thoroughly with a clean cloth after oiling. The pen will feel completely dry, but will retain enough oil in it to insure protection.

In the event that the nibs become damaged through excessive use, or by dropping, they may be repaired. Open the nibs as wide as they will go. Place the inside (flat side) of the nib on a fine abrasive stone. If the opening between the nibs is too small and the stone too large, try using a piece of emery cloth, which can be stiffened by placing it on a thin piece of board, like a sandpaper pad. Keeping the surface perfectly flat, gently grind until the surface is bright and free from scratches. Do this with both inner sides.

Now close the pen and repeat the process with the outside surfaces. Since these surfaces are rounded, you must gently work around them, being careful to do the same amount of grinding on the entire area. Continue this until any damaged area is eliminated or until the nibs are exceedingly sharp, but of exactly the same length. Close the nibs as tightly as they will go. With *extreme* care, rub the stone over the joined edges of the nibs with a rolling motion—the way you would run a shoe brush around the toe of the shoe. Repeat this step only two or three times, even though you use the gentlest of pressures. The purpose is to even the nibs; but if they are ground too flat, a fine line will be impossible to rule.

If too much grinding is necessary to even the nibs, repeat the inside and outside grinding until any excessive thickness is reduced.

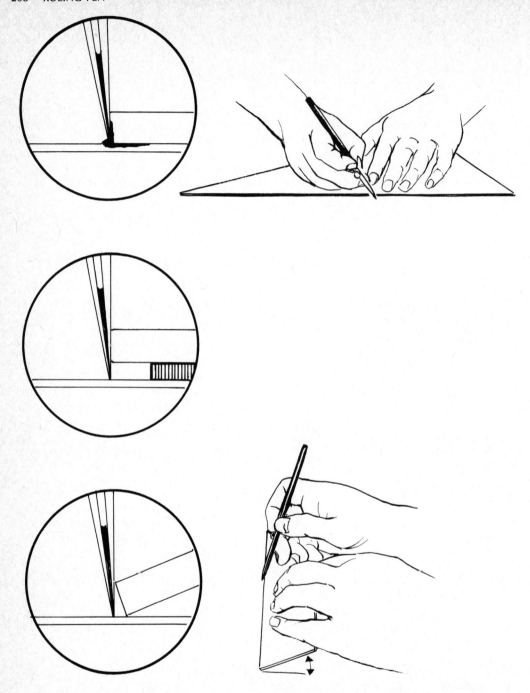

When pen point, straight-edge, and paper meet, ink can easily run under the edge and blot (top, left and right). Lift the straight-edge with tape, coins, another triangle, etc. to avoid blotting (center). Tilting the straight-edge by placing your thumb under the edge will also keep the pen point away from the edge (bottom, left and right).

Common Difficulties

Blotting. Too much ink in the pen, too wide a nib opening, imperfections of the paper surface, or holding the pen in one position too long will all cause the gravity-fed ink to flow too fast and blot.

Ragged line. Varying the speed of the line, changing the angle of the pen during the stroke, or working with damaged nibs will cause a line to be uneven and ragged. Paper surfaces can also cause the same trouble; dirt or excessive erasing are the main faults.

Clogging. If you are careful about the age, quality, and consistency of the fluid you are using, and the pen still clogs, check the nibs. If they are too sharp, they will cut into the paper fibers, which will collect in the opening between the nibs and clog there. If you are using paint, avoid going over the same line twice; the dried paint will pick up and clog the point. If there is clogging trouble with a new or just cleaned pen, moisten the nibs with ammonia or add a small amount of ammonia to the ink. Some paints will always clog; just keep cleaning frequently, and plan to work in short strokes. Minor clogging, the drying of a thin layer of ink on the inner surfaces of the pen, is too common to consider a fault. This minor block can be broken by stroking the edge of the nibs along any convenient scrap. This stroking will draw wet ink down from the nib to the point, will moisten and redissolve the ink at the point, and will start the flow again. If the clogged ink resists, try the same procedure on the back of the hand, or over a moistened finger tip.

Smearing and smuding. Be sure that the ruling edge is lifted slightly off the paper, away from the nib points; a beveled straight-edge is helpful. Be careful in removing the ruling edge from the paper.

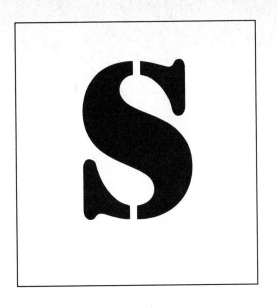

SADDLE STITCHING

The term used to describe the method of binding in which a wire staple is inserted into the spine of a folder by an automatic machine. The term derives from the saddle-shaped form which holds the assembled folder during the process and the wire thread used for such binding. Outside of hardcover books, whose individual signatures may still be thread sewn, the most common material used today is the wire staple.

Handmade samples may be prepared with a stapler. A commercial bindery, not the artist, produces saddle stitching, except for hand samples; but you must be familiar with the process so that you may specify it and understand it when preparing art of this nature. (See *Bindings.*)

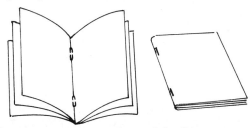

Typical example of saddle-stitch binding.

SANDPAPER PAD

A tear-off pad of a dozen sheets of sandpaper, about $1'' \times 4''$ in size, mounted on a small block of wood with a protruding handle. This block is a convenient means of sharpening or shaping pencil leads, pastels, charcoal, and crayons. The wooden handle prevents dirty fingers and a hole allows the pad to be hung out of the way when not in use.

Layout lettering, in particular, requires a shaped, chisel-pointed drawing edge that must be constantly renewed. When different colors are being used, the disposable sheets of the pad assure clean, as well as finely pointed, lettering tools.

There are many other uses for sandpaper that make it advisable for the artist to keep a sandpaper pad on hand. Cut edges of all kinds—cut-outs for mounting, mat frames, etc.—often have rough edges from improper cutting or faults in the paper. A few strokes with a clean piece of sandpaper will smooth out most of these irregularities. Ruling pens and other mechanical drafting tools may be cleaned, sharpened, or shaped with the fine grade of sandpaper that comes in the pad. An alternative is the metal pencil pointer. (See *Abrasives.*)

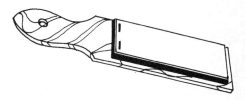

Pad of sandpaper sheets stapled to a piece of wood.

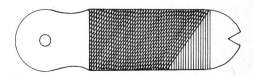

An alternative to the sandpaper pad or block, this durable metal file can be cleaned and reused indefinitely.

SARAL PAPER

This is a brand name for transfer paper used as a substitute for carbon paper in commercial art. (See *Carbon Paper.*)

SCALING WHEEL

A circular proportional scale used to obtain enlarged or reduced proportions of photographs and artwork. A readout window indicates the percentage of change. (See *Proportional Scales.*)

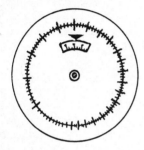

Scaling wheel with enlargement-reduction percentage readout window.

SCALEOGRAPH

A convenient device used for cropping photographs and drawings, the Scaleograph is made of two L-shaped pieces of plastic joined by an aluminum rod.

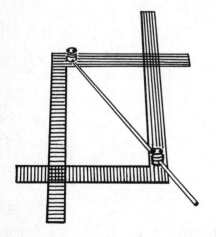

Scaleograph.

The angled pieces are adjusted to enclose a rectangle; turnscrews are tightened to hold the pieces firmly. One angled member can still be slid along the rod, permitting the enclosed rectangle to be enlarged or reduced without changing the proportions. Lightweight and easy to use, the Scaleograph is an alternative to the mathematical computation of rectangular shapes.

SCISSORS

For cutting, scissors are optional for artists. Many prefer razor blades or knives. Scissors should be tested carefully before buying. Loose blades or crude sharpening of the blades will produce ragged cuts. Blades that meet too snugly will be difficult to operate and will also produce unsatisfactory results. It is worth the extra money to buy the best pair you can get.

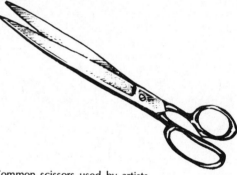

Common scissors used by artists.

SCOTCH TAPE

The generic name for all transparent, plastic tapes is also the brand name of the 3M Company. It is in such common use that it is easier to refer to it by this name than by any other.

Scotch tape (and the newer, invisible, mending tape) can be used for adhering, mending, and constructing almost all art jobs and materials. Many art papers will tear or discolor if you attempt to remove Scotch tape from them.

SCRAP FILE

Scrap is the name given by artists to pieces of reference material. Since it is impractical and expensive to assemble models and props for every illustration, or to keep acquiring up-to-date books with adequate design and type illustrations, prudent artists will tear out and save pertinent reference material whenever possible.

It is advisable to keep this material easily accessible. The simplest way is to collect such material by subject, place it in an envelope or folder, label it, and keep it on a shelf or in a file. Really thorough individuals will adhere each piece of scrap to a sheet of paper, label it with all the pertinent information, and maintain a separate filing cabinet for it.

Whichever method you find works best for you, get into the habit of acquiring such reference material and storing it so that it can be easily retrieved, when needed, or supplemented without creating a mess or damaging the material.

SCRATCH BOARD

Scratch board is a cardboard coated with white clay. When this surface is covered with ink, lines and areas may be scraped away with various tools, revealing the white clay underneath. In this manner, white-on-black drawings of high contrast and considerable detail may be produced which are excellent for reproduction in newspapers, etc., where halftone detail is easily lost. Scratch board is also a simple and inexpensive method of approximating etching and engraving techniques.

Most of the engraving tools used for block or lithographic engraving work very well with scratch board, and a number of simple scratch knives that fit into pen holders are also available. Multilining tools have rows of teeth that scratch several lines at one stroke. They are made specifically for scratch board and come in a range of sizes, each containing a different number of teeth.

Scratch board is sold in sheets of various sizes and quality. The better the quality, the thicker the layer of clay, which permits easier handling during the rendering and allows a certain amount of reworking for corrections. Scratch board also comes already coated. This eliminates one of the more difficult tasks of scratch board, but is not very helpful when large areas of the drawing must be white.

Common Difficulties

Uneven coating. If the ink is not applied smoothly over the entire surface, a number of problems occur. Basically, the ink cannot be removed evenly with a stroke of constant pressure, a fault that produces a line which is varied in thickness or interrupted when the scratch point does not dig beneath the inked surface. When additional pressure is applied to compensate, the line becomes ragged and the clay may crumble. These errors cannot be corrected easily.

To prevent this kind of difficulty, use India ink for the coating. Other inks tend to dry too slowly and thus seep deeply into the clay. Apply the ink with even strokes, trying not to overload whatever brush you use, so that too much ink is applied at any point. The best method to coat the surface is to spray the ink. This will insure that the ink does not soak into the clay and will produce an even coloring.

Mistakes. Drawing errors in scratch board may be corrected if the clay has not been removed completely by the scratching process. Simply smooth down the surface by scraping with the flat of a knife or razor blade, recoat the surface with ink, and repeat the scratch drawing. If care is taken, several corrections of this nature may be made.

SCREEN DETERMINER

A small plastic gauge which is used for discovering the screen count used in preparing a halftone. A graduated line pattern is printed on the gauge. Sliding the pattern portion of the gauge slowly over a halftone print will cause a distinctive four-pointed star to appear in the pattern. A reading may be taken where the points of the star cross a numbered scale. This reading will be the number of the screen used to create the halftone, and you may now match the screen or alter it in future specifications.

The screen determiner is a tool that is used mostly by production personnel. However, it is important that artists know of its existence, how it works, and that the information it provides is available from any production staff—in an agency or at the printers.

Additional features are the inch, agate, and pica rules printed on the edges of the gauge.

SCRIBER PENS

Hollow-nib pens mounted on a base that contains pins that fit into corresponding indentations on lettering guides to produce a form of lettering commonly used in mechanical drafting. (See *Lettering, Mechanical.*)

SEPARATIONS

The name given to the process of preparing art for reproduction. Art for each intended color in the finished piece is created or assembled separately so that the platemaker can make the printing plates directly from the art without further processing. (See *Overlays.*)

SERIGRAPHY

The name given to the silkscreen process, usually when referring to the fine art silkscreen and not to commercial silkscreen printing. (See *Silkscreen.*)

SHADING SHEETS

Line and halftone patterns that have been applied to clear plastic sheets, with or without a pressure sensitive adhesive backing. These sheets are available in a wide range of patterns and colors.

Shading sheets, when cut to shape and applied over line artwork, create simple values that simulate the effects of the benday shading process used by platemakers. The use of these sheets gives the artist, rather than the platemaker, control of the process and permits experimentation with the patterns, while eliminating this expense from the plate costs. A number of interesting variations and moirés can be made by combining several sheets in one area. (See *Top Sheet Shading Films* and *Zipatone.*)

Common Difficulty

Shadows. If the sheets are not adhered properly, they may create shadows when photographed for reproduction. These shadows will cause parts of the shading to be darker than others. Be sure that the sheets are fresh and that the adhesive is clean. Once the sheet has been placed, and the excess trimmed with either a knife or razor blade, rub the film firmly with a burnisher or other smooth surface. Your fingernails will do for burnishing if nothing else is available. When the sheet is fully adhered, the tone of the inked areas will be uniform and the plastic will be invisible. (See also *Burnishers.*)

SHELLAC

True shellac is composed of a resinous substance exuded by a small insect, although many shellacs are synthetically made today. In liquid form, it is used by fine artists to coat and protect paintings. For commercial artists, shellacs have been largely superseded by aerosol spray fixatives. (See *Fixatives.*)

SHOWCARD

An inexpensive cardboard covered with matte or glossy paper in a limited range of colors, used for creating signs and other displays. Also known as poster board, a full sheet of showcard is 28″ × 44″, although most art supply stores will sell it in several smaller sizes. (See *Papers and Boards.*)

SHOWCARD LETTERING

A form of single-stroke lettering for posters and signs. (See *Sign Writing.*)

SIGN CLOTH

An inexpensive cloth coated with a plastic facing used for sign writing. Sign cloth is identical to what used to be called oilcloth, which once was a staple in kitchens for use as tablecloths and shelving. The virtue of this cloth is its ability to withstand water. Just as it allowed people to wash off greasy kitchen surfaces easily with soap and water, sign cloth can last in the rain without deterioration. This inexpensive cloth is sold in rolls at stores carrying sign writer's supplies, and Japan color paints are used to letter on it.

SIGN WRITING

Sign writing, or showcard lettering, is the practice of creating one-of-a-kind display posters or signs by means of chisel-shaped brushes, pointed brushes held nearly parallel to the surface, or by metal pens with broad, slit loops. Such lettering is differentiated from calligraphy largely by the style of alphabets.

Most modern signs use contemporary lettering styles based on separated type characters. Calligraphy uses styles based on cursive, or handwritten, strokes. Most sign alphabets require the brush (or pen)

to be swiveled, to present a more constant angle of the chisel point toward the direction of the stroke. In addition, the materials used for signs require more permanent and colorful pigments and backgrounds. Sign writing is not considered a truly artistic form by commercial artists and few art schools provide instruction. The best method of acquiring skill is to follow the directions of a book on the subject, or better yet, to apprentice to a sign writer. (See also *Calligraphy.*)

SILKSCREEN

Silkscreen (or serigraphy, as the fine art version is called) is a stencil method of printing that has grown considerably in the last few years. Silkscreen is valued for its ability to use any medium whatsoever on any imaginable material or surface, regardless of contour. Simply described, silkscreen involves a stencil that has been adhered to a fine mesh cloth, stretched tightly over a wooden frame. Paint is forced through the stencil by the action of a squeegee drawn across the screen. The shape of the frame, the varieties of stencil technique, and the range of media allow for infinite variations in both the art produced and the objects being printed. These features have made silkscreen invaluable to both art and industry.

Artists should be aware of the silkscreen method for both commercial printing and for the creation of art. If you cannot study the technique in class, there are many fine books on the subject. Similarly, there are many small silkscreen kits with simple instructions that will permit you to practice the rudiments of the technique. Commercial artists cannot afford to be ignorant of this important process.

SKELETONS

For the commercial artist, a skeleton is usually a scaled-down, plastic reproduction of the human frame, assembled in an accurate position. Skeletons are available in flexible and inflexible forms and in a number of sizes. For the student, skeletons are a reference tool for understanding the structure of the human body and visualizing the action of any pose the body can take. Used in conjunction with a good anatomy chart, or a book on anatomy, a skeleton will help the student develop a thorough familiarity with the elements of figure drawing.

As with mannequins and anatomical casts, skeletons are reference material at best, and should be used only as a guide to understanding a pose taken by a live model, or a pose in a photograph from your scrap file.

Although the skeletons of men and women differ considerably in the size and position of the bones, it is not necessary to have both a male and female skeleton for reference. But such differences should be remembered and allowed for. A good anatomy chart or book will help. All of these items may be purchased at art supply stores. (See *Anatomical Casts.*)

SKETCH BOX

The sketch box is primarily a box for storing and carrying oil paints, brushes, and mediums. However, they are equally valuable to commercial artists for storing tools and equipment. Available in all sizes and arrangements of compartments, these boxes are carried by all art stores. Your imagination will allow you to find a multitude of uses for them.

Also suggested for this purpose are fishing tackle and toolboxes.

SLIDE RULES

A slide rule, in the strictest sense, is a mathematician's tool, made with sliding wooden and plastic parts, containing various mathematical ratios printed on the flat surfaces. Sliding the rule parts into different positions permits a trained slide rule operator to read out answers to com-

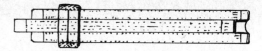

Typical construction of a slide rule whatever its scales or functions.

plex mathematical functions. Although these rules can perform simple multiplication and division, they are designed for the more difficult processes and are quite expensive. Many versions are available at mechanical drafting supply stores, but the user must be familiar with trigonometry, calculus, etc., and must have instruction in the proper use of the rules.

A simpler version, often less expensive, is sold at most art supply stores and performs only the simpler math necessary for rescaling artwork and photographs. These rules are usually referred to as proportional or scaling slide rules. The instructions for the operation of these rules are quite simple, and require little practice and no knowledge of math. Instructions are included with the rule. (See *Proportional Scales.*)

SOLVENTS

A substance that can dilute or dissolve another substance. Water is the most common solvent and, to commercial artists, the most valuable. Since most of your paints and inks are water-soluble, you will have little need for any other kind of solvent.

However, there are a number of other liquids you will use in conjunction with your art materials that are also solvents in a more limited way. Fluids like rubber cement thinner, ammonia, chlorine, pen cleaners, and acrylic brush cleaners are helpful and often necessary for the proper practice of commercial art. Since these solvents have rather specialized uses for the commercial artist, they are discussed in the sections where they are employed. If you are having trouble cleaning or removing a substance, check that entry for the best way to proceed.

A large group of commercial solvents are sold in paint and hardware stores that will work with the paint products sold in those stores. These solvents include acetone, lacquer thinner, mineral spirits, and turpentine. Since so many of today's paint products have synthetic bases, it is wise to check the can when you buy to find the recommended solvent. Most of the solvents cannot be used for conventional art mediums. But a few, like turpentine and acetone (nail polish remover is composed of acetone), are useful as general solvents.

A rather esoteric group of solvents includes benzine, naphtha, and ether. Although these may be available commercially, they are highly volatile and dangerous. In many cases their private use is restricted. These solvents do not perform differently from the paint solvents mentioned above, but they are usually more effective and quicker. As a general rule, it is wise to avoid them. Your paint or hardware dealer will be able to recommend substitutes.

The most common problems arising from the use of solvents involve the purity of the solvent, the amount used, and the effect it has on the drawing material. Always work with a clean batch of solvent in a separate dish or container. Throw it away when it is dirty. Don't pour it back in the container. Have enough on hand so that you can work quickly and avoid unnecessary repetition of steps. Most solvents will drive the pigment deeply into the working surface if allowed to stand. Have clean cloth, blotter, or absorbent cotton handy to wipe up the solvent quickly so that it will not sink in.

Always test the solvent on a separate surface first. Acetone will dissolve acetate sheets and plastic trays; chlorine can corrode metal and dissolve brush hairs and paper. Practice your procedure first, therefore, to be sure that you will not destroy your work.

Finally, use solvents where there is plenty of ventilation. Most solvents give off fumes that are extremely unpleasant and which may be dangerous.

SPEEDBALL

A brand name for a series of lettering penpoints that has become generic for all such pens and lettering styles used in showcard posters and sign writing. (See *Pen Points.*)

SPLINES

Flexible lengths of plastic used to create curves. The spline is held in place with lead weights which may be moved to alter the shape of the curve. Splines were originated for certain mechanical drafting situations that are not common to commercial artists; for example, long gradual curves several feet in length. However, there are times, in display work, etc., when such a device may solve a difficult problem, and the spline solution may be a good one to remember. The spline is sold in any length, by the foot, and the lead weights are sold separately. For smaller curves, most commercial artists prefer the more common French curve. (See *Curves, Adjustable.*)

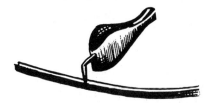

Length of flexible spline held by a lead weight.

SPONGES

Used by artists to apply clear water, create painting textures, and for cleaning. Either natural sponges or the synthetic substitutes are adequate for any of these purposes. Whatever preferences exist are the result of individual habits and requirements. As a general rule, natural sponges are more delicate and subtle, while synthetics are more durable.

Stretching watercolor paper, prewetting areas for watercolor wash, etc., require large amounts of fresh water applied quickly and accurately, qualities best found in a sponge. Be sure that the sponge is the right size and shape for the particular job—trim it with a pair of scissors if it is too large or too small. Both the sponge and the water must be perfectly clean. When finished, wring out the sponge and use it to blot up excess water.

For this kind of job, both the natural sponge and the synthetic sponge perform equally well. The size will be determined by the job. If you are working with large areas, use a large sponge. In small areas, a small piece of sponge, cut specifically for the job, will make it easier for you to work quickly within the confines of the area. The primary necessity is cleanliness. Use a new sponge each time, or keep one sponge for clean water only.

Dipping a sponge directly into paint and stippling the paint onto a drawing can create numerous textures. Altering the size and shape of the sponge; varying the amount, wetness, and number of colors of paint; and modifying the pressure and degree of overlap of the application will produce countless effects.

For these techniques, the synthetic sponges are usually preferred. Synthetic sponges are stiffer, more durable, and easier to cut into any shape. A natural sponge, for instance, will not hold a sharp edge or a fine point when it is wet; the synthetic sponge can do both. Even though you intend to cover a large area, keep the sponge small—maybe two or three inches square at the most. This size will permit you to exercise accuracy and control, but will fill a large area quite quickly. Overlapping the applications will eliminate any hard edges or differences in color and value. The smaller size will prevent the sponge from becoming overloaded with paint and bending, or drip-

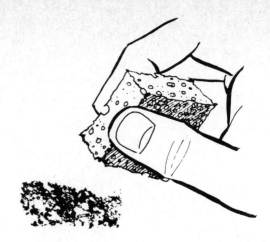

Creating texture with a trimmed piece of sponge.

ping, during its use. Any of these conditions can cause the sponge to apply color unevenly, producing less attractive results.

Once a sponge has become damaged, discolored, etc., it may still be used to clean working surfaces and tools. Here, the size of the sponge or its kind is relatively immaterial. If there are preferences, they will involve tools. Most artists and drafters use the softest, most pliant materials when cleaning metal drawing tools; there is less abrasive wear. Natural sponges are much softer and easier to force into small openings in these tools.

Common Difficulties

Crumbling. With age and use, any sponge will begin to deteriorate. This deterioration, which causes the sponge to become soft and crumbly, may be accelerated if paint or water is allowed to remain in the sponge. When you are finished, be sure that the sponge is clean and that any excess moisture has been squeezed out. Allow the sponge to dry completely before storing for future use.

Tearing. Any sponge that has been torn will, like a run in a stocking, continue to tear during use. Even a new sponge, if it has been carelessly cut to a new shape, may have an incipient cut that will become enlarged into a full tear. This does not mean that the sponge has lost its value. Only the area of the tear has been weakened. Such an area may be cut away carefully, or the sponge may be divided in two along the line of the fault. Both pieces will continue to work quite well with reasonable care.

SPRAY ADHESIVES

Term applied to any adhesive that can be sprayed from an aerosol can. Spray adhesives are quick and efficient, but they present problems if used improperly. The principal difficulty is in the permeating nature of the spray; spray tends to cover everything with a tacky coat that attracts dust and other particles and can last a long time. It is essential to use a particular, well-ventilated place to apply this adhesive, one well removed from your general work area. Try to spray in short bursts close to the surface. Spray against old newspapers and change them frequently.

The adhesive can clog the spray tip in a very short time. When you are finished, turn the can upside down and continue spraying until no adhesive appears. If the tip does get clogged, allow it to soak in a solvent, such as rubber cement thinner. Gently probe the very small opening with the tip of a needle.

SPRAY CAN HANDLE

The spray can handle attaches to any aerosol spray can. Pulling the trigger on the handle depresses the operating valve on the aerosol can, starting the spray. Once it has been installed properly, the handle prevents the spray can from being operated in the wrong direction. The easy trigger action is also less tiresome than holding the spray can tip in a depressed position when extensive spraying is necessary.

SPRAY GUNS

The slang name given to any atomizer, sprayer, or airbrush. It probably derives from the fact that the large sprayers are activated by a trigger in a pistol grip. (See *Sprayers* and *Airbrush*.)

SPRAYERS

A sprayer is any device capable of projecting a spray of liquid. At their simplest, sprayers may be no more than the L-shaped tubes of the mouth type atomizer. The most complex spray, of course, is the airbrush. In between these extremes are several devices that perform similar functions with slight variations.

The aerosol sprayer consists of a jar with a sprayer top that attaches to an aerosol can. This atomizer-action sprayer is inexpensive and adequate for any coarse spraying. The aerosol can is easily replaced and the uncomplicated parts are not harmed by the use of fluids that would clog or damage an airbrush. The spray is relatively coarse and suited only for broad area coverage.

Another variation is the electric sprayer. This sprayer works by vibration, agitating the fluid until it is vaporized, and then propelling the particles toward the surface. Here again, the action produces a coarse spray that is unsuited for detail work.

A third category is the commercial spray gun. These spray guns are capable of covering extremely large surfaces and they handle any medium. They must be used with compressors, and are suitable only for large display work, such as signs and back drops.

The sprayers mentioned here should never be considered for rendering. The spray produced is too coarse, the amount of fluid sprayed cannot be varied, and the shape of the spray is unchangeable. With the exception of billboard-sized work, these limitations are overwhelming.

However, any of these sprayers are excellent for applying fixative, shellac, lacquer, and any heavy, oil-based paint that would not pass freely through an airbrush. With any of these mediums, the primary function is coverage, usually of a fairly large area. Here the limitations described above do not apply. With only reasonable care, any of these fluids can be applied by a sprayer with perfect results.

Common Difficulty

Uneven coverage. The only fault with these sprayers, other than actual mechanical malfunction, is their method of use. Since their sprays are coarse and heavy, there is a tendency to apply the liquid too thickly. This may cause puddles, bleeding, or running streaks. Remember to apply the liquid at a proper distance from the surface. This distance is usually described in the operating instructions of the sprayer. If not, practice first on another surface until you have determined the best distance. Second, learn to keep the sprayer moving at a constant speed. Remember also that the liquid will build up at the end of a stroke as you begin to slow the movement prior to reversing the direction. A safer practice is to stop the sprayer before the end of a stroke, and start it again just after the next stroke has begun. This will allow the liquid to feather out at the ends, and a simple overlap of strokes will build up the proper amount, without accumulating any excess.

SQUEEGEE

A squeegee is a flat, rectangular piece of rubber set in a wooden handle. It is used to draw paint across the stencil openings of a silkscreen printing frame. Squeegees are provided with any silkscreen printing kit, and may also be purchased separately, in many sizes, from the same art supply stores.

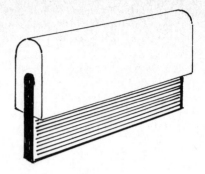

Squeegee, for use with silkscreen.

STAPLERS

The stapler or staple gun is not a specialized tool and should be familiar to you. The most versatile are the most valuable. In addition to the regular fastening chores, commercial artists need staplers for display work and binding comp folders.

In display work, the most desirable feature is the swinging base, which permits stapling to a large background. When extensive display work is necessary, the tacker is often preferred. The tacker, a variation of the stapler, has a trigger operated spring release which literally shoots the staple. This is a strong, positive action that assures a powerful bond, operates well in awkward positions, and reduces fatigue. The tacker is available in both the conventional double-pronged staple and single-pronged tack models.

When preparing comp folders, the stapler accurately simulates the saddle stitching most commonly used today. For this use there are staplers with extra-long arms which are capable of working in the middle of large sheets. Since these models are quite specialized, you may wish to avoid their considerable cost. Large folders can be bound with any size stapler if it has a swing out base. Place a sheet of cardboard under the properly assembled, *open* folder sheets. Place the stapler, with the bass swung open, over the spot which will be the spine of the folder. (A little practice may be necessary to determine the exact spot the staple will be delivered.) Release the staple gently, so that it goes through the sheets and halfway into the cardboard only. Lift the folder sheets together, pulling the staple into the final position and out of the cardboard. The prongs of the staple may now be bent closed by hand. Remember to drive the staple through the *cover* of the material, so that the staple closes *inside* the folder. Two or three staples, evenly spaced, will be necessary to bind a folder.

Staple tackers are also good for binding, except that the strong spring drive may force the staple through the cardboard and into the table, making the staple difficult to remove. To prevent this, use several thicknesses of cardboard, equal to the depth of the staple. Corrugated cardboard is best for this purpose, since the staple will pull out quite easily. (See *Tackers*.)

Common Difficulty

Jamming. Staples of the wrong size will jam a stapler. Use the brand designed for your stapler. Occasionally a properly filled stapler will jam. The most common reason for this is a loose staple. Staples are prepared in long strips and the machines are designed to operate with the staples close together. A loose staple or two may disrupt the spacing of the feed so that a staple will be in the wrong position when its turn comes to be ejected. Continued jamming of this nature can widen the opening so that normally-spaced staples will no longer feed properly. Such a stapler should be fixed or replaced.

STENCIL

Anything that serves to mask certain areas and allow paint to be applied in others. A stencil may be already prepared with specific openings (letter forms, for example), or may be cut from stencil paper.

Prepared stencils take many forms. In addition to letters, there are geometric shapes in the form of templates and guides which may be used as stencils. As opposed to a frisket, a stencil is not usually adhered to the working surface.

The purpose of a stencil is to allow color to be applied quickly and smoothly to one area while preventing the color from touching any other area. A stencil also allows a particular shape to be repeated accurately many times so as to create an overall pattern.

Paint is the most common medium applied with the aid of a stencil, although any other medium may also be used. Pencil, colored pencil, pastel, charcoal, inks, and dyes may all at some time be worked through a stencil opening onto an art surface. The stencil, itself, may be composed of any material (paper, plastic or metal) that can be cut easily into the required patterns. Similarly, a stencil brush, the normal tool for applying paint through a stencil, may be replaced by any brush, cloth, or sponge, etc.

Once the stencil has been prepared, either by assembling manufactured stencils or by tracing and cutting a pattern with stencil paper, it is placed in position on the art surface. The stencil is held in place by hand or with weights. The desired medium is then forced through the openings in the stencil. Paint is applied with an up and down, stippling motion, rather than a sideways, rubbing motion. Dry media are applied as they would be without the stencil. Outlines are obtained by tracing the drawing tool around the edges of the openings only.

Once the rendering is completed, the stencil is lifted carefully from the working surface to avoid smearing the artwork.

Hand-cut stencils are usually one of a kind, and are destroyed after using. Prepared stencils should be cleaned thoroughly after each use so that the accuracy of the opening is retained. Paint left on the stencil will also discolor future jobs.

Common Difficulties

Smearing. If a stencil moves, or if excess paint is forced under the edges while being used, smearing will occur. Hold the stencil firmly, use liquid sparingly, and always work toward the center of the opening. Use repeated strokes to build opacity rather than overloading the brush.

Buckling and tearing. Liquids soaking into a stencil will cause warping and buckling. Drawing tools can tear the edges of the stencil openings. In both cases, improper stencil paper is the fault. Make sure the stencil you are using is strong enough before you begin your finished art. If you are in doubt, create a new stencil with a stronger material.

Lack of detail. The thickness of most stencils, the unsecured edges of the openings, and the crude stippling action of applying the paint are not factors that lend themselves to fine detail. Where such control is imperative, use a frisket. Another factor that causes lack of detail is caking: dried paint that accumulates at the edges of the stencil openings. Keep stencils clean.

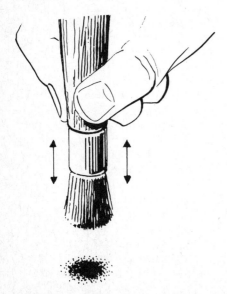

Use a stencil brush with the proper dabbing technique for stencil or stipple work.

STENCIL BRUSH

A coarse, thick brush used to stipple paint; that is, to apply the paint in a series of rapid, up and down strokes on the *point* of the brush, rather than the normal procedure in which the *side* of the brush is drawn along the paper. (See *Brush, Stencil.*)

STENCIL KNIFE

A thick-bladed, heavy knife used to cut oak tag, bristol, and other heavy papers and boards, with more control than a mat knife, which it resembles. (See *Knife, Stencil.*)

STENCIL PAPER

A stiff, durable stock that cuts easily and resists moisture are essential characteristics for stencils. Stencil paper, which comes in sheets or rolls, is cut with stencil knives or frisket knives. Oak tag, which is often used for stencils, is a more familiar name to many people. (See *Papers and Boards.*)

STENCILS, LETTERING

A form of stencil that contains the characters of the alphabet. Used for creating crude, rapid lettering on any surface. (See *Lettering Stencils.*)

STIPPLE BRUSH

A coarse, thick brush used to stipple paint; that is, to apply the paint in a series of rapid, up and down strokes on the *point* of the brush, rather than the normal procedure in which the *side* of the brush is drawn along the paper. Stippling produces a round area of color that grades off in smaller dots, caused by the paint deposited from individual bristles on the edge of the point. (See *Brush, Stencil.*)

STOMPS

A stomp is made of rolled paper (usually soft and coarse) or chamois and is sharpened to a point. Stomps are used to spread and smooth charcoal, chalk, and pastel. When rendering with these dry mediums, many artists prefer to smooth and blend with their fingers. However, fine detail and subtle tints cannot be obtained this way. The soft, coarse texture of the stomp carries the color evenly over the rendering, and can be controlled in the smallest areas more easily than the fingertip.

Color may be applied first to the drawing or placed directly on the stomp. Stroking the chalk or charcoal on a sandpaper pad will produce a powder into which the stomp may be dipped. In either case, the color is then rubbed into the paper with repeated strokes of the stomp. Practice will allow you to perfect many techniques of drawing and shading in this manner.

You can make your own stomps by rolling a small piece of blotting or Kraft paper. But the commercial stomps are very well made and inexpensive.

Common Difficulties

Dirty color. Dry mediums get very muddy if they are mixed too much. If you are doing a lot of work requiring the stomp technique, retain a separate stomp for each color. When a stomp gets too dirty, it can be cleaned by sanding the tip on a sandpaper pad.

Lack of detail. Continued use may blunt the stomp's point, making detail work impossible. Since the soft material tends to tear and fray when it is sharpened, destroying the fine point, it is usually better to use a new stomp.

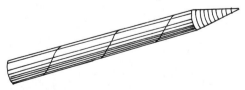

Rolled paper stomp.

STRAIGHT-EDGE

As the name implies, the straight-edge is a perfectly straight ruling guide for drawing lines with either a pen or pencil. Although straight-edges of various sizes and construction can be purchased in drafting supply stores, the name is also used to denote any ruling edge that is straight (that is, rulers, triangles, T-squares).

STUDIO MARKERS

(See *Markers.*)

STYLUS

In the broadest sense, a stylus is a writing tool of instrument. In a limited sense, the stylus is a tool for producing a writing stroke without actually creating a mark. As such, the stylus is used to create pressure: for making mimeograph stencils, for making copies through carbon paper, for applying transfer type, for following the guide in mechanical lettering.

SWATCHBOOKS

Swatchbooks are collections of samples prepared by various manufacturers so that artists may have a guide when selecting

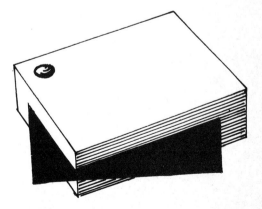

Typical swatchbook with metal post that allows pages to be fanned.

art materials, printing inks, papers, etc. These books are usually quite small, no more than the size of a file card, but they are made of the actual materials and are therefore quite expensive. Art stores sell swatchbooks containing samples of presentation papers and printed acetate. These are bound with a central pin or a chain loop to permit the individual sheets to be fanned. The sheets will be identified with a code number so that full sheets may be purchased to match. Art stores may also distribute sample sheets or folders provided by manufacturers to display their selection of pigments. If available, these samples are usually free.

The only difficulty with these swatchbooks comes with age. Most materials eventually become discolored or faded, making it difficult to select colors accurately. Obsolescence is also a problem. Many manufacturers add new colors or materials while discarding others. It is advisable to keep all referenced material up to date.

Many large art stores offer catalogs listing every item they sell, either directly or by mail order. Quite handsome and profusely illustrated, these catalogs contain a full listing of all product lines and their current prices. These catalogs are often free, or at least inexpensive, but they do not list every product available. It is wise to collect several catalogs from different firms to compare offerings.

Printing ink samples are presented in many ways, but usually they are shown in small swatchbooks with samples of each ink printed solidly and in several tints. These basic samples may be repeated on different paper stocks so that you can see how they will reproduce under different conditions. The more elaborate books, like the Pantone system, represent not just an ink, but the hundreds of colors that may be obtained by mixing these inks. A code number is assigned for every mixture which represents an exact formula which the printer can utilize when duplicating the color. The Pantone book contains several samples of each mixture, perforated and coded, so that they can be removed from the book and attached to a job going to the printer. (See *Pantone Matching System.*)

Paper samples are also presented in swatchbooks and folders. These range from small folders that contain samples hardly an inch square to large pads composed of many individual sheets that represent nearly the entire range of the manufacturer's output. Naturally these hand-assembled and hand-bound booklets are very expensive to produce. But the papermakers do not charge for them; they are offered free to potential customers to induce them to use the produce. Since they are expensive, however, they are difficult to obtain unless you represent an actual source of sales. There are occasions when legitimate educational groups can ask for and receive these samples when the manufacturer is approached directly. At other times you may find that paper distributors in your neighborhood will have extra copies of promotional material that they will gladly give you. A collection of these individual samples will offer you some awareness of the kinds of paper available, although they will not be as convenient as the swatchbooks.

Art materials are often represented by booklets and folders that show the colors or techniques of the various products, such as inks, paints, dyes, tapes, etc. Like the paper samples, these may be hand-produced and expensive. The art supply stores will have their own copies for reference, and you are always welcome to refer to them. Sometimes they will have extra copies that you may keep, but for the most part you must use their copies in the store or write directly to the manufacturer if you wish to obtain a copy for your own use.

Type is not actually shown in a swatchbook, but again, samples of type are compiled in folders and booklets by both the printers and typographers in your neighborhood, as well as the type manufacturers. Simple one-line specimens are usually offered free by your local suppliers. More extensive showings containing complete type fonts are usually bound as books and are sold at art supply stores, as well as by individual type firms. Once again, these expensive books are given free to customers whose business justifies the expensive preparations involved. (See *Type.*)

SWISS CHEESE

A slang term for a template, derived from the appearance of the plastic sheet with its numerous stencil openings.

SWIVEL KNIFE

A stencil or frisket knife, the blade of which is mounted in a revolving handle, so that the blade can follow intricate cuts without twisting the fingers. (See *Knife, Swivel.*)

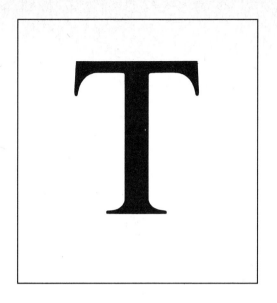

TABLES, DRAWING

A drawing table is a drawing board mounted on legs. The board surface may be tilted to any angle and the entire unit may be raised or lowered to various heights. The drawing table provides artists with a working surface at which they may sit and work comfortably and accurately. Drawing tables may be mounted on a single heavy post, or be supported by a sawhorse-style base.

Drafting tables are less flexible. They are built like conventional tables with four reinforced legs, and the top may be tilted, but not raised or lowered. Drafting tables are larger than drawing tables to provide the space necessary for the bigger blueprint drawings, and they contain small drawers which provide sufficient space for the lesser number of tools required by drafters. (See *Drafting Tables*.)

All these tables are available in a wide range of styles and sizes. Most stores will have models on display, and you should not select a table until you have had a chance to see and check them. A few pointers may be helpful in guiding your inspection.

Choose as large a table as space and finance permit. The larger tables are usually more stable, permit neater working conditions, and are capable of handling a wider range of jobs. Check the table for firmness and stability. A wobbly table is not conducive to good work.

Determine your method of working before you choose a table. For instance, if you work with a T-square, select a table that has a metal edge to insure continuing accuracy during the life of the table. If you are going to use a drafting machine or parallel ruling straight-edge, be sure your table has room for these devices without disturbing the working area.

Pick your auxiliary furniture at the same time. You will eventually need taborets, files, etc., and it does not hurt to anticipate their size and position when choosing a table to be sure that they will all work together efficiently.

Evaluate your future uses. If you intend to move frequently, it may be advisable to choose a portable model that will permit easy transfer. Some of the larger pieces are extremely difficult to disassemble and move.

Investigate second-hand furniture and office supply stores before making a final decision. Very often, fine tables and other equipment are available at a fraction of their original cost.

One final suggestion. Since the surface of the table will become dirty and disfigured with use, plan to keep a stock of cheap, thick cardboard, such as mounting board or show cardboard, on hand. Covering the table with this board allows you to keep the surface clean and smooth, providing a very satisfactory drawing surface at the same time.

TABORET

The taboret consists of a cabinet with drawers, shelves, vertical pad storage racks, and an uninterrupted surface on top. The size of the unit, the variety of individual features, and their placement allow for a number of styles, and few

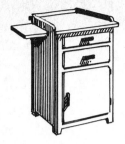

Taboret.

stores will carry more than a few of them. Taborets are used to store frequently used materials near at hand, and provide additional working surfaces as well.

Because taborets are rather expensive, many are tempted to improvise. You can construct one with inexpensive lumber, or a number of common items can be combined and transformed into taborets. For instance, filing cabinets alone or in groups may be combined with inexpensive night-tables from unpainted furniture stores, shelf units, and other similar items. Inexpensive drawer units are available in hardware stores that can be attached under drawing tables. Working in this manner, you can create elaborate taborets without being limited by the expense and style of the prepared units. To unify a collection of improvised units, cover them with a sheet of Masonite or Formica which you can buy at a lumber yard. These materials are attractive, difficult to damage, clean easily, and provide excellent working surfaces.

TACKERS

A term used to describe a form of stapler that delivers either a conventional two-pronged staple or a single-pronged staple. This staple does not hold by being bent back like the two-pronged staple, but drives straight into the backing surface. (See *Staplers.*)

TAPE, CELLOPHANE

An adhesive-backed, clear plastic tape that is more commonly referred to as

Scotch tape after the original product in this field. It is used for any number of adhering, binding, and mending jobs in the home as well as the commercial art field. (See *Scotch Tape.*)

TAPE, CHART

A series of adhesive-backed, plastic tapes that are useful for producing lines for graphs and charts, etc. These tapes come in a large range of widths from $\frac{1}{32}$" to one inch, in various patterns and colors. A dispenser that applies the tape directly and facilitates cutting is also available.

These tapes are applied directly to the artwork with a little pressure, the excess tape being trimmed away with a knife or razor blade. Since the tape itself constitutes the pattern or color, no additional modification is necessary. Thus, complex borders, dotted lines, etc., can be created with a minimum of effort, eliminating expensive hand work or type proofs. The quality is fine enough for finished mechanicals.

Charts, signs, and similar presentations which require extensive use of lines for graphs, etc., are other instances where chart tapes are indispensable. Here again, a suitable tape can be found that, laid directly on the art, will create a line of any thickness, color or pattern. This is obviously a much quicker and cheaper way of producing these lines with great accuracy and little hand work.

The tape is flexible and can be bent into curves, with some limitation. If the curve is too tight the tape will lift off the paper, rather than follow the curve. In this case, apply only a small arc of the curve, cut the tape, and repeat the process—overlapping the ends of the arc slightly.

TAPE, CLOTH

A strip of cloth with a water-soluble or pressure-sensitive adhesive on one side. Available in several widths and colors, these tapes are useful for sealing silkscreen frames, binding presentation material, repairing simple folder-type portfolios, and similar tasks. The tapes are strong and most of them are waterproof.

TAPE, CORRECTION

An opaque white tape, similar in all respects to drafting tape, with the exception of its surface. Where drafting tape is slightly rippled and tan, correction tape is white and smooth. The primary value of correction tape is its ability to cover mistakes and revisions with a clean, white surface. However, the similarities with drafting tape lead many artists to use it as a universal substitute whenever such a tape is needed.

TAPE DISPENSERS

Some drafting and masking tapes come in a package that may be used as a dispenser. The package has a cutting edge on one corner and is constructed so that the tape roll in the container turns freely. Since dispensing tape from the package requires both hands, most artists prefer some type of permanent dispenser that permits them to take a piece of tape with only one hand. There are many of these dispensers and you may take your choice. The most popular are the heavy metal desk stand and the lighter, less expensive, mounted unit that attaches to the side of the worktable. Both have firmly mounted cutting edges and movable cores that fit inside the roll of tape. The desk stand can, of course, be moved about at will, while the mounted unit is immobile, though conveniently out of the way.

A modified desk stand dispenser is available for two-sided tape. A spring-mounted roller presses against the tape roll and turns in the opposite direction. The covering for the two-sided tape is wrapped around this roller, and is automatically taken up as the tape is unrolled.

A specialized dispenser is provided for applying tape to the edges of booklet covers and other presentations. Called a manual edger, this dispenser contains a platform on which the material to be taped is placed, and a moving dispenser that applies the tape smoothly and accurately to the exact edge of the presentation. There is little need for such a device unless you work extensively with the preparation of material for presentation (such as booklets and charts), rather than for reproduction.

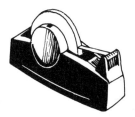

Weighted tape dispenser.

TAPE, DRAFTING

Drafting tape is manufactured by a number of concerns and therefore may have different names and properties. Essentially, drafting tape is used to hold a drawing to a board while the drawing is being worked on, and these differences between brands are not important.

However, you should remember that *cheaper* tapes, or tapes made for other purposes, may have an adhesive that will bind too firmly. If this happens, you will tear the paper or pull off the surface of the paper when you remove the tape. For this reason, stay with a product in the price and quality range of the so-called Scotch tapes (the best known brand) and specify a *drafting* tape. The most common substitute is masking tape; masking tape is made for frisketing with household paints and usually has too strong an adhesive for art purposes.

Drafting tape is excellent for mounting overlays and for taping artwork in a mat frame. Certain types of friskets are also made best with drafting tape and the method is fully covered in the section on friskets.

Try drafting tape as a pick-up, too.

There are many times when lint, dust, and other bits of foreign matter cannot be removed easily from a drawing without smudging. In such cases, make a loop with the tape, sticky side out, and use it with a gentle blotting motion to remove these particles.

Common Difficulties

Stickiness. First, the longer the tape is allowed to adhere, the more firmly it sticks. This is particularly important with frisket work. If the tape is allowed to stay for more than a day, it will not come off easily. If you are working on an involved job that cannot be finished in this time, and the frisket must remain for longer periods, make sure that you are using a high-quality paper or board. The better the paper—the more durable the surface—the easier it will be to remove the tape without damage.

Bleeding edges. The other difficulty is that the slightly crinkled texture of the paper tape itself prevents the tape from making *too* complete a bond, so that the tape can be removed. When tape is being used as a frisket, however, this slight irregularity of the tape may allow paint to seep under the edge. To prevent this, press the tape down very firmly with some hard-edged object. But do this only about $\frac{1}{16}$" from the edge, or the tape will not come off easily. Also avoid excessive paint strokes at the edge of the tape; do not force the paint against the edge. As you paint, move the brush *away* from the edge of the tape and towards the bare paper. This technique will also prevent too much paint from building up at the edge of the tape, leaving torn and ragged paint edges when the frisket is removed. (Always wait until the paint is thoroughly dry before lifting the tape.)

Finally, if your tape is too sticky, you can make it more manageable by adhering it to a clean surface and removing it several times. This will take some of the adhesive action away, making the tape easier to work with. (See *Correction Tape.*)

TAPE, GUMMED PAPER

The common brown paper tape with a water-soluble glue on one side is very inexpensive and can be used easily in a dispenser specially designed for it. Gummed paper tape comes in a variety of widths, the selection of which depends on your particular needs. Use gummed paper tape for sealing artwork in mats, for stretching watercolor paper, for sealing silkscreen frames, for wrapping and sealing packages, and for many other similar functions.

TAPES, PHOTOGRAPHIC

Both the surface and the adhesive of this tape are black. In all other respects, the tape is the same as masking tape: It has a very firm grip and is much stronger than drafting tape. Photographic tape is used to assemble negatives and produce masks in all photographic processes. As such, it is desirably lightproof and thus relatively costly. There are many cheaper black tapes on the market, costing about the same as conventional tapes. However, these are not lightproof, and any mask made with them may require a double layer. Be careful: even cheap tapes may be labeled "photographic."

TAPE, TWO-SIDED

Both cellophane tape (Scotch tape) and drafting tape are produced in a form that has adhesive on both sides. These tapes, sold in the same stores that carry the conventional tapes, are a neat, clean, and convenient alternative to other adhesives for bonding paper and cardboard. The rolls that contain these tapes have a backing strip that lightly adheres to one side of the tape. You cut a piece of tape from the roll with the backing tape intact, place the sticky side on the art to be mounted, and peel away the backing strip. Now the art can be placed on the mounting surface and adhered with firm pressure. The tapes are strong enough to hold paper and cardboard for extended periods, but heavier objects will fall off easily. Also avoid using this method in strong sunlight or other temperature extremes, as they will reduce the tapes' holding ability, causing the mounted object to fall. (See *Adhesives; Tape, Drafting;* and *Scotch Tape.*)

TECHNICAL PENS

Any of a group of hollow, round-nibbed pens used for both freehand and mechanical drawing. (See *Pens.*)

TEMPERA

Tempera is the general name for a group of paints that use an emulsion for a binder. The name derives from the ancient practice of tempering: the preparation of a careful blend (or emulsion) of water and an oily, fatty substance that would produce an adequate binding fluid into which the pigment could be mixed. Actually the term applied to both water- and oil-based paints, but has been limited to water-soluble products in recent years. Egg tempera is an example of this process. The oily egg yolk supplies the binding power, and makes an excellent emulsion when mixed with water. Most modern tempera paints are misnamed, since there is no tempering. A water-soluble glue, such as gum arabic, serves as the binder, and glues are not emulsions. Properly, they should be called gouaches. The general qualities of these paints are so similar, however, that the name is used interchangeably.

Temperas dry very quickly and eventually are completely waterproof. This characteristic has encouraged a fine, crosshatch technique that almost eradicated tempera as a modern medium. Several fine artists have reclaimed the technique in recent years, and more conventional methods are being employed. This has led to a modest revival in the medium.

There are no hard and fast procedures for applying tempera. You are limited, literally, by your imagination. Tempera works well with any kind of brush technique, with sponge stipple, in airbrushes, ruling pens, and in just about any other device or technique you can invent.

Like watercolor, tempera dries quickly and a painting with tempera should be planned well in advance. If you try to work with too much paint on your palette, it will dry out before you can use it. Once tempera has dried it can be dissolved again with water, but it loses some of its consistency and opacity. And a lot of time is lost trying to get the paint to the proper working condition again. Paint cups and egg crates permit you to mix each color, as it is needed, and prepare the proper consistency. The cups will also prevent the paints from running into each other, and the smaller surface exposed to the air will slow their evaporation.

TEMPLATES

Plastic stencils containing many sizes of commonly used shapes and symbols. They are used whenever these shapes must be drawn frequently, thereby providing accuracy and saving considerable time. Most of the shapes prepared on these templates have a direct use in some form of engineering drawing—electrical symbols, for instance. However, a great many of them, such as circles, squares, and hexagons, are used by the commercial artist as well. Templates are available wherever drafting supplies are sold, and you are advised to examine the selection offered to see if any of them may be suitable to your work. Although templates are not essential to artists, they are extremely convenient.

The template should be placed on the drawing and moved until the opening with the proper size and shape is in an accurate position. A pencil is used to trace the outline of the shape by guiding it around the edges of the opening. When inking with a template, it is best to use a Rapidograph pen or a similar India ink pen.

Templates may be used directly as stencils or friskets, too, with the paint being applied with an airbrush or a stipple brush. However, the adjacent holes should be covered with paper or tape to prevent the paint from discoloring other areas.

Templates are made of plastic and must be kept clean in the same manner as triangles and other plastic tools. Similar care should be taken in storage so that the fragile plastic does not warp or become nicked.

Common Difficulties

Blotting. Even with the proper pen, ink tends to run under the edges of a template when the drawing tool moves too close to the edge. Be sure that the template is raised above the surface of the paper by placing something underneath it while working. The common professional solution is to tape coins on the underside of the template. However, a triangle will work just as well. Place the triangle so that the open portion in the center falls over the area to be inked. When the template is placed upon the triangle, it will be supported firmly without interfering with the working area. Since it is difficult to keep the inking tool at a constant angle when the template is raised in this manner, inked lines may be inaccurate. Therefore, draw the shape first with pencil. This pencil line will act as a visual guide when inking with the template.

Nicking. Templates, being plastic, are easily nicked. Do not attempt to use a knife with a template to cut a form. Draw the desired shape with a pencil and the template. Remove the template and cut the form freehand. If some guidance is necessary to make the cut, keep an old triangle on hand and use it only for such cutting.

TEMPLATES, LETTERING

Plastic sheets containing letter forms which must be traced, one character at a time, by moving a drawing tool along the edges of the openings. (See *Lettering Templates; Lettering, Mechanical;* and *Lettering Stencils.*)

TEXTILE PAINTS

Water- and oil-based media that are designed specifically for application on cloth. With the exception of limited display and presentation instances, such paints are useful only as a hobby, and have little use in the commercial art field. Textile paints are easy to apply by brushing directly on the fabric, stencilling, hand-blocking, silkscreening, and airbrushing. Extenders, thinners, penetrators, blocking mediums, and cleaners are sold for use with these paints at most art and hobby stores. Instructions, which are easy to follow, are provided with textile paint sets.

TEXTURED BOARDS

A rather arbitrary, though descriptive, classification for a number of pebbled drawing papers mounted on cardboard. Ross and Coquille board are the outstanding examples of this type of board. The texture imparts a distinctive character to any drawing done on the board, which is highly desirable in line reproduction. (See *Papers and Boards.*)

TISSUE PAPER

Many art supply stores now carry packages of assorted tissue papers in a wide range of brilliant colors. Their only use in commercial art is to produce collage designs. This is accomplished by adhering the tissue to a white board with any cement or glue. Tearing the edges or crumbling the paper will create exciting textures, and overlapping the translucent sheets will produce additional variations. (See *Papers and Boards.*)

TONGS

A form of tweezer with broad, flat, gripping surfaces. The most common tongs are stamp tongs. Pikcing up small paper stamps and gummed hinges and placing them accurately in stamp catalogs is very similar to handling small pieces of art and type when you are cementing them to a mechanical. For this reason, stamp tongs have become quite popular with artists and are available at many art supply stores, in addition to stamp and hobby shops. The flat blades of these tongs can be sharpened on a whetstone so that they will slide easily under paper cutouts. (See *Tweezers.*)

TOP SHEET SHADING FILMS

Halftone patterns printed on plastic sheets that are cut out and added to line art before, rather than during, the platemaking process. (See *Shading Sheets.*)

TORTILLONS

Imported French stomps, made of soft gray paper rolled and pointed at one end. For blending charcoal, pastel, etc. (See *Stomps.*)

TRACE WHEELS

Small wheels with sharp points used to punch holes in paper through which powder may be forced. The process, called pouncing, is used to transfer designs from a paper layout to any material. (See *Perforating Wheels.*)

TRACING BOXES

Boxes with glass covers containing a light unit. A drawing or a picture is placed on the glass and covered with a fresh sheet of paper. Light from the box allows

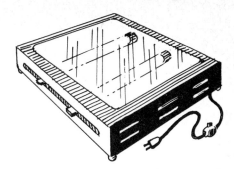

Tracing box, with two movable fluorescent tubes.

you to see the image through the top paper and trace it with any drawing tool. (See *Light Boxes.*)

TRACING CLOTH

A strong yet translucent material used by drafters to prepare drawings that will be reproduced by the blueprint method. The cost of the cloth, as compared with the cost of tracing papers and vellums, and the fact that artists rarely work with blueprints (except in proofing plates) prevents commercial artists from finding much use for this material.

The one time that this cloth is valuable to artists is when they must do considerable work by tracing and need a material that will resist erasing, tearing, and stretching or shrinking.

Tracing cloth is sold in rolls at drafting supply stores, although some retailers will sell you a portion cut from a roll.

TRACING PAPER

A light, highly transparent, onionskin paper used in the creation of layouts and for copying directly by tracing. Sold in pads of many different sizes. (See *Papers and Boards.*)

TRANSFER TYPE

A rather arbitrary name for any of a series of type alphabets that come on sheets of transparent plastic and are transferred to the work surface by rubbing one character at a time. No universal generic name has ever taken hold; these sheets are either called by one of the more common brand names (such as Prestype—one of the earliest), or by descriptive names, such as rubdown or pressure graphics. Transfer type is used to create lettering on layouts and mechanicals, and is a quick and inexpensive substitute for conventional typography and photolettering.

Each sheet of transfer type contains the elements of one complete font of type. Both upper and lower case letters are included on one sheet, unless the type is too large, in which case, two sheets are necessary. Numerals and punctuation marks are included with each alphabet. As in a font of type, there are usually more of the most frequently used characters (that is, vowels) than the less frequently used letters. These alphabets are available in opaque black and opaque white, while some manufacturers offer a limited range of colors. Each manufacturer of transfer type provides its own selection of type faces; you may choose a particular face from catalogs available from the manufacturer or the art store.

In addition, a number of prepared patterns (lines, dots, textures, symbols, etc.) are available from the same manufacturers. These patterns are shown in the same catalogs as the type. However, few stores will stock all the patterns or type faces shown, particularly in all of the colors. It may be necessary to place an order for less commonly used specimens, and allow time for their delivery. (See also *Shading Sheets* and *Zipatone.*)

Historically, there have been a number of methods that might be categorized as transfer type. These have included pads of letters printed on opaque stock that were assembled in a form before being Scotch taped together and trimmed. Although most of these products have been short-lived, you may still find some of them in art stores or on the job. They are not difficult to master.

One of these variants is still available—cut-out transfer type. It is identical to rubdown type with one notable exception. The individual characters must be cut from the master sheet with a sharp knife or razor blade, and the film and its characters adhered to the art together. The advantage is the durability of such a letter. It is virtually impervious to handling. However, the excess plastic can create an ugly halo effect on certain presentations and even mechanicals. Extreme care and neat trimming is necessary.

The assembling of transfer lettering is facilitated by a guide line printed underneath each character on the sheet of many brands. These lines may be used as a guide for positioning the sheet during the transfer process. First draw a light pencil line on the work. Make sure the line is the same distance below the desired position as the printed line is below the characters on the sheet. Now place the sheet so that the character to be transferred is in its desired position. If the two guide lines do not correspond, shift the transfer sheet slightly until they do. Now transfer the character, but *not* the guide line.

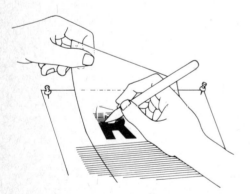

When applying transfer type, hold the sheet firmly with the heel of the hand. Gently lift the sheet with the free hand during or after burnishing. If transfer is incomplete, the sheet can be replaced accurately and further burnishing applied. Note that the backing sheet has been inserted to prevent the heat of the hand from producing unwanted transfer.

Another method is to transfer the character *with* its guide line on a separate sheet. Once all the desired characters are transferred, they are trimmed and adhered with glue, rubber cement, or Scotch tape, on the finished art with their guide lines intact. The line of characters may now be straightened by aligning their guide lines with a straight-edge. This method is particularly useful when the finished line of lettering is on a curve, or other unusual shape, since it allows you to experiment with the positioning. Naturally, in these cases, you will align the letters with a French curve or with a light guide line on the finished art.

Once the lettering has been properly placed, the guide lines may be cut away, painted, or covered with correction tape, etc. To avoid disfiguring display presentations, do not transfer the guide line itself, and draw the layout guide line in such a manner that it can be removed without damaging the art. A piece of drafting tape will work quite well and can be easily and harmlessly removed.

Another very satisfactory method of assembling transfer type is accomplished by tracing an accurate layout of the type with tracing or visualizer paper. In this way spacing can be corrected or unusual effects, like "bouncing" or curving the line of lettering, can be created. The layout is then placed on a light box, and a sheet of single ply bristol is adhered with tape over the layout. The individual characters may now be applied directly over their corresponding figures made visible by the light of the light box shining through both sheets of paper.

This method of producing unusual lettering is an important advantage of transfer type, since corresponding effects in typography and photolettering are extremely expensive.

Common Difficulties

Cutout type. Just about everything that goes wrong with cutout transfer type is related to the adhesive backing. If the sheet is too old, or if it has been subjected to temperature extremes, the adhesive will adhere poorly or not at all. The only way to correct this problem is to heat the sheet slightly. Working on a light box, for instance, will provide just about the right amount of heat from the light fixture. This heat will tend to soften and reactivate the adhesiveness.

Similarly, the sheet can pick up dirt or lint which will discolor the final art. In both these cases, it may be easier to throw out the faulty sheet and use a new one.

Rubdown type. Some of the common difficulties of rub-off type are listed below:

1. Torn letters. If the pressure is insufficient or uneven, if the wax is too old, or if the complete character is not covered by the rubbing, parts of the letter may not come free from the sheet when it is lifted off. If you suspect that the sheet you are using is too old, try a sample letter before working on the finished artwork. A little heat may increase the ability of the wax to affect a proper bond. Make sure that the entire surface over the character has been rubbed sufficiently, and lift the sheet off very slowly. If you keep a steady hold on a part of the sheet not being lifted, when the character does not come free, you may replace the sheet accurately and repeat the rubbing until the transfer is completed. Another cause may be an improper burnisher. If you are not using the recommended tool, practice first to determine which alternative works best.

2. Poor adhesion. Even if you observe the proper procedures described above, the letters may still be difficult to transfer. In this case, the problem may be in the surface of the artwork itself. Paint may not be thoroughly dry, pastel may be too chalky and dusty, and the paper, itself, may be dirty or greasy. In these cases, rubdown type will not adhere. Make sure all surfaces are clean and dry, and improve their receptiveness with a coat of fixative.

3. Waxy halo. On certain materials, notably acetate, Color-Aid, or Colorama, a residue of wax may be left around the letters. This residue may be unsightly in itself or it may attract dirt and destroy the appearance of a presentation. There is no way to remove this wax residue without removing the letter as well. For this reason, learn to apply the rubbing pressure only to those parts of the sheet directly over the inked character.

4. Corrections. Broken characters and misspellings can be easily corrected with drafting tape. Cut a narrow piece of the tape and attach it firmly. Slowly peel the tape away. If all the ink is not removed, repeat the process with a clean piece of tape. Usually, two or three applications will complete the job. If not, take a fresh, clean razor blade and gently scrape the surface. Be careful not to damage the paper. It is desirable to assemble transfer type on a good quality bristol or illustration board. If done carefully, the repaired surface will be receptive to a new character and will not show any sign of repair.

TRIANGLE

A triangle is a mechanical drafting tool made of plastic, metal, or wood. All drafting triangles are *right* triangles; one angle is always 90°, and comes in two shapes: 30°-60°-90°, and 45°-45°-90°. Triangles have an interior opening that makes them easy to pick up and convenient to hang on a hook, but this interior shape is not accurate and cannot be used for any mechanical purpose.

There are many sizes of these two triangles. The size is determined by the length of the longest side adjacent to the right angle. Personal preference will decide which size you choose, but 12″ is probably the most popular. This size affords you a reasonable length without becoming too cumbersome to handle. Any artist who uses the triangle frequently will keep several sizes on hand.

One of the basic items of commercial art equipment, the triangle is used in virtually every operation artists perform. It is mandatory that the triangle be used with a T-square or parallel ruling straight-edge for all exact work.

The main function of the triangle is to construct regular geometrical figures: the triangle, square, rectangle, hexagon, octagon, etc. Similarly, it is used to draw verticals and diagonals of 30°, 45°, and 60°. But its easily handled form and accurate straight-edges cause the triangle to be used for practically every straight line the artist draws, inks, paints, or cuts. This versatility explains why the plastic model has all but replaced the wood or metal versions. Wood is too easily damaged and metal is too heavy, although, for cutting, some prefer the durability of metal. But remember, for use as an accurate mechanical tool, be sure that you always place the triangle on a steady and accurate T-square or parallel ruling straight-edge. Only if the base of the triangle is true can the work done on it be correct.

When inking with a triangle, make sure that the point of the pen does not touch the base of the straight-edge where it meets the paper; the ink will blot under this edge. Plan your work so that the triangle will not have to come close to a freshly-inked line. When you rule over a line that has been inked, take special care that the stroke of the pen does not linger over the juncture of the two lines and allow the ink to spread to the edge of the triangle, where it will smear. Learn to pick up the triangle carefully so that it does not slide into the newly-inked lines and smudge them.

The triangle has one last function. Since it is always handy, the triangle is just the thing to place under T-squares, curves, and other triangles when they are being used for inking. The interior shape offers an excellent platform with even support all around when inking with ellipse guides and other small template forms.

Triangles of all materials are subject to damage and must be carefully cared for. Provide a storage place for triangles to protect them from being hit and nicked. Avoid high temperatures and humidity; both will warp and distort plastic and wood. Keep your triangles clean by wiping them frequently while you work. Occasionally wash plastic triangles with mild soap and lukewarm water. Dry them immediately to prevent warping.

Metal triangles can be cleaned with rubber cement thinner, and protected by wiping with a rag that has a small amount of light oil on it. Wipe off any excess oil so that you will not stain your drawings.

Avoid using a good triangle for cutting. It is almost impossible to keep from nicking and thus destroying the straight-edge. Save an *old* triangle for cutting only. Even metal triangles *can* be nicked.

Common Difficulties

Ragged lines. Check the edge of the triangle to see if any paint or other material has accumulated. If the edge is clean and still produces ragged lines, inspect the edge carefully for nicks. In rare cases, a nick can be smoothed down by lightly sanding the edge. Most often, such damage cannot be repaired and the triangle must be discarded for accurate work. Don't throw it away, however; keep it for cutting and other rough jobs.

Smudging. The triangle is just dirty. Clean it and keep it clean.

Inaccurate lines. In time, a triangle may begin to produce lines that are perceptibly not parallel, or which are inaccurate as to proper degree of angle. You will usually notice this in the verticals. Perhaps a line that you have drawn with one triangle will not agree with the line produced by another. In such an event, check your triangle by drawing a vertical line while the triangle rests firmly on a

stationary straight-edge. Then, turn the triangle over so that its base is exactly on the line you have just drawn. If the side of the triangle diverges from this line, make sure that the edges of the triangle are free of dirt and nicks. If the triangle is still not true, it has probably warped, so that one or more of the edges is no longer straight, but slightly curved. Nearly any material will become distorted with age, and there is no way to correct it. Such a triangle should be clearly marked as defective and kept for cutting and other rough chores. Triangles are relatively inexpensive and it is wise to replace them, whenever you suspect a defect, rather than risk an inaccurate job.

TRIANGLE, ADJUSTABLE

The adjustable triangle combines the function of a right triangle and a protractor. The hypotenuse leg of the triangle pivots and can be locked into any position determined by the protractor.

There are no special instructions for using the adjustable triangle. Once it has been set to the desired degree, it is handled in the same manner as the triangle. Read that entry and you will be able to proceed with no additional help.

The adjustable triangle is a precision tool and should be cared for as such. Keep it in a safe place, free from temperature and humidity extremes that can warp and distort the plastic edges. Avoid dropping, striking, or nicking these edges; there is no way to repair or replace them if they are damaged.

Dirt may be removed from the plastic by washing with soap and water, but take care not to wet the metal parts. These should be kept as clean as possible and oiled lightly to prevent rust and to insure smooth, accurate movement.

Common Difficulty

If the adjustable triangle is not damaged there should be no operational difficulty. Any inaccuracy is highly unlikely, and

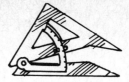

Adjustable triangle with two hinged sections and a sliding scale.

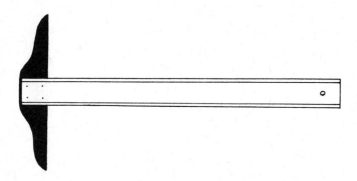

Typical T-square. T-squares may be made of metal, plastic, or wood.

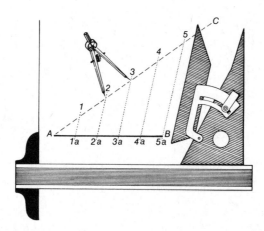

Step 1: To divide line AB into an odd number of identical divisions, draw line AC away from line AB. The angle of line AC does not matter.

Step 2: Using a ruler or divider, mark off a number of equal divisions on line AC; the same number as the desired divisions of line AB. The size of these divisions on line AC is unimportant as long as they are equal.

Step 3: With the triangle held firmly against a T-square, adjust the edge of the triangle until it aligns the last mark on line AC and point B.

Step 4: Slide the triangle to each division mark on line AC and draw a line crossing line AB. The resulting divisions of line AB will be equal.

can only be checked by comparing the settings with a protractor that is known to be exact. Since the adjustable triangle is used infrequently, it should last a lifetime.

T-SQUARES

A straight-edge with a headpiece mounted at right angles to the edge. Aligning the head against the edge of a drawing board permits artists to construct any number of parallel lines by sliding the T-square along the edge of the board.

T-squares come in many sizes and materials. The cheapest are constructed of wood and are the least satisfactory. Better models have a transparent plastic edge that is more durable and permits a clear view of the working area. Some of these plastic edges are slimmer than the body of the T-square so that ink from the ruling pen will not blot and run under the edge. The most durable T-squares are made of metal and are quite expensive. The metal edges have been beveled to prevent ink blotting, and the metal will withstand hard usage.

An adjustable T-square is also available. The head is not set permanently against the body of the straight-edge and may be set to any angle, so that angled lines may be constructed, each parallel to the other.

Common Difficulties

Warping. All wooden T-squares, with or without plastic edges, will warp in time, making it impossible to draw an accurate line. There is no way to repair this fault and a new T-square must be purchased. For this reason, buy the finest T-square you can afford. In the long run, it will be less expensive.

Cracking. The plastic edge of the better T-squares will sometimes crack or shatter, ruining the T-square. This is usually caused by extremes of temperature or humidity, which force the parts of the T-

square to expand or to contract at different rates. The stress will cause the plastic, which is more brittle, to break first. Once again, the T-square cannot be repaired. Prevent such troubles by keeping the T-square at a constant temperature in a dry room.

Nicks. Using the T-square for cutting may produce small nicks in the straight-edge. These nicks will disrupt the movement of a pen and produce ragged lines. Small nicks may sometimes be smoothed out by careful sanding above or below the nick, but *never* on the face of the straight-edge. However, in most cases the T-square will again be useless. Therefore, do not use a T-square for cutting. If you must, keep two T-squares and use one exclusively for cutting.

Smudging. Repeated movement of the T-square over a drawing surface will cause the body of the straight-edge to pick up graphite and other media which will be smeared as the T-square is moved to a new position. Keep the T-square clean by washing it in cool water with soap. Do *not* use hot water or harsh detergents, because they will warp, discolor, or damage the surface of the T-square. Wipe the T-square thoroughly after cleaning and allow it to dry completely before using. Metal T-squares may be cleaned in the same manner, but they should also be wiped with a light oil once they are clean. Always follow such procedures by wiping the utensil with a clean cloth. This will remove any excess oil which might mar the artwork, but will also leave enough to protect the surface.

Discoloration. Repeated cleanings and aging may cause the plastic parts of the T-square to become discolored. In most cases, this will not harm the T-square. However, it is usually a sign that the T-square is nearing the end of its usefulness. It is good practice to check such a T-square against an accurate straight-edge to be sure that no warping has taken place. If it has, replace the T-square.

Unparallel lines. The first part of most T-squares to malfunction is the head. The screws that hold it tight may develop "play." This causes the angle of the head to vary when it is pressed against the side of the board. You can check this by drawing a line with the T-square, and holding the head firmly against the side of the board. Try to move the opposite end of the straight-edge up and down on the surface of the board. (Make sure, of course, that the board edge is exact.) If you see any movement, tighten the screws in the head. If "play" is still visible, replace the T-square.

TURPENTINE

Turpentine, also referred to as essence of turpentine or spirits of turpentine, is the product of distilled resins from certain pine trees. Turpentine is a solvent for most oil-based paints and is the normal solvent for most fine art oil painting. (See *Solvents.*)

TV MATS

Inexpensive black card stock, die cut to provide openings identical to the white spaces on TV pads. These mats permit storyboard layouts to be prepared separately on any material and framed in the appropriate openings. Similarly, they permit corrections and revisions without disturbing the overall presentation. Because the die cuts weaken the structure of the board, it is common practice to attach another piece of stock, of exactly the same size, to the back. This also covers the ragged appearance of the many different panel inserts. (See *TV Pads.*)

TV PADS

TV pads contain sheets of light bond paper divided by shaded borders into a number of boxes shaped like television screens with smaller, rectangular boxes beneath. The pads, which are used for preparing storyboards for television and film continuity, are handled the same as any other layout paper.

The artists draws the pertinent illustration in the larger screen area and prints the action or dialogue in the box beneath the image. Perforations allow each frame to be removed from the sheet and assembled separately, or a sheet may be rendered intact.

TV pads vary in their overall size and in the number and size of frames per sheet. Small pads contain only one frame on a page.

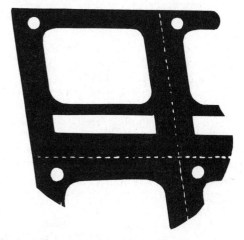

Portion of a TV pad showing the circular frame number panel, the screen-shaped illustration panel, and the rectangular copy panel. Note the perforations that allow each frame to be presented individually.

TWEEZERS

Commercial artists are required to handle many small pieces of cutout art, type, and photostats while producing comp layouts and mechanicals. To do this, many artists insert the point of a razor blade under the cutout and pinch it with their thumbs. This method is not difficult to learn, but has many problems. The sharp razor blade can cut or puncture the cutout, or dirty fingers can smudge it. The tweezer is a much neater and more convenient tool for such an operation. A number of tweezer styles are usually available at art stores, including sharply pointed and blunt rounded ones. Perhaps the most versatile style is the flat-ended, broadly spatulate one (illustrated here), once exclusively referred to as stamp tongs. This tweezer, with its generous grasping area, is ideal for handling both large and small pieces. To facilitate removing rubber cemented cutouts from a mechanical, the ends of the tweezer can be filed on a sandpaper block or a whetstone. It is true that rubber cement thinner quickly loosens the bond, but the plastic-coated papers commonly used in copying processes and type proofs resist the penetration of the thinner, and the plastic coating is easily separated from its base when wet. If you are not very careful, you can easily damage such a cutout. This will require some time to repair or may produce a smudged and dirty mechanical. The filed tip of the stamp tong is easy to slide under a cutout, and the broad blades provide a firm grip even when the surface is slippery with wet cement. If your art store does not carry tweezers, look for them at a hobby center, or variety store.

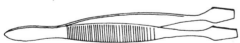

Flat-ended tweezers for small cutouts.

TWO-SIDED TAPE

A cellophane or drafting tape that has been prepared with adhesive on both sides. This tape is used as an alternative to rubber cement and other adhesives when mounting art on backgrounds. (See *Tape, Two-sided.*)

TYPE

Type as we know it today was invented, along with the printing press, by Gutenberg in the 1500s. For a long time, typography involved making metal copies of master characters that had been la-

boriously hand engraved. We know many of these typefaces by the names of the people who engraved them. In the last century, technological advances permitted the development of machines that could cast whole lines of type from individual molds assembled into a single form. Not too long ago, the rising costs of metal, wages, equipment, and rent made this form of typography, called hot type, prohibitively expensive. The advent of the computer, coupled with photography, created the cold type processes that are used almost exclusively today. In them, an operator types copy into a computer that has been programmed to deal with such considerations as type style, size, word and column spacing, hyphenation, and justification. The computer then transfers this assembled information to a printing device that photographically composes the type by optically modifying individual characters from a master negative. The completed sheet is then developed. Additional copies, if desired, are produced using a high-quality photographic reproduction system. An inexpensive photocopy is also provided for galley corrections or for use in preparing a dummy layout.

Type is perhaps the most important element in modern commercial art. Virtually no piece of communication whether printed, filmed, or videotaped, is without type in some form. As such, typography becomes the most vital subject for the new artist to master. Art and professional schools offer courses in typography, and there are many excellent books on type style and design. These range from histories to catalogs of the more popular typefaces in use today. It is difficult to find a single source that shows every typeface, since there are literally thousands of them. In addition, there are books on handlettering—both calligraphy and reproduction lettering—that all art students should study to gain a true understanding of the aesthetics and design of typefaces. All artists should be able to 'spec' type; that is, to provide written instructions to a typesetter so that a sheet of typewritten copy can be converted into composed, reproduction-quality type. Once located chiefly in large cities, typographic services are now available in a growing number of localities. The variations of equipment and the personal procedures of the operators make it important that you work closely with them to ensure complete understanding of spec instructions. (See also *Calligraphy* and *Handlettering*.)

Common Difficulties

Errata. With the demise of hot metal facilities, many of their valuable services have been abandoned. Principal among them is proofreading: checking against the original for errors and even correcting inadvertent mistakes of the authors. Similarly, the highly trained and experienced union typographers have been replaced by untrained typists, who have little, if any, knowledge of the aesthetics of type. These economies place a heavier burden on commercial artists, who must provide the design, spec the type as thoroughly as possible, and check the final proofs for errors in both content and style.

Damage. Many type services will provide only one proof. Accidents will happen and often the proof will become torn or dirty, as revisions are made in mechanicals. It is wise to order at least two proofs to cover such situations. As an alternative, do all your practice and experimentation with a photocopy, and do not use the proof until you are completely sure of the final layout.

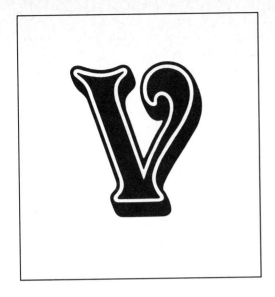

VAN DYKES

A simple paper negative copy similar to a blueprint, used by printers to proof their plate negatives prior to the plate-making process. (See *Blueprints*.)

VARNISH

The name given to a group of natural oils and resins, or synthetic plastic liquids that dry to form a hard, transparent covering. Used by fine artists to coat and protect finished paintings, varnishes serve as the base for most of the aerosol spray fixatives that are popular with commercial artists. (See *Fixatives*.)

VELLUM

The name for a high quality, commercial printing paper similar to bristol. In the art field, the name vellum is used to describe a very fine, transparent, tracing paper. Tracing vellums have much more strength than onionskin tracing papers, and will not wrinkle as much when wet. Vellums may be purchased in sheets or pads of varying sizes. (See *Papers and Boards*.)

VELOX

A photoprint of a continuous tone subject that has been transformed into line art by means of a halftone screen. The velox print may be placed in position on a mechanical as finished art, ready for the platemaker's camera. No other processing is necessary; the print will reproduce as line art.

The virtues of the velox (which merely duplicates the step the platemaker would normally take) are lower cost, greater control, and ease of correction. The cost is less, since the platemaker must photograph the continuous tone material separately and strip the resulting negative into a master negative containing the line art material. This stripping is expensive and subject to error. Since you position the velox print yourself, error is eliminated; and a velox print is line art, so there is only one plate negative produced—eliminating stripping.

Control is greater in that you may order a velox print in various sizes and degrees of contrast. You may compare the prints to select the one which will reproduce best. Although the platemaker can also vary his exposures and sizes, you will not be around to observe the results, and the platemaker's decision may not agree with your own.

Correction is easier since you can see from the velox print exactly how the final reproduction will appear. Screening continuous tone material always results in a loss of detail, so that it may be necessary to strengthen some areas of contrast. This may be accomplished with India ink and opaque white. These corrections will also be line art and will not affect the reproduction process.

The limitations of the velox are the time involved and the distortion that always results from adding an extra copying step. Velox prints are regular photographs; it takes time to process them, particularly if there are special instructions or effects. And the fine dots may weaken or fill in when they are copied again.

A velox is ordered in the same way as a normal photograph. That is, the material should be clean and flat, and the enlargement or reduction should be indicated. In addition, there are a number of technical effects that can be selected. These include the nature of the screen—the line count of the dots, or the substitution of other screens that produce varying textures instead of dots—and the choice of several hand alterations—silhouetting, highlighting, or a combination of solid line and highlighting with the conventional dots in the gray areas.

These variations are listed, with examples, in the promotional material of the photo studios that produce veloxes. A price list is usually available which will contain the average price for the work in different sizes. Since hand work is often involved, these costs may vary considerably from the price list. If you are in doubt, consult the photographer before you order the velox.

VIEWERS

Specific term applied by the Goodkin firm to distinguish its line of enlarger-reducers. The typical viewer is a large, freestanding, bellows-type camera without a film holder. It has an adjustable object board, bracketing lights, and a clear glass backing. An optional hood permits its use in normal light. The artist places an object or piece of art upside down on the board. Controls permit the board and lens to be moved independently to calibrated settings to provide enlargement or reduction of the image. A sheet of thin paper is placed on the glass backing, and the image is traced.

Common Difficulties

No image. If the model has a glass viewing plate, no image will be visible until a piece of paper is placed upon the glass.

Fuzziness. Paper that is too opaque will diffuse the image so that it is difficult to see detail. The most satisfactory paper for such machines is tracing paper. Another cause of fuzziness is in the adjustment of the table and lens. Even following the adjustment instructions exactly may not provide a clear image, particularly when you are copying a three-dimensional object. In these cases, additional fine adjustment of the positions can only be accomplished by trial and error.

Upside-down image. Like any camera, the image on the glass is always inverted. The subject must be placed on the table upside down. The directions will be reversed, too, when you wish to move the subject.

Distortion. No lens is capable of providing perfect images at all distances. Even with the finest models with the best lenses, some distortion results in extreme focuses, particularly at the edges of the image. Where extreme accuracy is required, it may be necessary to draw only one portion of the object at a time, moving the object between drawings so that each portion will be in the center of the field and thus not subject to the distortion. With practice you will discover the limitations of your particular machine and begin to be able to allow for them.

Hot spots. The bright lights, though shielded, may cause intense areas of illumination on the subject that produce glare on the viewing glass. In these areas no detail will show. Try moving the lights and/or the object until you eliminate or minimize the glare.

Too large or small. Most of these machines have a limit of four times enlargement or reduction. This is adequate for most of the work you will do. If further alteration is necessary, merely take the tracing produced with the maximum ratio, place it on the subject table, and repeat the process.

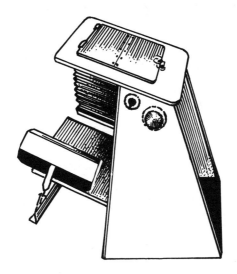

A specialized viewer with a film holder for producing
photographic negatives and prints.

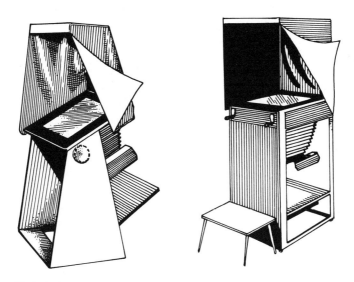

Typical viewers.

All other difficulties stemming from use of these machines involve their size and expense. They are not difficult to use, however, and just a few hours practice will enable you to use them to their fullest advantage.

If you do not have such a machine available, investigate the alternatives. Some of the alternative devices and procedures you can use are covered in the entry for *Enlarger-Reducers*. (See *Opaque Projector; Camera Lucida;* and *Photostats*.)

VINYL FILMS

These are some of the newest plastic films on the market. They are expensive and may be difficult to find in local art stores. However, their qualities of dimensional stability and resistance to water make them worth trying. Orders for these films can usually be placed through your art supply store. (See *Plastic Films.*)

VISUALIZER PAPER

A light, semitransparent, onionskin drawing paper used in the creation of layouts or "visuals." Possessing more tooth than tracing paper, visualizer paper is excellent for any dry medium, but shrivels when wet. Also known as layout paper, visualizer paper comes in pads of many different sizes. (See *Papers and Boards.*)

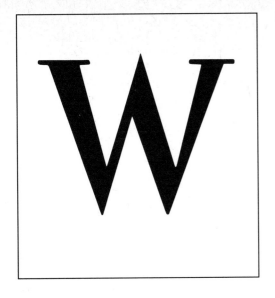

WATERCOLOR

These paints are noted primarily for their transparency and purity, qualities that make them highly suitable for fine art, illustration, general rendering, and layout. It is the name given to any waterbased paint. The colors intermix well with a minimum of the muddiness caused by excessive ground found in most other paints. Watercolor is one of the least expensive media, since the wash-technique usually practiced uses little paint. (See *Paint.*)

Watercolor paints come in tubes or open pans (or trays) and work equally well in either form. Tubes keep the paint soft and clean, but pans are always ready for use, providing they have been kept clean. It is a matter of personal preference which form you choose.

Watercolor paints can be applied with any brush, airbrush, or inking tool such as a ruling pen. But the paper should be strong and absorbent to resist the stretching caused by the large amounts of water that are used with the medium.

Like oil, watercolor is primarily a fine art medium. If you will reread the introduction, you will see why such subjects are avoided in this book. But watercolor is used extensively for commercial art, and general characteristics and techniques should be discussed.

Watercolor is a "one-shot" medium. The entire effect is destroyed if the painting is corrected or worked over. Even a painting that requires dozens of overlaying washes must be done quickly, directly, and spontaneously. For this reason, a watercolor needs the maximum of planning, both in the drawing itself and in the preparation of the materials.

Make several small sketches to test the composition and to determine the desired colors. These will allow you to make your final pencil guide with a minimum of lines, which remain visible in such a transparent medium. They will also allow you to plan your palette, so that the proper paints are mixed and handy at the proper time. In addition to a flat palette, it is advisable to have a number of paint cups or egg crates so that diluted colors can be mixed ahead of time in ample amounts.

Where soft edges or large areas are to be covered, wet the paper with clean water and a clean brush. Be sure to keep the amount of water constant over the entire area. Now tilt the paper so that it slopes toward you. Apply the paint in rhythmic, horizontal strokes, refilling the brush as necessary. Always allow the strokes to overlap, so that the brush picks up the remaining paint from the preceding stroke and carries it along, which will insure leaving an even amount of color as you proceed. The tilted paper will allow the excess paint to collect at the bottom of the stroke, where it can easily be picked up. Continue smoothly until the entire area has been covered. Clean the brush and wipe it dry. Pick up the excess of paint that has collected on the bottom stroke. Allow the painting to dry thoroughly before attempting any further work.

With practice, you will find that this procedure will let you apply smooth and even washes of color in any kind of area.

Once this technique has been mastered, it is relatively easy to acquire the ability to apply unusual effects or accents within this area while you are laying the flat color.

Although watercolor paint remains soluble, it is possible to lay succeeding washes over a painted area if the same careful technique is followed. In fact, it may be desirable to wet one of these painted areas before adding another wash. Simply use clean water and a clean brush and float the water or paint without scrubbing. These gentle actions will not disturb the paint beneath.

When the basic values have been applied, detail and accents may be added in any manner with a dry or loaded brush, or with any other technique you may wish. The whole key to watercolor is maintaining a smooth, steady rhythm while you work, and without going over any area while it is still wet, except to apply accents.

Common Difficulties

Streaking. Despite the best procedures, streaking in a flat area may still occur. These streaks are caused by uneven amounts of paint applied during the wash. This can be caused by uneven wetness in the paper, uneven amounts of paint on the brush, errors in the stroke or rhythm of the brush during the wash, and by settling the diluted paint in the cup. Practice will take care of any irregularity, whether in the wetness of the paper or the stroke of the brush. Remember to maintain a constant pace. Varying the speed will automatically involve varying the conditions under which the paint or water is applied. For instance, if there is too long a pause before the brush returns to make a stroke, the paint that has been applied previously will have extra time to drain away from its area into the excess at the bottom of the stroke. Or varying speed will allow certain areas to dry more than others so that more

paint will "take" in some areas better than in others. Make sure that you stir the entire contents of the paint cup *each* time you load the brush. This will prevent the paint from settling, which causes the brush to take more water than paint. These procedures do not, however, correct a wash that has turned out wrong. For the most part, there is nothing that can be done with such an error. In some cases, succeeding washes may hide the irregularity. But if no other wash is to be applied in that area, take a very clean ink eraser and rub it gently over the darker spots of the streak. Since the paint has been floated on, it will not have penetrated too deeply into the paper. If the eraser is handled properly, it may be able to remove some of the excess without destroying the surface of the paper or smudging the remaining pigment. Only attempt such correction when the paint has had a very long time to dry. *Never* attempt to make such a correction with a wet paintbrush.

Uneven gradations. One of the more charming effects of watercolor is the smooth fading away of a color. This is done by gradually adding more water to the wash with each succeeding stroke. However, it is probably the most difficult part of the technique to learn. Practice is the only answer. To correct an improper gradation, try gentle erasing as described above.

Muddiness. One of the principal virtues of watercolor is the sparkling brightness that results from using transparent color over white paper, an effect that closely approximates what can be obtained with printing inks. To have this brilliance destroyed by muddy colors is one of the tragedies of amateur watercoloring. Most muddiness will be caused by mixing colors improperly. Since the widest palette will not have all the values you need, it is necessary to mix pigments at times. To insure the greatest success, start with the purest pigments, the highest quality paints. But even the superb pigments will not mix with impunity. Use as few colors as possible to create the tint you wish, and, by all means, make sure that the brushes and water you use are *clean*. Watercolor requires more clean water than any other technique. Be sure that you have ample amounts on hand.

Dull highlights. No amount of planning or execution will insure that you leave the right amount of white paper to produce the required highlights. For this reason, it is necessary to go into a painting after it has been completed to add white. This can cause a lot of trouble. Either the opaque white causes a jarring conflict of techniques or the color beneath will bleed through. To prevent these problems, use a high quality opaque white, and use it sparingly. Another method is to use the flat edge of a sharp knife or razor blade and scrape away the color. This must be done with the same speed and directness as the application of the watercolor paint. Such action will insure that the effects resemble the technique of the painting itself. True, such vigorous action will gouge the paper and will not remove *all* the paint. Nevertheless, the results will be surprisingly consistent with the painting and produce the most satisfactory highlights.

Wrinkling or buckling. Since the medium is extremely wet, it is necessary to use heavier than average paper for watercolor. Otherwise, the paper will expand unevenly, causing high spots and depressions into which the paint will drain and which will cause pronounced irregularities in the coloring. To avoid this, use a proper watercolor paper or illustration board. Both of these materials have been designed for use with watercolor and will produce excellent results. If a lighter paper must be used, even if it is a watercolor paper, stretch it first. To do this, get a clean board that is slightly larger than the paper to be used. Soak the paper thoroughly in clean water. Your bathtub will do if nothing else is available. Place the wet paper on the board and smooth it out. Coat the edges for about one-inch with vegetable paste, making sure that the paste has the consistency of cream. (See *Adhesives*.) Next cut four strips of two-inch wide gummed paper tape so that they will cover the four sides of the paper with one-inch overlap. Wet the tape and press it firmly along the edges of the paper so that it covers 1″ of paper and 1″ of board. Make sure that the tape is wet enough to make firm contact at *all* points. Set the board aside and let it dry *naturally* for several hours. The drying will cause the paper to shrink, but the tape, reinforced with the paste, will prevent it from doing so. The result will be a piece of paper that is as taut as a drum. No amount of wetting will make this paper buckle, since any stretching will merely tend to relieve the pressure under which it is held. Naturally, you should plan to stretch paper well in advance of the time you need it. As a precaution, it is wise to stretch more than one piece in case of rendering errors. Old drawing boards are ideal for this purpose.

WATERCOLOR PAPER

A heavy, textured paper made specifically for use with watercolor paints. These papers are available in a number of weights and surface textures, and can be bought in sheets, pads, blocks, and mounted on boards. Watercolor is primarily a fine art or illustration technique, and these papers are used primarily by these artists. The less expensive illustration boards are sufficient for most of the water-based paints used in commercial art. If your interests are more inclined to fine art or illustration, you should use the better watercolor papers as their fine quality produces far better results. (See *Papers and Boards*.)

WATERCOLORS, DR. PH. MARTIN RADIANT CONCENTRATED

This rather unwieldy name is the brand name of a series of liquid watercolors, packaged in small dropper-capped bottles, and usually sold in sets. In contrast to the conventional watercolors, these colors are more aptly described as dyes since they are infinitely more brilliant, stain deeply, and tend to be less permanent when exposed to light for any length of time. (See *Dyes*.)

WATERCOLORS, DR. PH. MARTIN SYNCHROMATIC TRANSPARENT

A liquid watercolor sold in small stopper-capped bottles. These watercolors are similar to, but less brilliant than, the Radiant Concentrated Water Colors prepared by the same organization. (See *Paints* and *Dyes*.)

WATERCOLORS, LIQUID

Liquid watercolors are similar to drawing inks, but come in a wider selection of colors and are not waterproof when dry. The most popular of these liquid watercolors are the Dr. Ph. Martin Synchromatic Transparent Watercolors, not be confused with Dr. Ph. Martin Radiant Concentrated Watercolors, which may be more accurately referred to as dyes. (See *Paints* and *Dyes*.)

WAX COATER

A machine that coats the back of any piece of paper with a film of wax, permitting it to be attached by simple pressure to another surface. Material that has been treated in this manner can be assembled on mechanicals more quickly and with greater ease than with rubber cement. The pieces do not need to be dried, are not excessively sticky, and may be picked up and moved without using a solvent like rubber cement thinner. Also,

the wax is applied to only one surface, unlike rubber cement, which must be applied to both surfaces.

However, the wax adhering procedure is not particularly flexible. The machine does not handle small pieces well, the wax bond is not as strong as rubber cement, and repeated moving of the wax-coated material destroys the adhesion and discolors the working surface. Wax that has been left on the finished art is almost impossible to remove completely, and the residue will pick up dirt and smudges, creating a dirty mechanical.

Only studios and other large organizations that do a lot of mechanicals will find the cost of the machine economical. (See *Rubber Cement*.)

WAX CRAYONS

The common, soft-wax drawing crayons available in small boxes or large sets, used primarily by children for school drawing. (See *Crayons, Wax*.)

WELDERS, HAND

Used to apply heat-activated bonding sheets in the dry mount process, hand welders resemble soldering irons with small, flat heating units set at an angle to the handle. The hand welders may be used to bond the entire sheet, themselves, or to tack a large sheet into position before being inserted into a dry-mount press. (See *Dry Mount*.)

WHETSTONES

A whetstone is used to shape and hone metal. For artists, a stone is handy for cleaning and sharpening dulled drafting tools and knife blades. Some stones have different surfaces on opposite sides for coarse and fine work.

One of the finest whetstones available is carborundum. This material is very hard, accomplishes the job much faster, and does not wear out as quickly as stone.

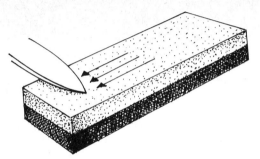

Two-sided whetstone with coarse and fine surfaces.

(See also *Carborundum* and *Abrasives.*)

When sharpening, first moisten the stone—preferably with oil—then grind the metal with firm, circular strokes. Once the metal has been ground to the desired shape, it is honed by drawing the cutting edge over the stone in one direction only, *away* from the edge. The same applies for cleaning or shaping drawing tools, with one addition. To prevent the edges of ruling pens from being too sharp or uneven, the drawing edges are *lightly* honed at right angles to the stone after the shaping is accomplished. Two or three strokes, if done properly, will suffice. (See also *Abrasives* and *Oilstones.*)

Common Difficulty

Wear damage. Most artists, not experienced in using stones, tend to oversharpen. It is extremely easy to ruin fine drafting tools and knife blades by reducing their working surfaces too much. A few *light* strokes are usually sufficient. Remember, it is always simpler to repeat a few strokes than to replace a damaged tool.

WRICO

Brand name for a hollow-point drawing pen and a mechanical-lettering scriber set.

The Wrico pen is a simple tube-shaped holder with interchangeable points. Wires of matching size are sold with the points and screw into a sliding rod within the body of the holder. These wires start the flow of ink, which is loaded into a simple open reservoir in the handle of the pen.

The Wrico scriber is similar to other scriber systems which are described in the mechanical lettering section. (See *Pens.*)

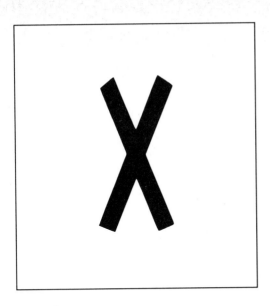

X-ACTO KNIFE

Brand name for a series of hobby knives with many variations of handles and blades. Not all are useful to commercial artists, but the few that are have become so standard that the name is used generically, despite their limitations. Refers to what are more properly called frisket or stencil knives, or mat knives. (See *Knife, X-Acto.*)

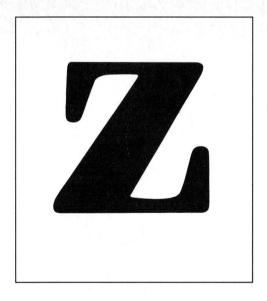

ZIPATONE

Brand name for a series of halftone patterns printed on adhesive-backed plastic sheets that are cut out and adhered to line art to create value tones. As this was one of the original products of this type on the market, the name has become generic, referring to any top sheet shading film. (See *Shading Sheets* and *Transfer Type.*)